BRITAIN'S GREATEST GENERATION

BRITAIN'S GREATEST GENERATION

*How our Parents & Grandparents
Made the Twentieth Century*

SUE ELLIOTT
AND STEVE HUMPHRIES

BOOKS

1 3 5 7 9 10 8 6 4 2

Random House Books
20 Vauxhall Bridge Road
London SW1V 2SA

Random House Books is part of the Penguin Random House group of companies whose
addresses can be found at global.penguinrandomhouse.com.

Penguin
Random House
UK

Plate section 1: 'Armistice celebrations' Topical Press Agency/Getty Images; 'Cenotaph'
Topical Press Agency/Getty Images; 'Flu pandemic' Everett Collection Historical/Alamy;
'Empire Day' Imagno/Getty Images; 'Cable Street' David Savill/Topical Press Agency/
Getty Images; 'Jarrow march' Fox Photos/Getty Images; 'Abdication headlines' Allen/
Topical Press Agency/Getty Images; 'Scout camp' Fox Photos/Getty Images; 'ARP tests'
William Vanderson/Fox Photos/Getty Images; 'War declared' Fox Photos/Getty Images;
'Local Defence Volunteers' Keystone/Getty Images; 'Dunkirk evacuation' Popperfoto/
Getty Images; 'Hawker Hurricanes' Popperfoto/Getty Images; 'Blitz firefighters' Fox
Photos/Getty Images.

Plate section 2: 'Factory worker' Keystone/Getty Images; 'Jean Valentine at Bletchley'
Arthur Edwards/WPA Pool/Getty Images; 'Arctic convoy storm' © Imperial War
Museums (A 14890); 'Desert war' Keystone-France/Gamma-Keystone/Getty Images; 'Von
Thoma surrender' Popperfoto/Getty Images; 'Surrender of Singapore' Paul Popper/
Popperfoto/Getty Images; 'Vera Lynn in Burma' Bill Lovelace/Daily Mail/REX; 'D-Day
landings' Lt. Handford/IWM/Getty Images; 'Butlin's bicycle' Hulton Archive/Getty
Images.

First published by Random House Books in 2015

www.randomhouse.co.uk

A CIP catalogue record for this book is available from the British Library.

ISBN 9781847947468

Typeset by Palimpsest Book Production Limited
Falkirk, Stirlingshire
Printed and bound in Great Britain by Clays Ltd, St Ives plc

Penguin Random House is committed to a sustainable future for our business, our readers
and our planet. This book is made from Forest Stewardship Council® certified paper.

MIX
Paper from
responsible sources
FSC® C018179

Dedicated to Jim Humphries

and in memory of

Lily Ann Elliott (1920–96)
Tom Elliott (1922–2010)
Marjorie Heppelthwaite (1920–2000)
Marjorie Humphries (1924–92)

Contents

Acknowledgements

Our first and most heartfelt debt of gratitude is due to all those who shared their stories and family photographs with us, whether or not they appear in these pages or in the television series which the book accompanies. They are too numerous to mention, but they made this project what it is. Sadly and inevitably given their great age, some of our featured contributors have since died, among them Hetty Bower, Charles Chilton, MBE, Ellen Elston, Major Freddie Hunn, MBE, Russell Margerison, David Mowatt and Donald Overall. We are grateful to the many families who helped us ensure that all these stories were documented.

We would like to thank all the people at the BBC who enthusiastically backed the project from the moment it was pitched: Janice Hadlow, Martin Davidson, Cassian Harrison, Don Cameron, Dawn Cleaver, BBC2 Controller Kim Shillinglaw and Director of BBC Television Danny Cohen. We gratefully acknowledge the hard work, imagination and determination of the talented team who worked on the project at Testimony Films in Bristol. Thanks to David Long for his many original ideas on this subject, and especially to the research team of Emily Sivyer, Pete Vance, Lizi Cosslett, Rebecca Hoskins and Sara Archer, who between them identified and spoke to so many contributors. Producer/editors Nick Maddocks and Andy Attenburrow made a major contribution throughout and we'd like to thank the principal cameramen who filmed much of the series: Michael Sanders, Stephen Brand, Eric Huyton, Nic Cartwright and Richard Cook. We salute Mike Humphries for his superb production management throughout.

Jan Faull at the BFI National Film Archive, Jane Fish at the Imperial War Museum and Paul Davis, Linda Reeve, Kevin Smalley and Nicole Wilkinson at the BBC/Getty Archives provided invaluable assistance on archive matters, and it has been a pleasure to work for the first time with Helen Foulkes, Sharon Hepburn and Caroline Cherry Roberts at BBC Learning, and with Paul Gerhardt, director of education at the BFI, Gemma Starkey and Abby Carswell on the BBC Learning/BFI/Into Film initiative to encourage children to make their own films about the greatest generation. Take 1 Transcription turned round the filmed interviews swiftly and unsung hero Barrie MacDonald compiled the index.

Our special thanks to the editorial and marketing teams at Random House who have given enthusiastic encouragement and valuable guidance from the start, as has our splendid agent, Jane Turnbull. The attentions of Publishing Director Nigel Wilcockson improved the final result immeasurably; any remaining errors or infelicities are entirely our own. Finally, loving thanks to our long-suffering partners Bevan and Sally for their patience and support during this all-absorbing project.

Introduction

This book was completed at the end of the centenary year commemorating the start of the First World War and written in anticipation of the seventieth anniversary of the end of the Second in 2015. The last combatant in the 1914–18 war died in 2009, aged 111; the youngest surviving veterans from 1939–45 and those who also served on the home front are now approaching their nineties. It seems the right time – perhaps the last time – to capture some of their untold stories and celebrate their achievements, not just during the most devastating war of the twentieth century, but also across the following decades and into grand old age.

Although a few of the people who appear in these pages are better known than others, the majority bear only the distinction of living through, and responding to, the most extraordinary of times. They represent the generation born roughly between 1915 and 1925 who endured much, experienced much and built much of the world we know today. They are the last eyewitnesses to, and players in, some of the most momentous events in the history of these islands in the twentieth century. We believe that, as a generation, they deserve recognition and celebration whilst they are still here to tell us first-hand about their lives and to receive our thanks. That's what the BBC series *Britain's Greatest Generation*, made by Testimony Films, and this book set out to do.

When interviewed over the latter half of 2014 (a small number of interviews were held before that), the youngest of our subjects was 89, the oldest 109. Selected primarily for the richness and variety of their personal experiences over eight, nine or ten decades and their ability to tell their stories fluently, they also represent many backgrounds and regions of the UK. Some were already seasoned interviewees; others were talking publicly for the first time. In every case the emotional power of their testimony deeply affected us as interviewers and writers. The interviews, conducted over one or two days and usually in their own homes, often appeared as rewarding for the subject as for us: talking about their lives offered the opportunity to recall happy times and come to terms with former pains. Though the experience could be emotionally draining and there were often tears, our subjects valued the chance to talk at length about times long gone but never forgotten.

Memory, of course, plays tricks on us all. Wherever possible the testimony of these now very elderly people has been checked against authoritative sources. Dates can be notoriously slippery – someone remembered meeting Aneurin Bevan at least a decade after his death – but we came across no substantial 'errors of memory'. The oldest memories often shone the brightest.

Quotes are taken verbatim from interview transcripts, edited only for clarity where necessary. These, with all their idiosyncrasies, not only reveal individual character but carry the bigger story.

So is this really Britain's greatest generation? We believe so. The reader will judge, not only from what follows, but from their own knowledge of people near and dear to them who were part of it. Children of the Edwardian age who grew up in the shadow of one catastrophic war and then had to fight another, they went on to make a post-war world that stretched from the atomic age to the digital age and beyond. They had their faults and their virtues. Without the universal benefits of education and access to limitless information, they were arguably more biddable, more patriotic and less cynical about their leaders than we are today. They put up with more and made do with less. Their lives, marked by hardship, turmoil and danger, nevertheless now seem – to us and to them – so much less complicated than our own.

Of course they may share characteristics born of different times but they are not a homogeneous group; they remain individuals, bound together only by birthdate and by history. They are our parents, our grandparents, our great-grandparents. We should value their experience and learn from it.

For us, as children of Britain's greatest generation, it has been a unique privilege to record their story.

Sue Elliott and Steve Humphries
December 2014

I

Memories of War

1914–1919

I didn't like what I saw. I couldn't have put it into words. I only knew there was something wrong about adults killing each other . . . That doesn't achieve anything except death and sorrow.

Hetty Bower, aged eight in 1914

For no generation of Britons in modern history has war been such a defining feature as in the lives of those born just before, during and soon after the First World War. Those who remember little or were born too late to have known anything about the war itself will nevertheless have had their childhood and adolescence irrevocably shaped by its legacy in the years that followed. War was the formative event of their growing up and, 20 or so years later, of their adult lives too.

Memories from these very early childhoods, related now in old age, are those that have survived a long lifetime. They are necessarily impressionistic, the detail is scant, sometimes apparently trivial, but the impact is always profound: these are the memories that remain embedded even when what happened yesterday or just now escapes too easily into oblivion. Very often they are memories inextricably linked with love and pain. Emotions too deeply felt to be articulated or perhaps even understood, they can only be conveyed through snapshots of events, snippets of conversations, long-remembered songs.

From the very oldest of this generation we have the last eyewitness accounts of the impact and legacy of the First World War, seen through a child's eyes. These are not, of course, the familiar stories of trench horrors or men in action but of families at home waiting for news, struggling to survive, grieving their losses. Among them are strong memories of happy times with loved parents, but early experiences of bereavement, family disruption and disability, hardship and hunger linger long in the memory too. Simple pleasures and the deepest of sorrows mark the child-hoods of this generation and so shape the people they go on to become.

———◆———

In the early years of the war, while the country was still caught up in a mood of patriotic fervour, children took their cue from their parents: war with Germany was an exciting adventure, there was no question that Britain would emerge victorious – probably by Christmas – and those brave fathers who responded to the recruiting propaganda would soon return to them. In the mean-time, there were fascinating new spectacles on the streets to enjoy.

Vera Price was born in Bristol in 1904 into an extended middle-class family. At the age of 109, she recalled seeing men marching off to war in August 1914.

> We had friends who lived in Bath and they were coming over to spend [August] Bank Holiday Monday with us. They had two little boys and my parents had two little girls and we were great friends for years. We went to Temple Meads to meet them from the train. And they were just then sending the army men to Portsmouth by train to go over to France. And I can well remember that on the bridge over platforms one and eight I saw these little white spats on the soldiers going by the trelliswork of the bridge and I was absolutely fascinated by these little things, brilliantly white . . . Oh, I well remember my father saying – the men were all chatting, you know – 'Oh, it's nothing very much. All be over by Christmas.' And of course that was the 4th of August.

Another young girl who watched the men marching away in 1914 was Londoner Hetty Bower. Her Orthodox Jewish family was politically engaged and she took an interest in what was going on around her from an early age.

There's a song that we used to sing:

> Lord Roberts and Kitchener, General Buller and White
> They are the leaders for a terrible fight
> When the war is over, we'll buy a lollypop
> And send it off to Kruger with a Kaiser on the top.

I was nearly nine years old. We were told the schools would be closed as they were going to be used as recruiting centres. Well, we thought that was lovely, not having a school to go to. But it could be very boring, very quickly, and we were damn glad when our schools came back to us and we could go to school once more. I saw men leaving for the front because we passed the railway line at Dalston Junction on our way to school. We were up on the pavement and the railway was down there and we could wave and cheer them.

The pride and excitement of seeing the marching men was dispelled when, as the war progressed, she saw the injured and limbless return to the streets of London.

And then we saw the results of the war when the men came back with trouser leg rolled up because there was no leg to put in it, arm sleeve hanging down because there was no arm. I didn't like what I saw. I couldn't have put it into words. I only knew there was something wrong about adults killing each other when they should be sitting round a table [talking] about what they wanted and what they didn't want. Not killing each other. That doesn't achieve anything except death and sorrow.

Her sense of injustice stirred, Hetty resolved to become a pacifist.

At the outbreak of war Ellen Elston was six and her father was already a regular soldier, a company sergeant major in the East Surrey Regiment. He didn't go straight to the Western Front but started the war training recruits in Kent.

> I remember going with my mother and brother on a visit to see my dad at Dover Castle. Dad had to drill the men and it was exciting to see all the soldiers lined up and our own dad taking them through their paces. We thought that was marvellous, watching through the narrow slits in the wall. Afterwards all the men clustered round him and us: [we] were the sergeant major's kids, and we were carried around the square on the men's shoulders. One or two of the men put their new stiff hats on our heads, and others gave us a few coppers in change, so that we had lots to talk about when we went back to school.

For some of these children, their earliest memories are also some of the most dramatic. John Harrison was born a month before the outbreak of war in Farnborough, Hampshire, where his father held a senior position at the Royal Aircraft Factory. One of his earliest memories, probably in 1917, is of going with his mother to meet his father from work and passing the nearby prisoner-of-war camp where captured Germans were put to work cleaning aircraft engines. And as a young child he would be taken to see the aeroplanes in action:

> My father came home one morning and said, 'We're going to see a brand new aircraft. It's got three wings, it's called the Tarrant. It's a bomber.' We went down there and there was this huge aircraft, with three wings and six engines. It trundled across the grass, lifted off, there was a great roar and it dived straight into the ground. What they didn't know in those days, because they'd got no testing facilities, was that if you put twin props in the front

and four-bladed props at the bottom and turn them on full bore just as you get off the ground, it tilts you up. And that's what it did and killed the two pilots.

Bombing raids by German aeroplanes and Zeppelin airships plagued London and Britain's east coast towns between 1915 and 1917, causing thousands of deaths and injuries. Hetty Bower recalls their rudimentary sheltering arrangements in Hackney:

> The runners would be running down the street shouting, 'Down to the bottom of your houses! Down to the bottom of your houses!' And what good that would have been with a direct hit is nobody's business. But we had a very large mahogany dining table and we used to take our pillows so we had a soft pillow to sit on. My eldest sister's husband had an HMV gramophone which he put on top of that large mahogany table and he would play lovely records in order to drown the anti-aircraft gun . . . It was my first introduction to Beethoven's symphonies.

Despite the havoc and horror they wrought, a Zeppelin airship was a momentous sight that stopped traffic and people in their tracks. Gus Bialick was a very young child being wheeled through the streets of east London by his father, on leave from the army, when they witnessed an extraordinary spectacle.

> In those days there weren't any sirens to warn you of enemy aircraft. There were policemen on bicycles with a megaphone shouting, 'Take cover! Take cover!' And a policeman on a bike came round a corner and shouted, 'Take cover!' and my father was pushing me in a pushchair towards the basement of a house. On the way there he said, 'Look up into the sky!' And there was this Zeppelin in flames drifting slowly over London. It had been shot down. It landed in north London in Barnet. It was an amazing sight because it was drifting slowly but it was ablaze. As a child, it made a great impression on me.

Though Gus, now over 100, remembers this as happening in 1917, it is more likely that he and his father were one of the hundreds of thousands of Londoners to witness the celebrated shooting down of the *L 31* in October 1916. It could be seen for over 35 miles in every direction before it finally came to earth in Potters Bar, just north of Barnet. The hero of the hour was Royal Flying Corps Second Lieutenant Tempest, who buzzed around the giant ship firing his machine gun until his incendiary bullets finally set the Zeppelin ablaze. *The Times* reported 'a gigantic pyramid of flames, red and orange, a ruined star falling slowly to earth. Its glare lit up the streets and gave a ruddy tint even to the waters of the Thames.'

Such acts of conspicuous and possibly foolhardy bravery were widely celebrated on the home front at a time when the news from Flanders was grim and would only get grimmer. Letters home rarely revealed the true rhythm of life in the trenches: hours of boredom and fruitless 'bull' in often appalling conditions interspersed with intense periods of bloody warfare. When fathers came home, the realities of war were unlikely to be shared with wives and sweethearts, much less with children. But there were inevitably occasions when inquisitive ears weren't far from adult conversations. Vera Price remembers one occasion that made a lifelong impression on her.

> My uncle was talking to my father – he must have been on leave from the front. They were talking and I was sitting way back. The war was going terribly badly for us and an order went out that no prisoners should be taken. They had to be shot. Uncle came across a German boy who begged him not to kill him. He was his mother's only son. Uncle said he was nearly in tears himself but he had to kill him, and he rammed the bayonet in. This affected me terribly but I knew I mustn't let it. I felt I just had to accept it.

A visit from a father on leave – even if granted because of an injury – was a rare occurrence, a cause for celebration and an event that even very elderly people remember clearly. Londoner Ellen Elston's father came home on leave in 1916.

In 1916 he was wounded on the Somme and I remember him coming home. We had a gramophone in those days and I can remember him getting me on his knee and singing a song that was very popular then:

> And when I told them
> How beautiful you are
> They didn't believe me!
> They didn't believe me!
> Your lips, your eyes, your curly hair
> Are in a class beyond compare.

Later generations were to become more familiar with the devastating parody of this gentle ballad that accompanies the closing scene of Richard Attenborough's 1969 film *Oh! What a Lovely War*, based on the stage musical of the same name:

> And when they ask us
> How dangerous it was,
> Oh, we'll never tell them,
> No, we'll never tell them . . .

Not all the men who went away were combatants. Bill Frankland's father was a country parson in Cumbria. Bill, born in 1912, was a young child during the war but he remembers clearly his father's coming and going. The fact that he wasn't in the front line made Bill no less proud of his father.

One of my first memories of the First World War was my father going off as a padre. He went to France to begin with and I think he was there for about 18 months. I know my mother was delighted when he came back. I remember him having an injection, I think it was a TB injection, which caused a very sore arm and as a small boy I thought he'd been wounded. He finally went off to Alexandria and later Cairo, where he was in a hospital ship. He used to send these lovely postcards of the Sphinx and the Pyramids and they were very beautiful.

He had what's called a Sam Browne [belt] as an officer, that I inherited and wore at the beginning [of the Second World War] whenever I could, including when I got married. To me, wearing it was carrying on a tradition that there were things worth fighting for. We were told to fight for our country, and this is what we were doing. And I was lucky that I was an officer and so it was to me a privilege to wear something that he had worn in the First World War.

Vera Price's father was a skilled engineer with his own business and, though called up late in the war, he never served abroad. Vera and her siblings were fortunate to have him at home, but they were encouraged to make their own contribution to the war effort by cheering up injured soldiers in Bristol General Hospital.

Some of us girls – we were about 12 years old, I suppose – five or six of us used to go and sing patriotic songs to the men. They were in their blue hospital uniform, and I can remember the looks on their faces and how thrilled they were, that these little children . . . Because they probably all had children of their own . . . That was awfully good, we did that for quite a long time.

She still remembers snatches of the songs she sang: 'Keep the Home Fires Burning', 'It's a Long Way to Tipperary' and 'Pack Up Your Troubles . . .':

> Pack up your troubles in your old kit bag
> And smile, smile, smile!
> What's the use of worrying?
> It never was worthwhile.
> So, pack up your troubles in your old kit bag
> And smile, smile, smile!

Smells are sometimes as powerful as images in the memory: Donald Overall, born in 1913, has a striking memory of his father.

> I remember Dad coming home on leave and he used to sit me on his instep and hold my hands and rock me up and down on his leg in his army uniform. And he smelled of khaki and tobacco because he smoked a pipe. He'd carry me upstairs on his left shoulder and I'd have my head on his shoulder and I remember smelling his khaki uniform and his tobacco.

Much as the War Office letter or telegram was dreaded, uncertainty about the fate of a loved one was worse. The chaos of war and the difficulty of identifying badly damaged or decomposed bodies, compounded by clerical errors and communications problems, meant that some families were left in despairing limbo without a head of the household and without news of him. At a time when it was rare for mothers to work outside the home this made for financial as well as emotional distress. Many families experienced hardship. The lucky survived on charity; the destitute had only the workhouse.

Not all the families who faced hard times were poor and working class. By spring 1917 naval blockades of British merchant ships by German U-boats meant that imported food – which before the war had made up two-thirds of the country's needs by calorific value – was dangerously reduced. Meat, grain, sugar and fats were all in short supply and prices shot up. Even if mothers had the money, the goods often weren't available in the shops. A voluntary rationing scheme proved a dismal failure. Urban families fared the worst: if they couldn't grow their own food or rely on occasional supplies from friends or family in the country, they went hungry. Even middle-class children were sent early to 'bag' a place in long queues outside shops rumoured to have a new consignment in. Vera Price was one of them.

There were big food shortages during the war. We used to hear
– goodness knows how we heard it – but these rumours used to
go round: there'd be margarine at Maypole [grocer's] today and
people used to come from all over Bristol. At six in the morning
they used to send their children into a queue to wait for their
parents until it was time to go to school, when all the parents
turned up, took the places the children were holding and waited,
probably till midday . . . And you were very lucky if you got to
the door and found there was any margarine left.

Enid Wenban also was born into an affluent family in Surrey in
1920 and her father had a reserved occupation with the GPO
during the war, but the impact of food shortages in 1917–18 nevertheless resonated through her family down the years:

My mother used to talk about how awful it was not being able to
get food. She was reduced sometimes to giving my father carrots
on toast for supper. She said if her parents hadn't sent her food
parcels from time to time, she didn't know what she would have
done. There was no rationing till right till the end of the war. You
just couldn't get things. When the Second World War was looming,
my mother started stockpiling tins of food like nobody's business.
It really stuck with her. She talked about it a lot, so it made me
realise what an awful business it was.

If experience of hardship and hunger had a lasting impact, so
surely did the loss of a father. Of the nearly 900,000 military
fatalities in the 1914–18 war, up to a third were fathers. At least a
quarter of a million families were affected. The moment the news
arrived is still a vivid and painful memory for this generation of
war. News of the death of Donald Overall's father arrived in 1917.

I remember this distinctly. Mother opened the telegram, read it,
and collapsed on the floor. What was in the telegram I never knew,
but she collapsed on the floor and I was holding on to her skirt.
I tried to wake her up. I couldn't work out what was wrong . . .

She said, 'Your father's dead, he's not coming back. You'll have to be the man of the house.'

Ellen Elston recalls the moment the news arrived of the death of her sergeant major father and how family life changed for ever:

> I think we nearly forgot we had a dad, we didn't see much of him. Until one Sunday morning a telegram boy came and we thought, Ooh, a message from Dad! All excitement, all clustering round. And it was a telegram for my mother, saying my dad had been killed in action. Mum was upset all the time. I could hear her wandering round the house crying. I suppose she tried to put on a brave face, being the mother of six children. There was a big picture of Dad in a big gold frame, which she turned round to the wall. I suppose she just couldn't bear walking in the room seeing it.

For some children, there were no physical memories of their fathers at all. Charles Chilton was born in 1917 to a father who'd joined up underage, leaving behind a pregnant new wife. He was killed at Arras before he was able to meet his son.

> Reading his letters home, his one ambition was to get back from France in order to see his baby when it was born. And when I was born my mother and grandmother wrote and told him so, and he was eager to get leave. But he never did get leave and so he never saw me.

For young Charles, the excitement of war made more of an impression than the shadowy figure that was his father:

> A man came to our house and said he knew my father, served with him in the Sherwood Foresters. He said he saw my father just a few yards away standing up, and a shell exploded and he was no longer there. Nothing of him was found. Well, I boasted

about it to my friends, I'm afraid. I didn't know my father, I didn't have any feeling for him. All he was was a photograph hanging on the wall. I'd never seen him, touched him. Even my mother never told me much about him.

Death was a commonplace in many families but the grieving process was made more difficult by the absence of the traditional rituals associated with a funeral and burial. All dead combatants, regardless of rank, were interred where they fell on the battlefields of Flanders or in the distant theatres of this first global war. Remains of the dead were not, with rare exceptions, brought home for burial. There were so many, it would have been entirely impractical. In any case, for every body that could be identified and given a named grave in some foreign field, there was at least one other for whom identification could not be made or whose remains were missing altogether. For those fortunate enough to have a grave, the Imperial War Graves Commission, established in 1917, had begun its herculean task but the cemeteries took years to complete and few widows could afford the time or cost of a pilgrimage to a husband's grave.

Bereavement without a body, or without a grave to visit, was doubly painful. Deprived of established ritual, grief could be prolonged, with no recognised public outlet. War widows had to conceal their tears for self-preservation and to set an example of strength for their families and the wider world. Children, who would in peacetime have been involved in family funerals, took the lead from their mothers, feeling unable to show their distress. Ellen Elston, the eldest of six, remembers her special sense of responsibility after the news of her father's death:

Good neighbours would come round and offer their sympathy, feeling sorry for us, bringing us sweets and biscuits to cheer us up. But that was all. In no time at all Mother had made black-and-white-check dresses with a black belt for all the girls, and I can see us now, all walking down the street together and people looking at us because Father was well known in the community. I never cried in front of other people. You are too proud to let people see that things reach you, you are taught that. I wanted to cry, inwardly, but you didn't want anybody to see it, especially being the eldest. I kept everything inside because I daren't let the other children see me break down because they looked up to me, so I waited till I got to bed, and then I had a good cry, just as I'm sure Mum did when she was on her own.

Suppression of emotion, perhaps instilled by a parent or learned at a time when the enormity of loss was so difficult for everyone to comprehend, is a common characteristic of this generation. Once embedded, for good or ill, this enforced stoicism lasted a lifetime.

The loss of a father often meant new responsibilities for the eldest child, even if they were still young themselves. When Donald Overall was told he'd now have to be 'the man of the house', he remembers responding with pride:

> 'What? Me, Mum?' Five years old. I had to stand up and be counted. I did. I did stand up straight because I wanted to be like my father. My younger brother was born and my mother said, 'You've got to look after him. He's your young brother.' I was the man of the house; I was ten feet tall.

Ellen Elston found herself mother to five siblings whilst her own mother went out to work.

> I was only nine and I was looking after the family because I was the eldest. I didn't mind it most of the time. The bit I hated most was when the baby cried. I used to make up what they called a sugar tit – a piece of material with some sugar in – and make a knob and stick it in the baby's mouth hoping that it would suck and be quiet. I'd end up crying as well when the baby cried. It worried me because you didn't really know what to do to make her stop, you didn't know what was wrong.

The kindness of strangers in times of difficulty made an impression on the children who witnessed it. An unknown woman took pity on Ellen and her brother the first Christmas without their father:

> My mother wasn't looking forward to Christmas, was she? I mean, killed in August, the first Christmas with us youngsters. I think she was making mince pies or something and my brother and I went for a walk and we stopped to look in this toy shop, admiring the things you knew you couldn't have. This lady came looking in the window too and she said, 'Why don't you go inside and look? It's cold out here.' So we went inside. She followed us in and all the different things we liked, she bought us! And my brother and I, we had a big bag full of all these lovely things. And she said, 'Now, you go straight home and you tell your mother that you met Mrs Christmas.'

When the war finally ended, it was a time for rejoicing but also for reflection and remembrance. Vera Price has a clear memory of 11 November 1918 as a beautiful day.

> We were all at home and I was making mud pies in the garden for my little brothers and all of a sudden the factory hooters and church bells and anything that will make any kind of noise began raging all over Bristol. I've never heard such a noise in all my life. It was terrific, and I rushed up from the garden, rushed into the door and I said, 'It's the eleventh hour, of the eleventh day of the eleventh month!' And it was . . . everybody was . . . It was wonderful. It really was.

The institution of Armistice Day from 11 November 1919 took on personal significance for hundreds of thousands of bereaved families. On this day they could be part of a communal ritual that allowed them to express their own, as well as a nation's, grief. The return from France of the Unknown Soldier for burial in Westminster Abbey on Armistice Day 1920 was the occasion for the greatest outpouring of mass grief Britain had ever seen. The anonymous remains, selected at random for burial among kings, stood for all 'the Missing': the coffin on the gun carriage could contain any bereaved mother's son or grieving widow's husband. The massed bands, pipes and drums, the gun salute, the slow-march procession escorting the cortège: they all stood for the funeral denied to so many.

Donald Overall was there with his mother on that momentous day. They were in Whitehall, close enough to see the unveiling of the new permanent Cenotaph by the King on the first stroke of 11 o'clock, the signal for the silence. The crowds in this area – 10 and 20 deep, all the women in black, all the men hatless – were mostly there by invitation, allocated in a ballot of the bereaved. The remainder, many of whom had been queuing all night, had been let in at 8.15 a.m. until the allocated space was full and the barriers closed. Even so, many were turned away disappointed. It seems likely from Donald's account that he and his mother were among those fortunate enough to have a personal invitation and therefore a ringside seat at one of the most solemn and significant events of the twentieth century.

> We went up there on that opening day, and we got there early and we were quite close to the Cenotaph and we saw the Unknown Warrior come through on his gun carriage and King George V came out and there was a small service around the Cenotaph and he pulled the string and all the flags dropped down like that, and there was the Cenotaph resplendent in all its glory, far better than what it is today because it was brand new. I just stood there dumbfounded.

And on every Armistice Day that followed, he remembers with tears in his eyes the silence at 11 o'clock being strictly observed.

On the 11th of November, it didn't matter what day of the week it was, everything stopped. Everything. Not even a newspaper blowing across the street. Nobody dared – nobody wanted – to move. And if anybody did move, the crowd would have lynched him. My mother used to stand there, holding us two kids, and I can remember . . . Yes, Christ, I can remember it.

For those born in the years immediately after the 1918 Armistice, the war still cast a baleful shadow, especially for those whose fathers returned with physical or mental injuries. Mabel McCoy was born in 1921 to a middle-class Manchester family. She remembers, as a five-year-old, watching the disabled servicemen in an Armistice Day parade:

It was appalling: some had no arms, some with crutches. And the men with no legs, that was the worst thing because they were on home-made little trolleys with wheels on. On this parade they had this soldier with them pushing them along, and the ones who were blind had a soldier leading them. And they weren't a proper marching column, they were shuffling. There were those who'd been gassed and who looked terribly unhealthy. This small child of five watching this great column of men who'd survived but who'd been terribly injured.

Well into the 1920s reminders of the war were everywhere. Frank Rosier, born in Chelsea in 1925, grew up in a close-knit family on a 'homes for heroes' estate in what was then a poor part of London, close to the Lord Roberts Workshop, a charity set up during the war to employ disabled ex-servicemen.

My father had been in the war and my big uncle Jack had lost a leg. I used to live near a factory where disabled people made furniture; my uncle Jack worked there. We were surrounded by the war – ladies in black walking about, and on the 11th of the 11th it was strictly observed – and if I asked Dad about the war, he'd tell me to shut up, it was such a dreadful war. I can never remember them ever talking about it, but you were surrounded by it. The wounded were treated awfully, put on a little trolley and pushed about.

Mabel McCoy's father had survived without physical injury but not without cost. He'd had a good job in the cotton trade but had joined the Lancashire Fusiliers at the outbreak of war and served until he was demobbed in 1919. The war had affected him in ways that troubled Mabel:

In bed he always slept with the sheets and blankets wrapped completely around his head with just his nose sticking out – I asked my mother about this and she explained to me that it was because he was terrified of the rats he saw during the war. He did a lot of things with me as a child, he'd take me for walks and we'd play word games and number games as we walked. On one of these walks behind our house we were going over a dry ditch and suddenly my father froze. He'd seen a rat down there, in the ditch. He was terrified, absolutely terrified. He recovered himself once the rat was gone. That was a long time afterwards, I would have been about 11, a good 15 or 20 years on from the war.

In common with many fathers returning from a difficult war, it was never spoken of.

It was very difficult for me as a child to understand why my father never spoke about his experiences in the war. My mother never encouraged him to, but I think that was because she had had a soldier upbringing from her soldier father. She understood that my father was traumatised by what had happened to him during his five years in France. But I did realise that when he was extremely emotionally upset he'd want to play his piano.

He came from a musical family. He had a Collard & Collard, very expensive, the best British piano you could buy then. When he came back from the war, he would sit for hours playing, but he tended to like music that was aggressive and noisy. When he was feeling particularly upset or down, he would sit there and play the Beethoven *Appassionata* at full throttle and I think it was his way of getting rid of the frustrations inside him. The music was talking to him, perhaps consoling him.

Striking in these testimonies about the effects on their lives of the First World War is the obvious affection these men and women felt for their fathers even if they were largely absent – or removed altogether – at a formative time in their young lives. Reading between the lines, the influence of strong mothers holding families together through the worst of times kept the memory of absent fathers alive for their children and helped them live with the men who returned, perhaps much changed. The mothers' role in influencing the attitudes, values and fortunes of this generation comes to the fore in the interwar years as they pass through childhood into adolescence.

Some common themes are already emerging: children having to adapt to the dislocation of family life caused by bereavement, disability and financial hardship; learning emotional control; taking on responsibility for others at an early age; appreciating help and giving it in return; dealing with loss, and accepting that life deals blows and isn't always fair. The stoicism, resilience and emotional reticence forged by these early experiences were all to become hallmarks of this generation.

Whatever they understood of the war – and little of substance was passed on at the time by fathers – parents, school and print media instilled in these children a strong sense of nationhood, of belonging in a country at the heart of a great empire of which they should be proud. Public ritual reinforced patriotism and a sense of being part of something bigger than self and family, even if this offered no tangible help in times of trouble. As Charles Chilton recalled: 'Most of us didn't have soles to our shoes and some of us didn't have shirts to our backs, but we were very proud of being British.'

Whether readily articulated, conscious or not, for all those born under its shadow, the 1914–18 war left an indelible mark. They witnessed its aftermath and experienced its devastating effects. These have never been forgotten. As Donald Overall said, when interviewed as a 95-year-old, of a father he hardly knew: 'I missed him as a boy and I miss him as an old man.'

In the following decades there would be many more challenges both personal and national to mould this generation of war.

2

Childhood

1920–1929

We are the King's Cross Boys
We know our manners
We spend our tanners
We are respected wherever we go
Eye-tiddly-eye-tie, eat brown bread
Ever seen a donkey drop down dead?
We are the King's Cross Boys.
        Charles Chilton, aged ten in 1927

While Charles Chilton and his gang marked out their childhood territory in the backstreets of King's Cross, the young Margaret Rhodes was practising her curtsey for the imminent arrival of Queen Mary for tea at her father's Scottish castle. The aftershocks of the First World War still convulsed the adult world in the 1920s: unprecedented political and financial instability, industrial unrest and social upheaval became hallmarks of the decade, though for the moment class divides stayed firmly entrenched. Against this tumultuous background, whether they were growing up in poverty or a palace, this was the time for our generation to form the interests, habits and values that would see them through a lifetime of unique challenges.

At ten, Charles Chilton wasn't yet able to articulate any of the personal characteristics implicit in his gang's anthem, but they are all there: pride, independence, giving and demanding respect, loyalty to friends and community, politeness and obedience but also a cheeky disregard for authority. Like so many children across the class spectrum at this time, he learned them young.

Struggling out of the emotional and financial shadow of the First World War, the period began with the 'Spanish Lady' and ended in the Wall Street Crash, both calamities that left lasting marks on families in Britain, as they did throughout the world. The rabid strain of Spanish influenza killed up to a quarter of a million people in Britain alone; the financial crash in America ruined families, businesses and livelihoods here too. The affluent were not immune to the former and were the most immediate victims of the latter. Money was no bulwark against these two great disasters at either end of the decade.

In between, unemployment, the scourge of the interwar years, was much more likely to affect the working and lower-middle classes. In 1922 the British Legion estimated that at least a million ex-servicemen were unemployed and many had never had a job lasting more than a few weeks since the end of hostilities. Improvements to unemployment insurance and Poor Law 'outdoor' relief had banished the Dickensian conditions of the pre-war period, but if there were no longer homeless urchins and child prostitutes roaming the streets of Britain's big cities, fear of the workhouse still held its grip and poverty characterised many children's lives.

This is not, though, what they most remember. Childhoods, whether materially deprived or affluent, are generally recalled with great pleasure as happy, fun-filled and free, especially when compared with what followed. Play hours were unlikely to be filled with elaborate toys or organised entertainments but they were rich in adventure, discovery and companionship. Carefree days amusing themselves with friends on the streets or roaming the countryside encouraged initiative, self-reliance and physical risk-taking. Children soon learned the limits of their own capabilities through rough-and-tumble experience. If they were warned about 'nasty men' – or were on the receiving end of their attentions – then they seem not to have remembered.

This idyll doesn't always sit comfortably with the facts of many children's lives. The war was over but death was still a frequent visitor to many families. Those diseases and conditions now a distant memory – scarlet fever, diphtheria and tuberculosis among them – were all potential killers. When Matthew MacKinnon-Pattison arrived at Quarriers Homes as an infant he was already critically ill with whooping cough which, together with diphtheria, killed 2,000 children every year. At the age of three, Jim Purcell in Jarrow had rheumatic fever and was given a week to live. Bill Frankland had TB as a child and was so unimpressed with the doctor who attended him that he resolved to become a much better one as soon as he grew up.

Well before the arrival of a comprehensive free health service, when health insurance was rudimentary and only accessible to working men with a reasonable wage, medical attention was beyond the reach of most families, so they self-medicated with quack remedies, patent medicines or alcohol. Sometimes the cure was simple and natural. John Harrison suffered from chronic asthma until he started skinny-dipping in a local pond.

> After two summers my parents found out and I got a thrashing. And I said, 'Well, wait a minute, I didn't get asthma last winter or the winter before.' They said, 'That's right,' talked among themselves and sent me for swimming lessons. And that was the start of my swimming, with a costume!

The wartime deaths of fathers were no less sad for being portrayed as heroic, but they were at least at arm's length. In the years that followed the war, children were likely to have experience of the dead and dying much closer to home. Vera Price was already in her teens when the flu epidemic took hold of the country in the months immediately following the Armistice. Despite her sheltered middle-class upbringing, this brought Vera face to face with death for the first time.

> The baby daughter of a friend of an aunt of mine died, and I was invited to see her little corpse, which my mother was very against my seeing. But my aunt thought it would be a very good thing

for me to see her and my mother gave in and allowed me to see this lovely baby who was nine months old I think, still very much a baby-in-arms. And she was lying on a deep purple velvet cushion and I thought I'd never seen anything so beautiful in the whole of my life. And ever since then, I've never been afraid of death.

Even young children were aware of 'the Great Flu': John Harrison recalls, as a boy not yet five, the 'big black horses' drawing the vans that came round to collect the dead.

They stopped [coming] and I said, 'Where are the horses now, Dad?' He said, 'The grave diggers and the funeral people are all dead. There's nobody to bury the bodies.' And that was a bit of a shocker because my friends went. When the schools did open there were a heck of a lot of spare places, it was that vicious. A class of 30, half or more would be dead.

My mother had heard years before that elderberry tea was good for the fever . . . so we cycled to Farnham, gathered all the blossoms we could of elderberry, brewed up the tea and drank it twice a day. We sweated all night, but we didn't get the flu. And as I say, about half the classes were empty when we did eventually get back to school. It was a very traumatic time, but it didn't register at a young age quite as it does now, thinking about it.

Childbirth and infant-rearing were routinely high risk, especially in working-class households. Deaths in childbirth had remained virtually unchanged since 1900. With the introduction from 1917 of infant welfare centres, infant mortality rates improved but families continued to be decimated by premature deaths. Russell Margerison, born in 1924, should have been one of six children.

I grew up in the backstreets of Blackburn, Lancashire, a very poor family, very poor. My father and mother had six children, three of whom died in the flu epidemic before I was born. I only knew one of them because another also died in my childhood, and then the other one died at 19, so I'm the only surviving member of my family. I can't tell you why this was and how they suffered. I suppose, in fairness, my parents kept it from me. My brother, who was five years older than me, he wasn't too well for a few years. I used to push him around in a wheelchair so I knew he was poorly, but I never knew what the matter was. At the end he became completely paralysed and that night he died. It was very hard losing a brother and him being the only one I knew.

Later the same year, Russell lost his beloved mother.

My mother died at 40. She had a very, very hard life. She seemed to spend all her life working, working, cleaning steps and washing flags, as they used to do in Lancashire. Whenever I walked in I'd never fail to get a wink or a smile from her, she was a lovely person, and I don't remember ever seeing her without her dust hat or apron, but she always had time for affection and love. I missed my mother tremendously.

Many children saw the burdens placed on mothers and the sacrifices made to care for others: these were practical manifestations of love that made a deep impression. They saw the struggles of hard-pressed fathers too, and parental responses to love and loss were also noticed and internalised. If there was hardship at home it was borne stoically: children knew no different.

The home life of the poorest, though cheerfully borne, was grim. Charles Chilton, born to a father killed at Arras, started and ended his childhood in poverty in King's Cross tenements. His mother was young enough and fortunate enough to find another husband, but this only made their living conditions worse:

My mother worked very hard to keep me and herself and of course when she married again she had two more children. So now we were five living in one room. No bath, no running water. If you wanted water you had to go down to the yard at the back and fill up a bucketful. This was normal life for me, I didn't think anyone else lived differently, but we were overcrowded, I remember it was a room full of beds and we had to sit on the beds to eat our meals.

Meanwhile, in cheap lodgings just behind the London Hospital in Whitechapel, Gus Bialick, born in 1914, was growing up part of this poor, racially mixed and sometimes volatile neighbourhood. His Jewish father had fled from persecution in Poland, his sights set on America. Instead, in 1905 he arrived in the Port of London without funds, friends or spoken English, part of an illicit cargo of immigrants bribing their way from Rotterdam. Like so many desperate new arrivals, he made his way to the East End, where the existing dockland community of Irish poor was gradually giving way to the new Jewish influx.

We lived in two rooms in a house in Newnham Street, which isn't there any more. My father worked in a wholesale costumiers in the workshop. My [maternal] grandparents lived at one end of the street and we lived at the other. Every time I fell out with my mother I would run to my grandmother. In her eyes, I never did any wrong and I was always right! But there was a great deal of poverty. There were soup kitchens organised by the community. I think the Rothschilds contributed quite a lot of money arranging for things like that. The majority of people were really poverty-stricken. Families had eight, nine children often. Once a year at Easter time, money was contributed by the Rothschilds to arrange for the poor boys in my school, the Jews' Free School, to have new clothes and they consisted of the same material every year. It was called Derby cloth – a grey, black and white material – and everybody knew who the poverty-stricken students in the school were by the type of clothes they wore.

The Bialick family were better off than most: father Isaac had a steady job as a skilled machinist and only left when his employers tried to reduce his pay and he decided to set up his own business. While he was getting established life was hard but he worked all hours and after a few years things got better. Life around them, however, changed little. The young Gus was much influenced by reading Dickens in the local library, and Hogarth's famous print *Gin Lane* also struck a chord with him.

> He shows you the dissolute women, their clothes in disarray after they'd drunk gin, which was so cheap, and there was a lot of drunkenness at that time. That affected my attitude towards the general population. I tell you why. Where I lived in the East End there was a lot of drunkenness and I saw fighting amongst men. In those days there were fist fights and the men were so drunk that they used to fall down at the end of the fight and lie in the gutters. The police would come along, with their flatbed trolleys, pick them up and wheel them to Leman Street police station and they'd come before the magistrates in the morning. I saw a lot of that. In fact I learned the facts of life at a very young age in the East End, I would say, amongst the foreign sailors that used to come in, in the ships in the Pool of London, almost every day. There was drunkenness, prostitutes, fighting – mostly at the weekends when the dockers got their wages. But life was like that.

Life in the Tyneside shipbuilding town of Jarrow, later to become the most potent symbol of Depression-era unemployment, was hard even for families where the breadwinner was in work. There in 1921 Jim Purcell was born, much loved, into a poor family.

> I was the oldest. I didn't have a pram because we couldn't afford it. We stayed in the back bedroom and I slept in a drawer, then when my brother came along, he slept in the drawer and I slept at the foot of my mam and dad's bed. They were really hard up but they tried hard to keep going. Dad used to mend our boots, when he could afford the leather. Sometimes we couldn't go to church because we had no shoes to put on.
>
> There was a second-hand shop that would sell shoes, but there might be a hole in the sole, so you'd have to scrunch up newspaper

and stick it in the shoe, but if it rained it wasn't too nice. When we couldn't afford shoes or boots we went without. It did toughen up your feet. We were walking on blinking concrete so our feet got hard, and our feet used to crack and we'd call this a stone bruise. You'd be walking along and there'd be tarmac and this dust that if you walked over it and you got a bit of that dust in the cracks in your feet you jumped like mad in the air. There was no refuse bins then, so people would throw their cigarettes on the ground – if you walked on one of those! But sometimes you'd find a spent match and you could use it to get the stuff out from the cracks in your feet. It was rough, I'll tell you now, it was really tough, but everybody being in the same boat, there was no animosity between anyone.

Poverty wasn't just an urban problem. On the Norfolk coast Freddie Hunn, born in 1919, the middle child of seven, lived with his parents and widowed grandmother. His father was a skilled man, a ship's engineer who would work on the boats in Great Yarmouth's dry dock when work was available, which wasn't often.

I slept in the attic with my three brothers, all in the same bed, three at the top and me across the bottom. The sheet wasn't white and there were bedbugs. We had a very basic diet: toast and marge for breakfast, stew and dumplings for lunch and bread and jam for dinner. If the cake shop was selling stale goods cheap, that was a treat. Summer and winter I'd wear a vest and jersey, a pair of short trousers, long socks and shoes with cardboard inside to cover up the holes. In the herring season we'd go down the town docks with a bag and pick up all the herring dropped from the baskets on to the floor and bring them home. That was wintertime and my hands would be chapped with the cold. The salt water from the fish made them sting like hell . . . This I used to do at least twice a week. I didn't put it down as a chore, I thought I was doing good, it was bringing food in and I never gave another thought to it.

Another country boy, George Montague, was born in 1923 and grew up in a tied cottage on a private estate in rural Buckinghamshire.

> We were, in today's standards, extremely poor. My father . . . managed to get a job as a gardener in this huge country estate and Mother managed to get the job as a laundress. Now we lived in an extremely primitive cottage joined on to the laundry. No bathroom, no proper kitchen, two little bedrooms, no toilet inside the house. We had to walk outside to go to the toilet and empty the bucket when it was full.

Children weren't usually aware of how others lived outside their immediate circle, so they never thought about being either rich or poor. They accepted their lot without comment or complaint because they knew no other. 'I thought everyone lived like us' was a common recollection. Often it was only in adulthood that those from impoverished backgrounds realised – or were told of – their disadvantage. Gladys Parry, who grew up in the back-to-back terraces of Hulme, a poor district of Manchester, only discovered she was poor in court when another woman stole her purse:

> And this is how I came to know I was poor. I didn't know until then. There was this magistrate on the bench and she was saying, 'How could you steal off these poor people?' And I thought to myself, That's me! I'm not poor! Not realising in a way, yes I was. But you didn't class yourself as poor. You just got on and did what you had to do.

At the time, Kit Sollitt never considered her family to be poor. Her father used to have his own small steel-grinding business in Sheffield, but they'd come down in the world after he caught a debilitating skin disease from working with metals. But they had her mother's fish-and-chip shop, a roof over their heads, were tidily dressed and had a bath once a week in front of the fire. There were others far worse off – and dirtier. Kit would have liked proper shoes, though: in the summer they all wore 'running slippers', and in the winter 'wellies'. Born in 1919, one of eight, she got little of her mother's attention.

> When you're in a large family, you're just one of a number. I can only remember my mother kissing me twice in my life, and that's true. There were so many, she'd get your name wrong – she'd go down about three names before she got to you.

After her mother's death, Kit realised what a 'walking wonder' she'd been to cope with eight children, an invalid husband and the family business. Only much later did children reflect on the relative poverty of their young lives – at the time it was all they knew. Loving parents were all that really mattered then. Children with hard-working mums and dads in a strong marriage learned that security and happiness depended not on material comforts or even enough to eat, but on an instinctive resourcefulness, enjoyment of simple pleasures, and a firm sense of belonging to family and community.

The home was where early moral values were instilled. Bill Frankland learned one important lesson from his parson father that would save him much distress later in life:

> I think I was six or seven. My twin brother had done something which annoyed me a great deal, I can't now remember what it was. We each had our own little garden to grow things and he was growing strawberries and I stamped on these strawberries. My father saw me and said, 'Why are you doing this?' And I said, 'Because I hate my brother. I hate, hate, hate him!' My father said, 'You must never hate anyone. If you hate anyone, it does *you* harm but it doesn't do any harm to the person you hate. If countries didn't hate each other there wouldn't be war.' I remember him giving me almost this little sermon about hate. He said, 'No. Christians love, love, love and that's what you must do: love.'

Children without parents to guide them had a harder hill to climb; they had to find love and security where they could. In the first half of the twentieth century thousands of unwanted children – the homeless, orphaned or illegitimate – lived in homes run by charities like Dr Barnardo's. If they weren't in charitable institutions they came under the care of local Boards of Poor Law Guardians and lived in workhouses or were 'boarded out' with families. In Scotland in the interwar period, over 9,000 children were under Poor Law protection; many more lived in voluntary institutions.

Matthew MacKinnon-Pattison, born in 1924, was orphaned as an infant. His mother died in childbirth and his father died two years later, putting his future in the hands of the Orphan Homes at Bridge of Weir outside Glasgow. At the time, Quarriers Homes, as it became known after its founder William Quarrier, was one of the largest voluntary institutions for children in Scotland. It accommodated up to 1,500 orphaned, destitute and sick children at any one time in a 'children's village' containing a school, hospital, church and 'cottages', each housing up to 30 girls or boys. A Christian couple acted as house-parents and the children called them Mother and Father.

> When I went there I was a year and 11 months and I couldn't walk or talk. The couple that looked after me came from Cumbria. She'd been a nurse and she nursed me though measles, chickenpox, diphtheria, the lot. I had the bundle, so naturally they grew close to me. We had boys coming and going all the time. Some had been taken away from their family by the police, others were abandoned. I looked upon the house-parents as my real parents, because I knew no different. Home is where you grow up, it's where love is.

Fred Glover would agree with that. Born in 1923 in the Kentish Weald, Fred had no idea who his natural parents were. He was informally adopted by another couple as a baby before legal adoption was made possible in 1926. His adoptive mother had lost her

first husband on the Somme; her second had been gassed in the
war.

> He died when I was seven and to everybody's amazement they
> had a gun carriage there. I ran along behind the cortège all the
> way to the cemetery. It was after that things were tough. My
> mother had a very hard time because her pension was pitiful of
> course, so she had to go out to work in a laundry. When I think
> of it now, bringing up four children, I don't know how she managed
> it. And yet we seemed to be happy.

The highlight of the year was their working holiday in the Kentish
hop-fields, where the children slept on straw in barns and went
scrumping in local orchards. Despite the hardship and frequent
'moonlight flits' from a series of rented rooms, Fred grew close
to his hard-working foster mother.

> Did I bother to trace my biological parents? The simple answer is
> no, because my mother saved me from an orphanage and gave
> me an upbringing and I didn't want to lose her.

The contrast with those who grew up in materially affluent or
privileged homes could not be more acute. Diana Athill, born in
1917 and the eldest of three, spent blissful holidays on her grandparents' Norfolk estate at Ditchingham where there were 'horses,
ponies, everything you wanted, and you felt it all belonged to
you'. The source of the family's wealth was mysterious: perhaps
it had come from land sold to build railways in the previous
century. It was considered vulgar to probe too deeply but there
were intriguing clues.

> Mother told me that when they went up to Yorkshire, Gramps
> had a little key on his watch chain that meant that he could stop
> a train at any station he wanted, so he must have been a major
> shareholder in the railways or something.

Life was extremely comfortable, though this wasn't to last and home life was potentially problematic for Diana and her siblings: their parents were ill-suited and did not have a happy marriage.

> You made the best of it in those days, but there was an underlying tension in their marriage and as children we felt it, though of course we didn't know what it was. This could have ruined our childhood. It didn't because we had the advantage of living in biggish places with lots of lovely people around us – nannies and servants and lovely people who liked us – like a buffer state around us. We could escape quite easily.

The life of a young girl growing up in 'the last days of a long-lost world of seemingly unassailable privilege' was of a different order again from those of comfortable upper-middle-class families like Diana's. The Honourable Margaret Rhodes was born in 1925, the youngest daughter of the 16th Lord Elphinstone, and spent much of her childhood at the family's Scottish estate outside Edinburgh, the perimeter of which she discovered took two hours to perambulate. Here it was de rigueur for house guests to change their outfits three times a day, shooting parties on the grouse moors received silver-service luncheons from liveried butlers, and Queen Mary came to tea.

Margaret was intimately connected to the royal family through her aunt, Elizabeth Bowes-Lyon, later Duchess of York. Her aunt became Queen Elizabeth when George VI came to the throne following Edward VIII's abdication in 1936. The Princesses Elizabeth and Margaret Rose were her first cousins and among her closest childhood companions on the long summer holidays at Birkhall, her aunt's Scottish home.

Even so, the family weren't untouched by the 1929 Crash and her father had to give up their London house 'because something happened to Swedish matches'. But Margaret remembers that 'very little of it actually permeated to the nursery, though I do remember notices up all over the house saying "Turn Off the Lights"'.

The hardships, such as they were, of a life of privilege were very different from those of other children. Scottish castles were cold and draughty, protocol had to be strictly observed (as Margaret discovered when she fluffed her kiss-and-curtsey routine with Queen Mary) and it was a matter of luck whether your parents took much interest in your welfare or upbringing. This was a job for nannies and governesses.

Parents were relatively remote compared to now, I suppose. On the whole one was dressed in one's best party dress and one was taken down at teatime by Nanny and you stayed down until six or six thirty when Nanny came to fetch you and you went back up and had supper and to bed.

Whether conveyed explicitly by parents or servants, the children of upper and middle-class families were acutely conscious of the values and standards expected of them. Despite having a wealthy family, Diana Athill knew 'you weren't supposed to be silly, vain, boastful or show off'. Physical courage was valued, as was the ability to cheerfully withstand the cold. Attributes instilled by her mother included politeness, cleanliness, honesty, aspiring to be good through willpower and self-control, and the 'good Christian values' of treating thy neighbour as thyself, turning the other cheek and not being obsessed with material possessions.

Being British was important. As a child, Diana felt sorry for the French and people from other countries because Britain was 'the best country in the world'. This was reinforced by maps showing large areas of the world salmon pink, something mentioned by many of this generation. This pride and strong sense of belonging gave confidence and self-assurance. On the other hand, she also learned 'the English way' of dealing with unpleasantness of any kind: 'If my family didn't like something, they just wouldn't talk about it,' a bitter lesson she determined not to put into practice in her own life.

Values imbibed in chilly Scottish castles have lasted Margaret Rhodes a lifetime:

I was brought up very much to consider that unless one went out and did something constructive in the afternoon, one was being a bit amoral. [My parents] always cited a family they knew whose children stayed indoors and read the *Tatler* and I can't remember what the other things were they disapproved of, but that sort of thing. We were always pulling up ivy or making bonfires. My generation grew up to be obedient, respectful and also tough.

Obedience was a common requirement across the class spectrum. For large families in cramped accommodation it was essential if chaos was to be avoided; in middle-class homes it more likely reflected the strict upbringing parents themselves had experienced. Enid Wenban grew up in the leafy suburbs of south London.

Mother had a very Victorian upbringing and she was a bit like that with me. 'You'll do as you're told. There's nothing worse than a disobedient child,' she used to say. Spare the rod and spoil the child. I did feel this was unfair at the time. They were always there, and we were taken out, but there was no outward show of affection. And in those days, of course, adults didn't show affection in public to each other, let alone to their children.

Of course, children weren't entirely biddable all the time: naughtiness and an independent streak are evident in many testimonies, but it is also apparent that these children soon learned which rules were inviolable and which could on occasion be bent. Punishment for transgressions was harsh by modern standards. Matthew MacKinnon-Pattison recalls how the belt was in use at Quarriers Homes:

a long strip of leather with a split up the front of it. And if you didn't behave yourself or you did something wrong: 'Hold out your hand,' and belt, belt, belt. That wasn't necessarily exclusive to Quarriers, and it didn't happen all the time. They weren't sadists. It was only done when you stepped out of line.

In many families, like Enid Wenban's, it was the mother who dispensed discipline; fathers were more likely to be apart from their children for much of the time and so be inclined to indulge them when they came home.

My father was one of eleven and he was a very tolerant man. Mother was the disciplinarian but my father ameliorated this. A lot of my father's enthusiasms rubbed off on me: the natural world, gardens and gardening. He was a great example. We used to go out catching butterflies.

In Manchester, Mabel McCoy came from a similar background and had a similar experience of sharing delight in the natural world with her father. Despite his mental fragility, she felt a close relationship with him but, as in many middle-class families of the time, this was not a tactile one.

We used to go on walks together and he was always very helpful to me in pointing out flowers and birds and natural things. I can remember him taking me to a place near Rochdale and we were lying on a hillside watching the skylarks. We had such a rapport, but he was of the age when you kept things to yourself. There were no hugs and kisses. My father would walk along with me, but wouldn't hold my hand except perhaps when we were crossing the road. But we had this great understanding of each other.

Parents were rarely demonstrative except with their very young children and constant protestations of love would have been considered unnecessary, showy or vulgar. The absence of outward demonstrations of affection seems not to have caused children to doubt that they were loved, nor diminished the love and respect many felt – and still feel – for their parents in return.

There is another explanation for this apparent lack of warmth in families where the daily grind of paying the rent and putting food on the table was the major preoccupation. Joan Wilson describes her lower-middle-class childhood in Croydon in the 1920s:

They were good, law-abiding people but it wasn't a warm family life. We were well fed and comfortable but not close. There was no physical contact and no confidences. We didn't sit down and chat, perhaps because of lack of opportunity. It was a typical family then. People were concerned about just living.

———◆———

In an age of deference to one's betters, social class mattered. Divisions between and within classes were sharply defined, particularly in the status-conscious suburbs. Jimmy Perry, born into a middle-class family in 1923, who went on to write *Dad's Army* and a string of other popular class-based comedies for the BBC, claims that the first word he learned after 'Mummy' and 'Daddy' was 'common' because his mother used it so much. In a defining moment of his childhood, he was reprimanded for helping a boy drag driftwood from the Thames, near to where he lived.

> Everything went back to class. There was a boy, an urchin with scanty clothes, toes through his shoes, dragging a wet sack of wood. 'Mister! Gi's a hand with this?' I helped this boy along to the end of the road towards the slightly inferior areas of Barnes where he lived. He said, 'Thanks, sir!' A little boy. Never forgotten it. When I told my mother, 'Oh!' she said, 'that was dreadful! You might have caught something from him!'

Jimmy also remembers a general election – probably in 1929 or 1931, soon after universal suffrage – when his aunt was visiting. Their maid came into the room to tell Mrs Perry she was going off to the polling station. When she'd gone, his aunt was outraged: 'Vote? A servant girl? No business to be allowed! Somebody should do something!'

In the countryside landowners held sway. Joy Lofthouse, born in 1923, grew up outside Cirencester where she recalls the lord of the manor throwing his uneaten sandwiches to the village children on his way back from the hunt. Here, even minor authority figures demanded respect. If you went to the village school as Joy did, 'you practically saluted' the local policeman, the schoolmaster and the vicar. George Montague, growing up beholden to the landed gentry on a country estate, learned to resent his parents' masters:

> My father had to touch the peak of his cap every time he saw them. We children had to make ourselves scarce, to be seen and not heard, or not even seen when the gentry walked round with their children. We lived in a tied cottage, right? Which meant that if either my mother or father got the sack, within one week we'd be homeless. So that was it. I hated them.

There were racial distinctions too, though few children were aware of them at the time. Like many city communities, London's docklands were tight-knit. They were also full of immigrants. Sid Graham, born in 1920, grew up in Canning Town with his English mother and Barbadian father. Though he experienced discrimination later, he recalls none in his childhood: 'Africans, West Indians, Chinese, everybody got on.' In nearby Limehouse, London's nineteenth-century Chinatown, Connie Hoe was born in 1922 and spent her first eight years with her English mother and Chinese father. The opium dens of old Limehouse had long gone and the area was more racially mixed, but the community was still close.

> Everybody knew everybody else and we were like one big family. If your friend was called in for their dinner, you went with them and just sat down at the table and ate with them. You shared everything. Shared their worries and their happiness. No friction at all. I can't remember anybody being aggressive or being racist, not at school or at home.

Nevertheless, Connie attracted the attention of the British Eugenics Society and was given an IQ test. In the 1930s it was widely believed that some races were intellectually, morally or physically superior to others, and proponents of these eugenic theories proposed that 'defectives' should be eliminated by selective breeding.

I was told to go to this place, this Chinese restaurant, where they had a room upstairs. In those days when you were told to do something, you did it. There were these two English ladies and they measured my face and neck and took details of my appearance and intellect. The outcome of it was that they found the children of mixed race were more intelligent than the other children they examined!

When Connie was eight in 1930, her mother died of meningitis. Soon afterwards her father returned to Hong Kong for a family bereavement and never came back. Connie was left in the charge of a childless neighbour:

I just moved from number 41 to number 12. Nobody asked any questions, no social services, no vetting to see if Auntie Kitty was suitable. However, she must have been because I lived with her until the war broke out.

Though she had lost her family, she remained curious about her Chinese heritage.

Auntie was very Victorian, very British, and I felt very British but I had black hair with a fringe and everybody used to say how I was like the Chinese-American film star Anna May Wong . . . I read every book in the library about China but most of the books were written by missionaries that had retired so they were writing about China [long ago]. I wanted to know about it, but there was no one to ask . . . I was quite proud to be Chinese. I still am.

———◆———

If behaviour was strictly regulated at home, children had a degree of freedom outside the home unimaginable today. Despite having to kowtow to the estate gentry, when George Montague was off the leash he could revel in the countryside all around him, make his own adventures and, strongly influenced by Baden-Powell and the Scouting movement, practise fieldcraft.

It was a wonderful childhood because it was deep in the countryside. Mother said to me one morning, 'Oh dear, Daddy's not well and we've got nothing for dinner.' So I didn't tell Mother, I didn't tell anyone. I knew where Dad kept the gun and cartridges and I went out into the park – I'd been out with my father many times – and I went upwind so that the rabbit didn't smell me, and I waited and waited very quietly and I shot this huge great rabbit. Took it back, gave it to Mother. One of the proudest moments of my life, I was only 12, maybe 13, at the time.

Even young girls of eight or nine could be out all day, playing alone or with friends, so that the mother could do her housework, and be required only to be 'back for tea', as Enid Wenban remembers:

There was a certain freedom in those days, children could go out and play and we'd go out cycling. This made me adventurous, I've always liked taking up a challenge. On holiday on my aunt's farm in Devon I could run wild, but even in Purley I could go out on my bicycle without necessarily being asked where I was going. Life was fairly free and easy.

Fergus Anckorn, born in 1918, describes his idyllic childhood growing up in Kent as 'heaven on earth'.

I don't think it could have been much happier. Of course, at that time I didn't realise how happy I was. It was normal for me. I loved the countryside. I knew the names of all the plants, I could go out and pick mushrooms and know which ones I could eat and which ones I couldn't. If I heard a bird singing I knew which bird it was and if I found a bird's egg I knew who'd laid it. I was always happy in my own company. I could spend all day wandering around on my own with my doggie, so it made me quite independent of the rest of the world. Every day was a lovely day for me, so I lived my little life on my own and I didn't know there was anything nasty in the world.

Play was invariably outdoors unless the weather was bad, and the simplest pleasures entranced even the most privileged of children. Margaret Rhodes loved her annual visit to stay with her aunt and cousins at Birkhall on the Balmoral estate, where she and Princess Elizabeth 'used to play a lot of being horses. We galloped round and round fields and neighed and pranced and did all the things that horses do.' (At night, though, she remembers being kept awake by Princess Margaret Rose in the next room singing 'Old Macdonald Had a Farm'.)

For urban working-class children like Charles Chilton and Gus Bialick, the streets were their playground. Improvised hoops, tag and chasing games, and races with home-made trollies filled the empty roads. Kit Sollitt, born in Sheffield in 1919, played all the usual street games with her siblings: hide-and-seek, shuttlecocks, whip-top. But there was another more intriguing source of entertainment:

> Opposite was a pub with windowsills we could climb on and look in. And once a week it would be for men dressed up as women. I'll always remember it. There were quite a few in Sheffield. And we used to watch their antics in this pub. They were singers. There'd be a piano and they used to come in taxis every Thursday. Well, it was amazing for us . . . they'd wear feathers and all sorts. We couldn't hear what they were singing, but that were our Thursday-night enjoyment.

This was a time for the introduction to interests that would last a lifetime. When Fergus wasn't enjoying the countryside he was entertaining his parents and brother and sisters with magic tricks. His father, a Fleet Street journalist, had given him a simple box of tricks for his fourth birthday. From then on, he was fascinated by magic. Every birthday he would get a new box and his pocket money would go on new and more complex tricks to perform for family and friends.

Charles Chilton's passion was music. His stepfather worked in a piano shop in London's Euston Road.

They also sold gramophones, so we had a gramophone with a big horn and lots of records, and one of my earliest memories is listening to these records, memorising them and then performing them. We sometimes didn't have enough to eat, but we always had music.

In the 1920s, well before the age of television when even the 'wireless' wasn't in every home, families made their entertainment around the piano. John Harrison's parents were both musical and encouraged his piano-playing as well as his swimming. By 1919 he was performing in churches and village halls around his Farnborough home.

My father used to take me, sitting on his bicycle crossbar to the concerts. It was quite interesting, but bloody cold coming back at night on the front of a bike.

Vera Welch, born in 1917, started her own musical performances young:

I grew up in East Ham, in the Working Men's Club. It was the social life around the club, it's all we had in those days, so I started singing there when I was seven. Dad was a member of the organisation of the affiliated clubs so he had free access to go in any of the clubs. So I used to go with [Mum and Dad] and sing at their concerts. I never had a lot of friends because at weekends I used to be busy singing.

When at the age of 11 she started working with Madame Harris's Kracker Kabaret Kids, Vera Welch adopted a new, more mellifluous stage name: Vera Lynn was on her way.

———◆———

There were other diversions. Long before they reached adolescence, an interest in the mysterious world of sex started to grip

some children. Diana Athill was a bright inquisitive child, determined to get to the bottom of the mystery.

My mother always rather held it against *her* mother that she hadn't
been taught the facts of life, and felt that we should be taught
them but she didn't quite feel brave enough to do it herself. So
she let me read anything and everything. She had a little book by
Marie Stopes called *Wise Parenthood*. I found this in the bookcase
and opened it and lo and behold it was a book teaching people
about contraception. In the course of telling them, it gave very
detailed descriptions of sexual intercourse and little diagrams of
vaginas and things. I read this spellbound from end to end. It
dawned on me, *this* is what it's all about! Marie Stopes was very
high-minded so there was a lot about how beautiful it all was if
you really loved someone, so I took that in as well.

Later, there was another source of knowledge. Grandfather had
an enormous and wonderful library. Grandmother insisted on
spring-cleaning it every year, she went through every book, dusting
and polishing. I was with her as she did this in the smoking room.
There were three vellum-bound volumes with 'Ballads' on the
spine. I thought, Oh, ballads, it would be good to be admired
reading something so serious, so I reached out for one and she
said, 'Oh no, you wouldn't be interested in that one,' and of course
I was on to it absolutely in a flash, so later on I nipped in, picked
one up and it was the most wonderful collection of bawdy ballads.
That was a revelation because not only did it tell you exactly what
happened but it made it all great fun. So I was a pretty well-
informed 12-year-old by the time I got there. I had nothing left to
learn.

Unlike the precocious Diana, the majority of children were
ignorant of the facts of life. Hetty Bower was one of ten, so
pregnancy and childbirth were a regular occurrence at home. But,
contrary to what she'd been told there, babies were not delivered
in the doctor's black bag.

I had no knowledge of sex. There was a girl in our class who was telling stories. The doctor that came to Mum didn't carry the baby in the black bag, the baby came from the mum. 'What do you mean?' 'The baby was inside her and then it came out.' That was whispered information that went through our class when we were about eight. 'Your mum and your dad, they're together in bed and then soon after that the baby comes.'

Boys were no better informed. Teachers and churchmen favoured stern warnings about the physical and moral dangers of 'spilling your seed' and 'draining your body of precious fluids'. Jimmy Perry took these warnings seriously and recalls resolving to limit himself to 'two wanks a week with an extra one at holiday times'. George Montague decided to ignore them altogether.

Every boy did it. I don't know any boy that didn't. Baden-Powell said a Boy Scout shouldn't, it was only a street-corner yobbo who'd do that sort of thing. And I thought to myself, No, B.-P., on this point you're wrong. You might as well tell me to stop going for a pee as to stop what we were doing. So I never did.

————◆————

It would be wrong to say that by the time they approached adolescence this generation was well on the way to forming a unique character of its own. However, among their disparate personalities and backgrounds a particular combination of values, characteristics and experiences stands out: love and respect for parents as models for their own adult lives; the importance of family ties; intimate acquaintance with hardship, suffering and loss; a delight in freedom and independence; and, for all but the most urban children, a love and appreciation of the natural world.

Personal qualities of courage, initiative, obedience, honesty and fairness seeded by parents would continue to be encouraged at school, in church and by youth organisations as they left childish pursuits behind and prepared for adulthood. Pride in being British and a clear sense of their own position in the world were already firmly rooted; for some, a growing political awareness would take them in character-forming new directions. In the confusion of adolescence and in an uncertain world tumbling headlong towards another war, all of these qualities would be called on.

3

Growing Up

1930–1939

Because things were so difficult in the Depression, you had to be interested in new ideas. The fascists thought they had the answer to poverty, the communists thought they had the answer. We happened to be teenagers in the middle of it all.

Gus Bialick, 16 in 1930

'The really *bloody* thing about being poor,' Diana Athill's mother told her after having to lose her indoor staff, 'is that if you leave something on the floor when you go out, you know that when you get back it will still be there.'

Struggle and sacrifice were a novel experience for some in the Depression years, business as usual for millions of others. If the 1920s held out the promise of slow but steady recovery, the 1930s presented an altogether darker face. For the generation reaching adolescence and launching into their adult lives in this dangerous decade, these were watershed years. Values and habits learned in childhood were reinforced by family, church and state, but for the first time there was the chance – sometimes the necessity – for them to break away from the familiar embrace of home and community to make their own choices and forge their own way in the world.

As they reached young adulthood our generation couldn't but be aware of the titanic forces threatening the world's political and financial stability but, for the moment, their own universe remained small, secure and familiar: friends, family, church – and school.

The majority of Britain's children between the ages of 7 and

14 (15 from 1936, though a child could leave a year early to work
if the family could demonstrate hardship) were accommodated
in local authority or church elementary schools. The education
they offered was rudimentary, typically in large, sex-segregated
classes in three-storey Victorian buildings, the emphasis still on
rote learning, copperplate handwriting and a firm grounding in
Britain's glorious imperial history.

Empire Day was the occasion for patriotic ceremony and celebration for all schoolchildren across Britain's colonies and dominions. For this generation, the British Empire is still a potent
memory and part of their early lives. After more than 80 years,
Enid Wenban still knows the date:

> Empire Day, of course. May the 24th. Oh yes, the great British
> Empire. A lot of my friends' fathers would have been in the
> Colonial Service, West Africa, India, and my contemporaries later
> on, a lot of them had been born in India. We were very proud of
> the empire and leading the empire.

At St Pancras Church of England Elementary School in King's
Cross, Charles Chilton remembers the parody of 'Land of Hope
and Glory' they used to sing in the streets on Empire Day:

> Land of soap and water
> Mother, wash my feet
> Father, pick my toenails
> Whilst I eat my meat.

> We were supposed to be very proud of the fact that Britain had
> the largest empire in the world. We were very proud to be British.
> Our headmaster, he rather thought that our elementary school
> was really another Eton or Harrow because he wanted us to behave
> like one. We had a school motto and our motto was 'Play the
> Game'. And of course, playing the game to us was quite different
> from playing the game that he had, but anyway, we had this school
> song and I can still remember it:

> Play the game, play the game
> All true Britons do the same
> Win your goal by honest work
> Never sham and never shirk
> Play the game, play the game, play the game!

Bright children could take a scholarship to a grammar school at 11 or 13 and have the chance of a more academic education. Charles was a bright boy but his headmaster told him he'd disgraced the school.

The examiner had looked at my paper. Looked at it, mind, didn't read it, and said, 'This boy will not pass.' Why not? 'Well, look at the horrible writing, can't read it.' And that was my scholarship gone down the drain.

In Manchester, Mabel McCoy was thrilled to win a scholarship.

I loved school and I wanted to get on. You really have to put it in the times of the 1930s. Manchester was very keen on building schools and getting young people through because there was so little work for everybody, the better education you had, the better chance you had of getting a job, never mind a better job.

Conscientious as she was, conditions at home made it hard for her to study:

We lived in a council house that only had one living room. I had a brother two years older who was very spoiled. I think we had our first radio in about 1935 and all the time he was in the house we had the radio going with dance band music – Henry Hall – and it was impossible at that time for me to do my homework in the living room. The only place I could go to do my homework was the bathroom as it was the only other room in the house that was heated, by the hot water system. I put a tray on top of the washbasin to write. You had no choice.

Matthew MacKinnon-Pattison's education was untypical and probably better than most. Quarriers Homes, unlike many orphan institutions of the time, took education seriously. Matthew was bright and responded well to the solid, authoritarian schooling on offer.

> We had a very good education. We had a teacher there and boy, could she teach. Her name was McWilliams and we called her Pussy. She had a voice that could castrate an elephant at 200 yards and I'm not joking. And if you didn't get it right you got her tongue. But when it came to mathematics, she taught me and I came top of the class and she loved me for it because I never forgot her teaching.

Britain's long-entrenched education arrangements meant that the children of different social classes rarely mixed on equal terms. For children of the affluent, private education was a foregone conclusion, and girls in the upper and upper-middle classes like Margaret Rhodes and Diana Athill had their own governess. Boys were sent to local prep schools or to board at public schools from as young as seven. This could be a miserable experience for those who were shy, studious or different from the crowd. Bullying was rife. In London, Jimmy Perry went to the exclusive Colet Court, where he was called 'Pisspot Perry' and 'Mouse'. He once claimed he'd rather go through the war again than repeat his days there. Things didn't get any better when he went on to St Paul's,

> one of the greatest public schools in the country. I spent most of my time hiding in the lavatories. It was a nightmare; stayed with me for the rest of my life. The cruelty was extraordinary, because the boys took their example from the sadism of the masters.

Few remember their schooldays with affection and fewer believed what they learned there equipped them for life. Episodes of naughtiness and the corporal punishment that inevitably followed stand out but otherwise the words of Fred Glover stand for the experience of many: 'nothing much happened there as I recall'.

Impressionable adolescents learned as much from their involvement with churches and youth organisations as from their formal schooling. Though the established Church had suffered a decline in political and moral influence since before the war, 60 per cent of the population still professed to be 'C of E'. Even if they weren't regular churchgoers themselves, many parents made sure their children attended Sunday school or joined the youth organisations attached to the local church, if only to get them out of the house. Kit Sollitt and her many siblings found that they had a full programme of activities:

> Sunday morning to church and Sunday afternoon to church. Monday I went to the Brownies. Tuesday I went to the Band of Hope. Christian Endeavour on the Wednesday. Wherever Mum could get us in, we went.

By 1938 the Scout Movement claimed half a million members, ensuring that the solid Christian values and simple patriotism so prized by English educators continued to mould the character of succeeding generations. The Scout Promise – encapsulating concepts of honour, endeavour, duty, obedience, patriotism, Judaeo-Christian morality and service to others – said it all.

The recipients of this character-forming exercise were unaware of the bigger moral and nationalist agenda: to them it meant a weekly escape from the home where they could meet friends, learn exciting new things – often out of doors – and have fun. Many spoke warmly of their time in these organisations and in retrospect recognise their character-shaping influence. George Montague started young in the Cubs and was soon hooked.

> Every single boy in the village I knew of was either in the choir and/or in the Scouts as well. I joined the Cubs at the age of nine and I was thrilled to bits with everything I learned from that. I read Baden-Powell's book and was enthralled with it because it really is a wonderful book on the basis of growing up as a child, to be a good human being, never to steal, never to tell lies, to be

useful and handy and do things, and to be able to survive with the minimum of luxuries, which I enjoyed. Camping, I loved it, and I became very high up, I became the troop leader.

Bob Frost joined the Scouts from Cubs and as part of the 15th St Pancras troop enjoyed its many outdoor activities.

Cross-country running over Hampstead Heath, going away camping, swimming, boxing . . . The camping and the going out and the freedom of being outside was a real boon in those days. It gave me the freedom to get out and about and meet other people, do things I wouldn't normally have done and learning a lot of new things as well: telling the time [by the sun] and points of the compass. My parents had enough confidence in me, at 15, to let me go away on my bicycle with a little bivouac tent on the back, for a week, and I cycled from London to Dorset and back. Later on, when I found myself on the ground and rather alone, all of that came into play. I owe much to the Scouts.

The local church was often the social focus for many middle-class families. Enid Wenban's local Congregationalist church in Purley was a formative influence, both socially and spiritually.

We had a big house and our church was very outgoing. There were always people coming to stay, people from other countries. If people needed accommodation, Mother would always offer; we had all sorts of people coming to stay with us, which was interesting, it helped me look outward, I suppose. I was a Girl Guide, I loved going camping; the company was attached to our church. Apart from the family, the church was the centre of our social life. Belief in God came later on.

For Matthew MacKinnon-Pattison, reaching adolescence in the Quarriers Homes, Scottish Presbyterianism was an integral part of life. The magnificent 1,000-seat Mount Zion Church dominated Quarriers Village.

The church was beautiful and all the windows were stained. Up above each window would be a text. And above where I sat was: 'When my father and my mother forsake me, then the Lord will take me up,' which was very poignant.

Matthew, like all the other Quarriers children, went to church twice on Sunday and at least once during the week, and learned by heart reams of hymns, psalms and Bible tracts, many of which he still remembers today.

Religion wasn't force-fed, it was given to you like a preventative medicine. If the good Lord had you, then the devil wasn't going to get you. So you got this church service on Sunday in the morning. Sundays in the evening. In the afternoon, being Scottish, you sat and read religious tracts because in those days you didn't dare do anything on the Sabbath. And on Wednesday we'd have another church service, a bit more relaxed, a slide-show from a missionary and all that sort of thing. Before breakfast you'd gather in the playroom and the father would read the Bible and say some prayers and before tea you had the same again. And we didn't mind it because you've always got to remember one thing: you don't know any different.

———◆———

At 14 or 15 most adolescents were expected to leave the security of childhood and move seamlessly into the world of work. This abrupt transition could be a release, a challenge, a shock or a revelation. Matthew tried his hand as a hotel bellboy in London, then returned to Scotland to work in a tough Clydeside shipyard. Here he was exposed to views and influences that challenged everything he'd been taught at Quarriers.

The Clyde wasn't called the Red Clyde for nothing. They were very, very red. Of course they started educating me on communism and I went in with both feet like nobody's business. By this time my church had been replaced by the cinema, but these lads start to teach me and I start to read books – Karl Marx, Thomas Paine – and I became very, very political. Now, this started me questioning about religion and I thought, Yes, Thomas Paine has got a good idea there.

In London 14-year-old Charles Chilton too was about to start moving in different circles after a first unhappy apprenticeship.

I worked for a company that made electric signs that used to hang outside shops, but I hated it, I hated the people who I worked with. Their idea of fun was torturing the little boy apprentices like me and carrying out absurd and disgraceful things on them and if they cried it was: 'Crybaby, can't take a joke, eh?' So I decided the first possible chance I got I'd leave this place and find something else.

I realised I was quite close to that new BBC building Broadcasting House which had just been opened by King George V so I thought, Well, they must need boys in the BBC – why don't I go in and ask for a job there? So I went in through those great bronze doors and went up to the reception. They soon sent me packing, but as I was walking out a commissionaire said, 'Listen, son, if I were you, I'd go home and write a letter.' So I went home and I immediately wrote a letter asking if there was a vacancy in their 'firm' for a bright young boy who'd just left school, and I got a reply inviting me for an interview. I had the interview and a week or so later got the offer of a job as a messenger boy with the BBC.

There in 1932, Charles says, his 'real education' began:

When I got to the BBC I was most impressed with the people I was working with. They were educated, friendly, kindly people. There was one man there particularly, he used to compile the serious music on gramophone records. I used to go and talk to him in his office and he used to give me lessons in music and tell me what books to read and things like that. I met a new society, learned so many new things. The BBC to me was wonderful.

But messenger boys were just that: as soon as they were 17 they got the sack in favour of a new batch of 14-year-olds. Charles's salvation lay in his passion for popular music and film scores: his stepfather worked in a record shop and his mother had been a cinema cashier. This got him a job in the newly established Gramophone Department. He was now on the first rung of his long BBC career.

Young people's labour was cheap. Even so, some found it difficult to get any kind of work on leaving school. Gus Bialick and a group of friends, driven by unemployment and a desire to better themselves, decided to use the opportunity to explore new pastures.

It was a time when there was very little work and a time when we were experimenting with different ways of life because we tried to break out from the ghetto of the East End and get to know about other things in life. We tried various things like listening to classical music to improve our minds. We tried vegetarianism, we tried socialism, we tried communism. The fact that we were young Jews made us drift towards the communists, for the simple reason that they were the ones who were fighting fascism the most and the hardest. Our lives were in flux, they were changing and we were learning things outside of school which were so different to our lives before. I became a vegetarian at the age of 19 which was about 80 years ago and I've been a vegetarian ever since.

A few of us bought an old tent and we took it up to Epping Forest. For three years we stayed there; not all the time – we had to come back on our bikes, eight or nine miles, to the labour exchange to sign on for our ten shillings a week which the government gave us to live on. I used to visit my mother, who put a pound of cheese and a loaf of bread in my saddlebag, and back we went to Epping Forest.

You couldn't stay at home in those days. Life was too irksome. You couldn't watch your father being unemployed, life was unbearable, so we went into the forest and lived that way. We used to steal potatoes and vegetables out of the farmer's grounds, we had berries and nuts and we lived there quite happily. We'd swim in disused quarries that were filled with rainwater. It was a beautiful, idyllic place to live. Those three years spent up there were the most wonderful years in my teenage life. We got toughened up living that way, because we stayed up there in the wintertime as well. We used to have plenty of wood to light bonfires so we kept reasonably warm. I was a really tough kid in those days. Well, you had to be.

———◆———

The 1929 Wall Street Crash started the pernicious Depression that was to haunt the decade. By 1931 three million were unemployed. But while the old industrial heartlands of the north of England suffered, some parts of Britain were booming. Speculative house building, light industry and the manufacture of new consumer goods all experienced an interwar bonanza. Around the periphery of London and in the south-east, new arterial roads and rapidly expanding industrial estates provided access to and employment for the growing suburban sprawl. Frank Rosier's family moved out from Chelsea, making a new start in Hayes on the edge of west London, where the massive Heinz and Nestlé factories drew workers from the city.

In these new suburban homes an array of desirable new labour-saving devices – promoted by the private electricity and gas companies – entranced (or entrapped) the modern housewife. A new salaried lower-middle class was colonising the leafy outskirts of Britain's cities and making its mark. It aspired to a 'comfortable' life in which home and family were the focus and there was money to spare for annual holidays, private schools and perhaps a small car.

'The gentry' were snooty about these suburban upstarts, as Diana Athill recalls:

The thing about class in those days was, from our point of view, you liked people who did things, like saddlers or who looked after animals, you didn't like people who lived in the suburbs. That was the bottom. That was the end. And that was very odd. We didn't know anyone who lived in the suburbs, it was generally considered to be beneath contempt. The working class were all right, you know, and there was a relationship there. There was something very peculiar about anyone who wasn't quite working class and wasn't quite the gentry. Shocking really.

In their own upper-middle-class lights, Diana's parents had come down in the world. For much of her privileged childhood Diana and her siblings had lived in their grandmother's 20-bedroom mansion on the Norfolk–Suffolk border with its small regiment of servants and surrounding thousand acres. Then in 1930, when she was 13, her father went to work in the City and the family moved to a much smaller house in Hertfordshire – though this still had six bedrooms. Her mother announced that, as they were now poor, Diana would have to lose her governess and make her own bed. She was told that they had 'lost all their money'. In fact her parents had simply been living beyond their means.

My mother was extravagant. There was a terrible time when the bank told them they mustn't cash another cheque. Panic stations all round. Because we didn't have much money. I remember being told as a child, 'You know you'll have to earn your own living?' Which struck me as being rather shocking, considering what I was surrounded by at the time. I thought, Oh well, I shall be married by then and my husband will keep me.

Used to such a cosseted existence, it was difficult at first for Diana to comprehend what being 'poor' really meant. It came home to her when she went to the larder one day and was alarmed to see that, once the next meal had been eaten, there was nothing for the meal after that: 'for a few moments, poverty had become real'. Food did reappear in the larder and the family adjusted to a more modest lifestyle, but Diana's parents had no solid marriage to see them through testing times. In smaller accommodation, the children were exposed to the tensions of a scratchy relationship and Diana often had cause to wonder aloud why they didn't just divorce, even though she knew that 'divorce was scandalous and very few people did it'.

By 1936, after a haphazard education at home and an unhappy stint at boarding school, Diana was reluctantly preparing to go up to Oxford. She'd failed to win a scholarship but an aunt was paying her fees. Bright, well read (especially on sex) and looking forward to living happily ever after with Tony, the older man she'd fallen in love with at 15, she was nevertheless profoundly ignorant of life. Inevitably, there would be shocks ahead.

For many young men, apart from joining the army or running away to sea, marriage was the only means of escape from the privations and restrictions of their childhood home. Charles Chilton was enjoying his new working life at the BBC, but life at home was becoming unbearable.

> I was tired of sleeping three, sometimes five, to a bed. On those occasions it seemed to me I was sleeping in a forest of legs because we slept two at the bottom and three at the top. I began to meet people who lived differently. I wanted a home of my own and to be free.

So in 1938 Charles married Bess, his best friend's sister from elementary school, and they started out in their own small flat in King's Cross. But Charles had already moved far from his humble origins in his tastes and interests and their relationship soon foundered.

> Bess was very much a cockney girl, a dressmaker. I went to the BBC and did things she didn't understand and she certainly didn't understand the people I worked with. When sometimes I used to bring them home she'd say, 'Oh, don't bring those people home, they're not my kind of people, they're not our class of people.' But they were *my* kind of people, I was working with them. She

felt she couldn't fit in with the kind of society I was beginning to work in.

Young women had a harder job breaking from home ties. Unmarried daughters were expected to stay at home to help manage the house and look after elderly relatives; marriage was usually the only means of escape. Hetty Bower had already demonstrated an independent streak, encouraged by her strong-willed older sisters. By the mid 1920s she had a responsible job as an accounts clerk and had joined a union, the Association of Women Clerks and Secretaries. Her sister Anita worked at the pioneering Finsbury Health Centre. In 1928, despite their mother's protestations, Hetty and Anita moved out of the family home in Hackney to live independently, but by then she'd already met her match whilst out collecting for the miners during the 1926 General Strike:

> 'Not an hour on the day, not a penny off the pay,' that's what they used to say. I was already a member of the Labour Party then. I was given this address, 60 Montague Road, and a little woman with bright blue eyes opened the door. 'Mr N. Bower? There's no one of that name here. What's it about? Oh, that's our Reg. Reg! There's somebody here from the Labour!' And this young, very good-looking man with a most charming smile came out, and my first reaction was, Oh, what a pity he's not Jewish! Jews didn't marry outside the faith, not if they were the children of Orthodox Jews like I was. Anyway, this lovely smile provoked a smile in return.

Hetty risked her family's disapproval but this was a true meeting of minds: she and Reg shared interests and political views and they soon fell in love. After a courtship rambling in Epping Forest, youth hostelling in Europe and visiting the International Workers' Olympiad in Vienna in 1931, Hetty and Reg married in 1932. They honeymooned walking in the Wye Valley, a precious private memory for Hetty as she recalled it nearly eight decades later.

I was devoted to Reg. He was a darling: loving, kind, upright. We wanted to be together all the time. We were very much in love with each other and we had a lovely time together and I'm not telling you anything more!

———◆———

For young people still living at home in areas blighted by unemployment, the pain of seeing fathers without work was hard to avoid. Rudimentary benefits, paid through local Public Assistance Committees, were subject to an intrusive Means Test, hated because it arbitrarily discriminated against those with a few precious savings or possessions.

Mabel McCoy's father's pride and joy – and his emotional crutch – was his pre-war piano; her mother's was their beautiful mahogany dining table. Before the war he'd had a good job in the Manchester cotton industry, but global economic conditions were changing.

Manchester was no longer the cotton centre of the world. The first firm he worked for went bankrupt. He got a job straight away but the second firm went bankrupt after a couple of years and that was 1932. There was very little work and he applied for unemployment benefit and was Means Tested. I was in the house when the men came [from Public Assistance] and they went all over the house looking at our possessions. They saw the piano, and they'd got my mother to get her Co-op dividend book with 17s 4d [about 85p but worth considerably more then] in it and said to my father, 'Before we give you any money you must sell this piano and spend the dividend money.' My father – he didn't show anger – said, 'No, I'm not selling the piano.' So they said, 'Well, no sale, no money,' so for the next however many months we went on without much money.

I can remember one Christmas for Christmas dinner we had bacon and egg and were delighted to have it, but we kept the piano. But my poor mother was worried about how we were going to manage. It was wintertime, we had a coal fire but no coal, we had gas fires in the bedroom but there was no money to feed the meter, so they chopped up the lovely mahogany table which was pure sacrilege. Their main concern was feeding themselves and us. Mother never chided my father or questioned how we would manage. She understood him perfectly and the desperate frustration inside him – released by going back to the piano and thumping out one of his favourite pieces.

Nearby in Blackburn, unemployment was endemic. Russell Margerison's father was without permanent work from the time he was demobbed until 1938.

There was no work round here whatsoever. Unless you were a tradesman you had no chance whatever. He was out of work all the time I remember of my childhood, it was purely living on the dole. You could just not get work. He was no scrounger, he really wanted to work and every day he would go out looking for work. Nothing doing. It must have been very depressing for him, but that's the way it was.

Russell's father finally found a job at Queen's Park Hospital, a former workhouse. Workhouses had been abolished in 1930 when the old Poor Law Boards were replaced by local Public Assistance Committees. However, the changes resulted in few improvements on the ground for the sick, the infirm and the destitute: the 'hospitals' that replaced them were housed in the same austere Victorian buildings. But Russell enjoyed his visits there.

His job was to look after the tramps when they came in. The tramps in those days were real characters. You had the sloppy and the dirty and the uncouth but you also got the other sort, there was one of them called the Knight of the Ward, he always wore a top hat and a bow tie and believe it or not, he used to polish his nails on his shoes, he was so immaculately clean. These people were nothing to be scared of. I probably learned quite a lot from them, they were so down to earth. My dad got very friendly with some of them. One he used to bring home regularly, called Dummy because he was deaf and dumb, and my dad learned sign language to communicate with him. He was a hard case but Dad had a soft spot for him. He brought him home the first time, and we didn't have a lot of money. Mother put a meal on and then she put a jar of jam on the table and he started crying. He said that was the first time he'd ever been offered jam.

His father's fortitude in the face of hardship made a lasting impression on Russell, and he loved his mother dearly. After losing five of her six children and struggling through much of the 1930s on the dole, by the end of the decade she'd contracted terminal cancer.

My dad was a tough guy, he took life in his stride. He wasn't a worrier, he got on with it. I admire him for that. He had a hard life, as did my mother. She was a lovely person, she never deserved it.

In the West Country, Joy Lofthouse's father had been a professional footballer in the 1920s – in the days when they were lucky to earn £5 a week – but by the early 1930s he was out of work and looking for casual labouring jobs.

My father finished his football career because of cartilage trouble at the beginning of the Depression and you couldn't just walk into a job then. There was unemployment benefit if you'd paid in, but unlike nowadays, if you didn't take the first job you were offered, it stopped. So Father was offered work in Guernsey picking potatoes and he had to go, or there was nothing to support the family. So yes, those were very lean years.

———◆———

Three major events which came to characterise those lean and fractious years all happened within days and weeks of each other in the autumn of 1936. Most young people would have learned about them from newspaper reports, word-of-mouth accounts or casual gossip, but a privileged few were eyewitnesses to the events – or their repercussions – themselves.

Jim Purcell had just left school in Jarrow, where over 70 per cent of working-age men were unemployed following the closure of its shipyard in 1933. On 5 October 1936, 200 of them set off on foot for the 300-mile march to London, a 'crusade' to plead for action on unemployment. Though there had been several 'hunger marches' before, Jarrow was the biggest and became the most potent symbol of the Depression decade. Jim watched them set off.

> I saw the Jarrow March . . . the dignity of them, they weren't screaming and shouting, they marched and they marched and they were welcomed in every town. The Jarrow March was a dignified march. They didn't shout their heads off. They marched and they sang and they played their music. Doesn't matter what happens, you canna get Jarrow people down.

The Bishop of Jarrow was there to bless their endeavour and the mayor and town council were all present, some of whom, as Jim remembers, joined the march. At their head was Jarrow's Labour MP 'Red' Ellen Wilkinson. Exactly a month later, after a rally in Hyde Park and an emotional speech by Wilkinson in the Commons, the marchers returned to the north-east empty-handed.

> It's only when they got to London that nobody wanted them. So they came home, by train, at the cheapest fare there was. But they were great men.

The Jarrow Crusade had made its mark in history but failed to move the government. Unemployment, devastating as it was, took second place to a very different and more pressing concern, one that precipitated a seismic event in the life of the nation, empire and dominions.

Stanley Baldwin's Conservative administration was absorbed by a looming constitutional crisis. The new (and as yet uncrowned) King's proposed marriage to an American divorcee threatened to destabilise the monarchy and split the government and the country. When the crisis finally broke a few weeks later with the announcement of King Edward VIII's abdication, 12-year-old Margaret Rhodes was in a dancing lesson in Edinburgh. She couldn't contain her pride and excitement.

> I can remember hopping round the dance floor saying, 'My uncle's king!' and being ever after deeply ashamed of myself. I thought it was rather jolly to have an uncle that was king. He stopped being Uncle Bertie and became Sir too at that time, which I suppose was right and proper.

Baldwin was credited with saving the country from a constitutional disaster but the abdication crisis cast royalty in a new, less dignified light. No longer morally unimpeachable, kings now looked both reassuringly human and surprisingly dispensable. It was one marker in the long slow erosion of Britain's culture of deference that would only gather pace in the latter decades of the century. But for the moment, with her cousins' newly acquired status as next in line to the throne, Margaret now had even more people to curtsey to.

Like the Jarrow March, a third significant event that momentous autumn revealed dangerous flaws in the social fabric at home and reflected worrying developments in Europe. Anti-Semitism, a discreditable if whispered feature of polite society, was now an open secret in the poorest areas of Britain's cities. A new political party, the British Union of Fascists (BUF), led by the charismatic aristocrat Oswald Mosley, targeted those across all social classes seeking a scapegoat for their economic misfortunes. Attacks on Jewish businesses and the appearance of the BUF's black-shirted brigades were becoming common sights in immigrant areas. By the mid 1930s tensions between Mosley's followers and local immigrant communities erupted in sporadic violence in many British cities. They came to a head in an East End street on the day before the Jarrow March.

Gus Bialick, a young man Jewish by birth and communist by inclination, was on his home territory of Whitechapel on 4 October when 2,000 of Mosley's Blackshirts attempted to march through Cable Street.

> We found that Mosley was getting more strength among the population, because they thought he was the answer to their problems. Mosley decided he was strong enough to march through the East End of London, which he knew very well was populated mainly by Jews and Irish Catholics. Well, when he proclaimed that march, the young Jews of all denominations, whether they were religious, or whether they were communists or socialists or Labour Party members, decided to come together and prevent that march through the East End. They were also joined by the Irish Catholic families who worked in the docks at that time. All those different denominations and people stood together to prevent Oswald Mosley and his march.

Controversially, the 6,000 police on duty that day – a third of the Metropolitan force – were instructed to protect the BUF marchers. The 100,000 protesters, whose slogan, borrowed from the ongoing Spanish Civil War, was 'No Pasaran' – 'They Shall Not Pass' – were inevitably involved in scuffles and hand-to-hand fighting with police. As a result, the London Hospital received hundreds of injured people and of the 85 arrests that day, 80 were of protesters. Gus was there on the streets.

> I wasn't involved in any of the fighting. Perhaps I was cowardly, I don't know, but I remember it so clearly, the police weren't exactly on our side. They were supposed to be neutral or to prevent disorder, but I noticed, as a young person, that they chose to attack the Jews and the socialists and the communists much quicker and with much more force than the Fascists.

Hetty Bower was also there and had no doubts about whose side the police were on:

> The chief of the London police was hand in glove with the leader of the Fascist party. Mosley was fully expecting his Fascists would be able to march into Whitechapel and east into the Jewish area, but it didn't happen. There was a ginger-headed lad and we were told to hold the fort at Whitechapel. If they got through at Gardiner's Corner then we were due to stop them. But they didn't even get past Gardiner's Corner. I remember this little ginger-headed chap coming along: 'It's all right! They didn't pass! They didn't get through!' And a great big cheer went up.

Though Gus may not have taken up bricks or thrown marbles under police horses' hooves, his convictions, echoed by Hetty, were firmly held.

> I felt that the whole world was being engulfed in a backward step from a civilised world as we ought to have known it. I was afraid for the older generation, my grandparents. They were afraid of what was happening in their lives. And I was afraid on their behalf because we never knew what the future held for us. Fascism was growing in different parts of the world in great strength at the time and it was a difficult period.

For Hetty, already a politically aware young woman in her twenties, the Battle of Cable Street only confirmed her pacifist views and political allegiance. Despite her Orthodox Jewish background and a father who disapproved of women involving themselves in politics, Hetty was a committed socialist on the left of the Labour Party. What she'd already seen in Europe and at home convinced her that, though war was an abomination, the evil of fascism had to be defeated.

By the latter half of the decade Nazi expansionism in Europe and the realistic prospect of another war preoccupied the adult world. Young people were not immune from these anxieties. In 1937 Bob Frost had a first-hand taste of Nazi Germany whilst still at school.

> My mother and father put the money together to send me off to Germany with my technical school. We took German, workshop drawings and things like that and went to Germany: Cologne, Trier and Koblenz. I saw Hermann Goering arriving at Cologne railway station and scuffles in the street between the Brownshirts and the *Hitlerjugend* and the locals who were opposed to the rising German Nazi Party. Remember, the Spanish Civil War had been going on as well, with the International Brigade and that sort of thing, so I was aware that there was trouble on the Continent, to say the least.

With limited rearmament, the services became an attractive prospect for young men looking for escape and adventure. Inspired by the patriotic poetry of Rudyard Kipling and desperate to leave the constraints of his life in Jarrow, Jim Purcell saw a better future in the army.

> You couldn't build dreams, the state we were in. A soldier, he had a life, he had clothes, he had money, and I thought to myself, That's the life for me, the attractiveness of the uniform and good clothes for girls. I wanted to be a man among men.

After trying unsuccessfully to enlist, Jim was accepted into the Territorial Army, with the Royal Engineers, in 1937.

> It was an adventure, you didn't know what was going to happen. My uniform was exactly the same as in the First World War: heavy boots, peaked hat. I was so thin and skinny, the hat didn't fit properly. But I loved it so much – the drill, the friendship, the uniform, everything. And I loved working with engineers, blowing things up. And my mother and father were very proud of me.

Another keen reader of Kipling, Freddie Hunn had left his elementary school at 14, but with little work available in Norfolk signing up seemed the only alternative. In 1937 his friend 'Dolly' Gray had just enlisted with the 12th Royal Lancers.

> He was a good-looking chap, curly hair, tall, and he knew he was good-looking. He came home in the 12th Lancers uniform: lanyard, bleachers, spurs and that sort of thing, and he said, 'Why don't you join us?' I said no, I wanted to join the marines.

But Dolly regaled him with tales of breaking wild horses and driving armoured cars around on Salisbury Plain. Freddie, who'd grown up with comic-book heroes and whose favourite poem was Tennyson's 'The Charge of the Light Brigade', was seduced. He lied about his age and was sworn into the Lancers at 17.

> So I got to Tidworth . . . and there was no sign of horses or armoured cars. And Dolly got five shillings from the regiment and three days' extra leave, so he was on to a good thing! I remember my first big parade with General McCreery. He was colonel of the regiment then. And we had Field Marshal Lord Birdwood coming round. He walked up to me and put his hand on my shoulder. 'How old are you, my boy?' 'Eighteen, sir.' And he turned to Colonel McCreery: 'He doesn't look eighteen, does he?' 'No, he doesn't,' said the colonel. And then they passed on.

Others pursued more peaceful paths in the uneasy final years of the decade. Fergus Anckorn had graduated from boxes of tricks to learning sleight-of-hand techniques from the president of the Magic Circle. By 18 he was its youngest member and performing to paying audiences. Determined to fulfil the early career decision he'd made as a child with TB, Bill Frankland was in the final stages of his eight-year training to become a doctor. Gus Bialick and his friends returned from their tented idyll in Epping Forest, drawn back to the East End by the prospect of work at last.

By 1936–37 Hitler had built up quite a strong army and this was beginning to filter into the minds of the British government and they started spending money on armaments too. Consequently there was more work to be had, and more money around, so we went back to our respective households and started work in our own particular trades again. We were too small a unit to produce uniforms. We did small things. In fact I remember we had a contract to make men's underpants.

After an adolescence marked by the country's shifting fortunes, Britain's young people could look forward to an even more unsettled future. By 1939 the only certainty was war. Our generation was now grown or growing up. They would be among the first into the front line.

4

The Outbreak of War
September 1939–June 1940

Everywhere you looked, it was just explosions, smoke and flame.
I took a last look at Dunkirk, and if there was a hell, that was it.
Sergeant Freddie Hunn, 12th Lancers, aged 21

The relief and rejoicing that greeted Neville Chamberlain's return from Munich at the end of September 1938 was short-lived. An older generation scarred by the First World War had understandable reason to support every means of keeping the peace, even if this looked increasingly futile in the wake of Germany's violent expansionism. Chamberlain's deal with Hitler over the Sudetenland could only mark a pause in his plans for *Lebensraum*, not a full stop.

In workless Jarrow and Great Yarmouth, Jim Purcell and Freddie Hunn joined up as Britain rearmed. In Gus Bialick's East End workshop, fashion garments gave way to government contracts, and in Purley Enid Wenban's mother started stockpiling tins.

Fergus Anckorn had just finished a shorthand-typing course at Regent Street Polytechnic and was planning to follow his father into journalism. He dreaded the prospect of war.

I'd heard terrible stories because I was born just after the First World War . . . about the Huns and the raping and pillaging and torturing – which was all propaganda but I didn't know that. I was frightened to death at the thought that there might be a war.

The last thing he wanted to do was fight, but by the start of 1939 he was 20 and called up for six months' compulsory military training.

> Well, I thought I would die, because I'd had nothing but kindness and no unpleasantness in my life, and here I was going in the army. I'd heard about these beastly sergeant majors that swear at you and get you out of bed at five in the morning and kick you around and curse all day. In our house you would never hear a swear word of any kind. And I knew in the army there was plenty of that and I didn't think I could survive long. But of course I had to go. I went off to Woolwich into the Field Artillery and I thought, well, I don't suppose I'll last six months.

War was set to disrupt Fergus's life and the lives of millions of others. Preparations for a 'national emergency' had in fact started years before. In the latter half of the 1930s, while young people enjoyed the outdoors and tasted the first fruits of adult life, their government was ordering a million coffins. Official anxieties were mirrored at the cinema: *Things to Come*, Alexander Korda's 1936 science fiction epic scripted by H. G. Wells, showed cities laid waste by bombing, mass panic, death and destruction in a new global technology-driven war without end.

Civilian deaths were uppermost in official minds. The 1915–18 experience of German air attacks on undefended areas had been a bitter lesson and the devastating German bombing of Guernica during the Spanish Civil War only confirmed fears of mass civilian casualties. Civil defence measures were discussed as early as 1935 and air-raid precautions (ARP) a decade before that. City authorities were urged to construct public shelters and put in place evacuation plans for mothers and children.

By 1938 an estimated £6 million had been spent on gas masks and £3 million on sandbags. In the same year in London, Fergus recalls seeing City office workers digging air-raid shelters in their lunch hour. In Bristol, the older boys in Bill Graves's Scout troop, like many throughout the country, were being trained as messenger boys for ARP wardens. In Manchester, Mabel McCoy played cricket on fields fringed with ack-ack guns, where barrage balloons were tethered with thick wire cables.

It had been a time of anxious wait-and-see, but after the invasion of Czechoslovakia in March 1939, despite the heartfelt convictions of appeasers, no one young or old could be in any doubt that war was inevitable.

A new influx of immigrants to Britain's major cities, mainly Jewish refugees from Germany and the countries it now threatened or already occupied, was another harbinger of the imminent conflagration. By September 1939, 40,000 Jews from Germany and Austria alone had come to Britain. Gus Bialick's father signed up to receive German Jews seeking refuge from Nazi persecution. Hetty Bower, now established in her own home in north London with husband Reg and a young daughter, volunteered for the Czech Refugee Trust and ran a hostel in north London. But it wasn't necessary to be Jewish to lend practical aid to those suffering in Europe at that time: hundreds of British families took in refugees.

Government's humanitarian instincts were tempered by privately voiced anti-Semitism and worry about the security risks posed by an influx of potential enemy aliens, especially those coming from Germany. Children, however, were a special case. Dispensation was granted for children between 5 and 17 to come to Britain from Europe without visas if sponsoring families could be found to take responsibility for them. The *Kindertransport* scheme brought nearly 10,000 Jewish children to Britain in the ten months before the outbreak of war, the majority of them orphans, homeless or whose parents had been sent to concentration camps. But the scheme was never going to satisfy the huge demand from parents desperate to get their children to safety and individual private arrangements and charitable and philanthropic schemes also contributed to the exodus.

Dorothy Bohm was the child of wealthy Lithuanian Jews who lived in what was then East Prussia. The rise of Nazism prompted the persecution of all Jews but especially successful ones. Dorothy's father, an influential industrialist and local politician, refused to flee: he had a large factory to run and workers to look after. He was publicly attacked on radio and named as a wanted man. The family's apartment was stoned and at school Dorothy was kicked and called a Jewish toad. In June 1939, when she was 15, her parents decided she must leave for Britain.

> Father's contacts with Britain were very good, he managed to get me a visa and an entry to a boarding school. My mother begged Father, 'Let her stay for the holidays.' But my father said, 'No, she's got to go now,' and he was right because if we'd waited I would have been too late. He was very interested in photography and he used a Leica at that time. As he said goodbye to me he took his Leica off and said, 'This might be useful to you.' I'm still marvelling [at that] because he knew I wasn't interested in photography – I didn't like being photographed, I was a dumpy little girl – but maybe he thought I could sell it if I needed to.

She was met by friends of the family and, with no English, installed in a small school outside Brighton.

> They'd never seen a foreigner, never mind a Jewish person, and they were wonderfully good to me, amazingly good. Obviously, in order to learn a language you have to be put in the deep end because that's the only way.

For families with strong connections to the English-speaking world, Britain was an obvious refuge. Andy Wiseman, born in 1923, grew up in Berlin but by 1934 his father's Polish-Jewish background and work for the British Embassy were a dangerous liability. Andy's school friend refused to be seen with him and was told his father had forbidden it because Andy was Jewish. Ostracism from school and youth activities followed and he witnessed German Jews being beaten up in the streets. The family moved to Poland but with the threat of invasion in August 1939 decided to send 16-year-old Andy to England. It was just in time: Hitler invaded on 1 September. The borders were closed and Britain declared war on Germany within 48 hours.

Memories of the warm late-summer Sunday on which Neville Chamberlain's doom-laden declaration was received by Britons on the BBC's Home Service are as fresh as ever after 75 years, such was its impact. Margaret Rhodes was spending her summer holidays at Birkhall as usual with her cousins, the Princesses Elizabeth and Margaret. They were all at Crathie Kirk that morning where the minister preached a 'highly emotional' sermon about peace being over. It seemed unreal to the girls, yet 'somehow rather exciting'. Fergus Anckorn had escaped to the local pool for a swim but the pool owner brought out a portable radio, telling swimmers: 'You'll want to hear this.' Fergus didn't: it would only hasten his call-up to face the dreaded sergeant majors.

After gaining her School Certificate in 1937, Enid Wenban had left school and entered the Civil Service. She found herself at work that Sunday:

> I have a memory as if it was yesterday. I was working by then at His Majesty's Stationery Office near Old Street Tube. Everybody used to work on Saturday mornings in those days, there was no five-day week, you worked till one o'clock. But we also had to do duty in the office on Sunday in case urgent work came in. I was on duty on Sunday, the 3rd of September 1939, on my own in the office, though there were other people in the building. We used to take things to do, like dressmaking. There wasn't work to do, you just had to be there in case work came in. At 11 o'clock, somebody had a radio in the building and I can remember as if it was yesterday Chamberlain's announcement: 'I have received no such undertaking . . . we are therefore at war with Germany.' I got the bus home at four o'clock and all the barrage balloons were up and I thought, I wonder if we're going to have an air raid before I get home. We didn't, and of course it was the Phoney War, but we weren't to know that. Beautiful weather it was, in September 1939. But everything just changed overnight. We were just waiting for something to happen. I think for the older

generation who'd been through the first war, well, they were rather nervous, but for us who were young, it was all a bit of an adventure. I wasn't scared, I was just waiting to see what would happen.

In fact, the sirens did go off almost immediately following Chamberlain's broadcast. Keen Scout Bob Frost, who'd grown up near London Zoo, was now working in the laboratory at the nearby Royal Veterinary College (though 'they soon moved out of London as we had sufficient bovine tuberculosis to do considerable damage if a bomb hit the place'). He'd responded to a government appeal for young men with bicycles to volunteer for the Auxiliary Fire Service as messengers in case bombs put the telephone system out of action. On Sunday 3 September he was on duty at his old school, converted to a makeshift fire station.

The very first Sunday of the war the sirens sounded and the people living in the houses in the street outside the school came across to the school to ask the firemen what to do. Nobody knew what to do, so they were put in a classroom and we waited. Nothing happened. Then, as the morning wore on, it was Sunday, joints were in the oven cooking, a woman said – and you'll pardon my French – 'Bugger Hitler, I'm going back to look after my Sunday joint,' and off she went. And that was how we started the war.

Sunday joints feature in a number of memories of that day. Sunday lunch – or dinner as it was called in most households – was the most important meal of the week. Jimmy Perry, just short of his sixteenth birthday, was at home in Barnes.

My sister and brother and I were in the house. My father, who was an antique dealer, had gone to Chiswick to look round an antique shop. And there was my dear mother – Chamberlain hadn't come on yet – and she said, 'I wish your father wouldn't go away like that, I've got the meat in the oven!' And then on the wireless we hear, 'I must inform you that we are now at war with Germany. Obey your ARP instructions and listen to the Home Service. God save the King!' And so my mother said, 'War's started! London will be in ruins!' We'd all seen, a few years previously, H. G. Wells's *Things to Come*, where there's an air raid on London and it's completely destroyed. We all had this idea that London was going to be flattened in five minutes, which, thank God, was totally incorrect. And so we had Sunday lunch and my father came home: 'Where have you been, Dad? War's just started!' 'Oh, they'll never get here! No, they won't last five minutes!' And so the war started. Instantly [there were] air-raid precautions . . . everybody had a gas mask. What people didn't realise is, we were better prepared than the Germans for this sort of war. Everybody thought it was inevitable for years, so we were well prepared. We weren't armed properly, but we'd taken care of the home front.

In Sussex, Dorothy Bohm was at her new school in an unfamiliar country and with very little English.

I remember standing in the playground and listening – 'We are at war with Germany' – and there were gas masks round our necks. I don't know what we felt, there was so much new that I had to absorb. Can you imagine?

David Mowatt's memories of 3 September are still emotional after the passing of so many years. From a close-knit rural community in the Scottish Highlands, David was getting the harvest in when he was instructed to go home, put on his uniform and report to the local recruitment office. This came as a shock. He and his friends had joined the Territorials for extra beer money without thinking too seriously about it – the war seemed so far from life in the Highlands. The news was an even bigger shock to his mother. David was her baby, the youngest of seven. She collapsed in tears.

In Frank Rosier's household in London, his father and uncle greeted the news with fury:

I never heard my father and my uncle swear before. 'What's the matter with the stupid so-and-so Germans? They want another

hiding, do they? We'll give 'em one this time they won't forget!'
They were so angry and Mother was shouting, 'For God's sake,
the children! Stop swearing in front of the children!' And that
anger was with us, right through the war.

Bill Frankland, now a qualified doctor, didn't wait for the declaration of war. He knew where his duty lay:

What were we fighting for? Well, we didn't like what was happening
in Germany. In fact, I signed up three days before war started. I
became a CMP, a civil[ian] medical practitioner, on the 1st of
September so I started early, but I thought it was my duty and
this was the place I should be. The country needed doctors and
that was what I was doing. Patriotism, I don't know how you
define it, but I've always been proud of being English, so here I
was fighting for my country.

Bill was attached to the Royal Army Medical Corps and sent to
Tidworth Military Hospital. The garrison town of Tidworth on
the edge of Salisbury Plain was all too familiar to Freddie Hunn.
He'd arrived there, a naive 17-year-old, in 1937 to do his square-
bashing with the 12th Lancers. Within a month of war being
declared Freddie, now trained and fit for combat, was in France
as part of the British Expeditionary Force's armoured car regiment.

Fergus Anckorn took his magic tricks with him when he went
to Woolwich to train with the Field Artillery. The sergeant majors
shouted and swore just as much as he'd feared, but in many other
respects he found army life unexpectedly enjoyable. It appealed
to his love of order and mastering magic had given him a respect
for intricate tasks completed to perfection.

Everything had to be done in the right way. Your kit had to be
laid out in a certain fashion, every last bit, so that if you looked
at anyone else's kit you couldn't tell the difference. If there was
one hair out of place you got into trouble. And I got to like this.

I thought, Well, this is lovely. I know how to do everything, and I took a pride in getting it all right. And of course for the first six weeks it was square-bashing. Marching up and down, a whole body of you. And I thought it was fantastic to get all these men marching along, left turn, right turn, about-turn, halt, all as one. I used to take great pride in this because eventually when we passed out in Woolwich we marched through the town just in one block and I liked all that, anything to do with discipline.

If Fergus responded well to army discipline, there was still plenty of scope to display his independent streak and gift for entertaining.

I had a lot of fun with the sergeant majors because, for some reason or the other, they didn't take to me. They thought I was a toff. They made fun of me all the time, and I made fun of them. I would always win because I had the word power they hadn't. All my battery used to wait for Anckorn and a sergeant major having a go. One day the sergeant major stuck his mouth almost in my ear and shouted out, 'Gunner Anckorn!' I said, 'There's no need to shout, Sergeant Major, I can hear you perfectly well.' So that was peeling potatoes for me. Another time he said, 'Gunner Anckorn! Did you give me a dirty look?' And I said, 'No, sir. You've got one, but I didn't give it to you.' More potato-bashing. But I loved that because while the rest of the fellows were out on Beachy Head in the pouring rain on the guns, I was in the cookhouse with two or three others peeling potatoes and the cook sergeant would always give us a cup of tea and some fruitcake. I used to look forward to my little forays with the sergeant major. I was always in trouble, but I liked it, and it was really only tongue-in-cheek.

The long-anticipated 'national emergency' had finally arrived and Britain was now on a war footing. Despite the absence of expected bombing raids the country settled uneasily into new routines involving blackout blinds, gas masks and ration books. The well-rehearsed and large-scale evacuation plans were put in hand: in the first three days of September, 1.5 million children, teachers and young mothers were mobilised by train and bus out of Britain's cities. A further 13,000 were sent abroad in the first year of the war.

Not only children and vulnerable groups but government offices and strategically important organisations were sent out of harm's way. At the start of the war the BBC stayed in London but later on its programme and some other departments were evacuated to the country. By 1939 Charles Chilton was a rising young BBC radio producer and presenter with a passion for jazz. At Broadcasting House, before his department was evacuated to Evesham, Charles met a young girl who was to change his life.

> I was writing and producing programmes and I went to look for some records. There was this beautiful girl sitting there all alone and I decided to make her life more interesting. I took her to Soho for a Chinese lunch and showed her how to use chopsticks. I taught her a lot about music, and jazz, which was supposed to be my forte. She became my protégée and we worked up this great friendship.

Sections of the Admiralty were evacuated to Bath and here Diana Athill found a lowly clerking job after leaving Oxford, marking time until she could marry her fiancé Tony. They had got engaged after her first year at Oxford in 1937 and had quickly become intimate.

> There'd been an enormous step forward between my mother's youth and mine. Before, they were driven about by my grandmother's chauffeur. You know, people say the sexual revolution started in the sixties. Nonsense. It began with cars. As soon as young men had cars and could drive girls back from a dance, there they were in this little capsule of privacy. That's how it began.

Despite the prudishness of the times, sex before marriage was not uncommon. Contemporary surveys of married women suggested that more than a third had had sex before their wedding day. For

Diana, as for many women among this number, an engagement ring was a prerequisite for intimacy. Tony was older than her and a pilot officer in the Royal Air Force (RAF): 'He would fly down from Grantham to see me. Terribly dashing!' Though their marriage plans were postponed after he was posted abroad following the invasion of Czechoslovakia, she lived for his loving letters and longed for the day when she could begin her 'proper' life as a married woman.

That September Diana and her sister listened to Chamberlain's broadcast through their tears whilst filling hessian mattresses for refugees. By then Tony's letters had become less frequent.

———◆———

During this period of Phoney War, young people could be forgiven for putting their country's situation a poor second place to the convulsions in their personal lives.

In Perth, Jean Valentine was enjoying her classics course at grammar school. She was an only child and her father's work in the motor trade meant that the family was comfortably off. Her academic future looked assured. Then the war changed everything.

> My father was very concerned . . . he was about to lose his mechanics, there were no new cars to see, and there was strict petrol rationing quite early on. He asked me if I would mind leaving school. The original intention was that I would stay on into the sixth form and probably go to university . . . but it never came to that because I said no, I don't mind leaving school.

So she left and spent the time at home helping her mother with two evacuees and the commando billeted with them, waiting until she could do something more useful for the war effort.

Everyday life was now fraught with petty restrictions; though some seemed mildly oppressive, none were unbearable. People grumbled and grew apathetic as the months wore on with little evidence of danger on the home front. All those precautions – the shelters, the gas masks, the fire drills and ARP duties – started to seem rather tedious and excessive. For those at home, the war wasn't yet real.

Even for the young men who'd joined the regular army to escape deprivation and in search of adventure, the war so far was proving disappointingly uneventful. Fighting fit and with high morale, they'd been primed for action. The first four infantry divisions of the British Expeditionary Force (BEF) left for France during September and October. Freddie Hunn went out in early October with the 12th Lancers. Jim Purcell followed with 233 Field Company, Royal Engineers in early 1940. Here things were relaxed enough for the inexperienced 18-year-old to be taught some facts of life.

> My mates thought I should be told how to have sex. They took me to a brothel and we were all sitting talking. Someone came along and knocked my hat and when I turned round it was one of the ladies and she said, 'No, no, no. Baby! Piccaninny!' So I didn't have sex with anyone then, and I thought I was going to have a horrible life. I loved girls, but I couldn't get one.

In France, all was relatively quiet on the defensive line of forts that made up the much-vaunted Maginot Line on the border between France and Germany, while Belgium maintained its uneasy neutrality. The BEF dug in along the line and the French–Belgian border waiting for a German attack, expecting to fight the same static trench-bound war as the last one.

David Mowatt, in the 4th Battalion, Seaforth Highlanders, part of the 51st Highland Division, had been transferred from the French–Belgian border, where most of the BEF was concentrated, to the Maginot Line in the south-east. Here he was occupied on recce patrols trying to discover what the Germans were doing on the other side of the line. At this stage of the Phoney War there was to be no firing on the enemy. This was frustrating: they were keen and ready for action but, in retrospect, 'of course we didn't have a clue'. Though the men were well trained and morale was high, up-to-date armaments and strategic intelligence were lacking.

After months of waiting and watching by the Allied and the Belgian armies, Hitler's highly mobile Panzer divisions and 'sickle stroke' attack would take them all completely by surprise.

Fergus Anckorn too had yet to see any action with the Royal Artillery: he was still in Britain. The best of the equipment had gone to France with the BEF. Troops at home had to make do with second best, or none at all. For Fergus' first sentry duty, guarding the petrol pumps at Woolwich barracks, his weapon was a pickaxe handle. During gun training he drove a commandeered furniture van with the gun tied on the back. But then he had an unexpected opportunity to make use of his other talents.

> One day our general, a wonderful man called Beckwith-Smith, decided to form an army concert party. Now, I don't mean a lot of fellows dressed up in tutus prancing around on the stage . . . they all had to be good performers, and of course I went for an audition.

Ten acts were chosen, with Fergus as the magician.

> We were a very good concert party and we did a show every night for two and a half years all over the country. Sometimes we would be performing in a field, sometimes in a NAAFI [Navy, Army and Air Force Institutes], standing on the counter. Even in theatres in different towns. When we performed in the New Victoria Theatre in Edinburgh the queue to see us went round two blocks. All over the place and all sorts of audiences. We would turn up at five in the afternoon in a ten-ton lorry with all our gear. We'd put the stage up and proscenium with electric curtains which were run by a motor we'd pinched out of a windscreen wiper on a car. By seven o'clock the curtains parted and we were in the show. It was a wonderful time, white tie and tails every night. The experience was invaluable.

By the end of April 400,000 British troops – regulars bolstered by conscripts, Territorials and reservists – were ready and waiting in France, but they were looking in the wrong direction and ill-equipped for the highly mechanised assault that was to hit them. In the early hours of 10 May, Hitler's lightning strike on the Low Countries began. Completely bypassing the Maginot Line, German tank divisions forced their way through the supposedly impenetrable wooded Ardennes region while ground forces and paratroopers quickly took control of strategically important positions in Holland and Belgium. France was about to be invaded by its back door, and the BEF and Allied forces sliced in two by Hitler's 'sickle stroke'.

With Belgium's neutrality shattered, Sergeant Freddie Hunn's armoured reconnaissance regiment, the 12th Lancers, was first over the border to see what the enemy was up to: 'Our job was to get close enough to see the whites of their eyes and report back to divisional HQ in Lille.' Strapped on the back of his Morris CS9 light armoured car was a basket of six carrier pigeons for use in case the radio failed.

The Lancers' entry into Belgium on 10 May was cheered by hundreds on the streets and they were showered with flowers and offers of wine. The unseasonably hot weather started to melt the tyres of their CS9s and they had to stop at rivers to throw water on them. But by 12 May, as they sought to slow the German advance over the River Dyle, they faced a rather different kind of reception.

> We were parked in a farmyard between two buildings. I saw two planes and one of them dropped something that looked like a beer barrel. I turned to the others just as there was a huge explosion of mud, rubble and dirt. 'It's a bomb!' I said to the others, but they'd already dived for cover.

Supported by a company of Engineers, the Lancers were blowing up bridges to halt the advance and protect the rear of withdrawing BEF forces now outflanked and being pushed towards the coast. But the Germans could not be held off for long: 'The speed of their advance was unbelievable.' The CS9 was nimble and effective against enemy motorcyclists but the design, based on a Morris commercial van, was no match for Panzer tanks.

By 15 May the Germans had broken through the French front and French and Belgian forces were in disarray. In the fog of war the strategic situation was confused and the Lancers were once more sent into the fray to recce German tank positions. The British HQ and a major supply dump at Arras now looked threatened. But their progress was hampered by roads choked with fleeing Belgian refugees and demoralised troops.

> Each town you came through, of course, there were hundreds and hundreds of refugees trying to get away from the Germans . . . loaded up, wheelbarrows, horse and carts, anything they could carry. Old women, old men, children in prams, and they'd be taking up the whole road. Imagine one of these main roads absolutely chock-a-block with that sort of thing, slowing everything down.

Worse were the indiscriminate attacks on fleeing civilians by German fighters and dive-bombers.

> Suddenly, out of the sky would come three Messerschmitts, and they would dive on these people and machine-gun them. Can you imagine it? Thousands of people walking the streets and suddenly, out of the sky, came these aeroplanes. It's terrible to see. These poor people, they couldn't get anywhere, they couldn't run off because they were all crowded in. And the screaming from that, and the terrified people . . . After they'd gone through, you'd see poor old ladies dead in ditches, women with prams upside down, and the slaughter . . . But there's nothing we could have done about it, nothing whatsoever. I mean, had we had our way, we'd have made sure those people were off the road, but you couldn't control that, you couldn't control what the Messerschmitts were going to do. You saw these innocent people dying and you think, Well, why them? We're the people who should be shot at. If that

had been us shot and killed, well, we're soldiers, we expect that.
But you don't expect to see innocent people . . . It was one of the
terrible things that happens in war.

On 26 May the Lancers had orders to defend the town of Ypres
and the Ypres–Comines canal, 30 miles from Dunkirk and a key
strategic line of defence. On this day Operation Dynamo – the
evacuation of the BEF – had begun and it was of vital importance
to protect retreating troops from German attack.

I parked my car by the Menin Gate. The town was completely
deserted and silent, very eerie. Here I was by this huge monument
to the British dead of the last war . . . I didn't feel at all comfortable
there.

The Lancers fought bravely and managed to hold the enemy off
from their section of the Dunkirk perimeter for three days as the
BEF made their 'fighting retreat' to the coast. But on 29 May they
were a few miles outside the small coastal resort of La Panne,
east of Dunkirk, and still under aerial attack.

We couldn't do our job as reconnaissance, so we were ordered to
destroy our armoured cars because we knew we couldn't get them
any further. The roads by then were one huge junkyard of scrap
vehicles . . . There weren't many [cars], we'd lost lots of them,
more than half, and half our men had been killed. We got to just
outside Le Panne and were told, 'Right, destroy your armoured
cars.' We drained the oil out of them, raced the engines till they
blew up, took the radio sets out, smashed them up with
sledgehammers, cut the tyres, then poured petrol on to a
camouflage net, put it inside and set fire to it. Anything we could
do to make it useless. And that was sad, to see all that. Then we
took our guns off – we weren't going to leave them!

Freddie now realised the seriousness of their situation.

Then William Browne-Clayton, who was my squadron leader, he got the squad, what was left of us, and said, 'Right, you fight to the last man and the last round.' So straight away I went to the ammunition truck for my .38 pistol; they had little boxes of ammunition, 12 in a box. So I got loads of them, and filled all my pockets and I could hardly walk, I was carrying so much. But I imagined myself, you know, last man, loading up my pistol with six rounds. I'd imagine myself standing there, bang, bang, bang, bang, bang, shooting Germans and still they were all around me, and not a mark on me. I never got a thought about me being shot before I even got one round off. I just imagined all the Germans would be piled up around me! And that, I think, is a good way to look at it, because if you're thinking that way, you're not thinking, Well, I'm going to run away. You know, you're going to fight to the last man, and the last round . . . And I think that's the way, if you've got to go, to go. Because that was the only way we were going to get off Dunkirk beach.

Despite their desperate situation, in a rare moment of calm Freddie had his photograph taken by a comrade. In common with many in combat situations, he never entertained the possibility of dying.

It's always the same. You think it's somebody else going to get it, not you. I've had people killed standing by my side, but I never thought I was going to get killed. It's probably stupid, but that was the way to look at it, because if you thought you were going to be killed you'd be a nervous wreck, you couldn't do your job.

Without transport and laden with guns and ammunition, Freddie and the remnants of his squad marched the five miles on to the wide sandy beach at La Panne. They had been in action since 10 May and under almost constant aerial attack. They'd slept when and where they could and eaten little. They'd helped secure the perimeter around the evacuation area long enough for thousands of BEF and French troops to get through. They were battle-weary and exhausted but the job wasn't over yet for Freddie and what remained of the 12th Lancers.

Sapper Jim Purcell, a Territorial with the Royal Engineers attached to an infantry unit, had been in France only a few months. Since 10 May his job had been to blow up bridges to impede the German advance. Now he found himself on a 154-mile fighting retreat, marching smartly but retreating nevertheless. And like Freddie Hunn, he was constantly under air attack.

> Everybody got the order to evacuate. The Germans were coming down, we were just retreating in front of them all the way. Stuka bombers, they used to dive all the way down and you could hear the screaming, it made you deaf, and then they released their bombs and went straight up. After that, we were just on the roads. We marched properly, all the way. Being attacked, we lost a few blokes and then we were told we were going to Dunkirk.

On the beach at La Panne, where the 12th Lancers had arrived on 30 May, BEF troops were massed awaiting evacuation. Though activity in the port of Dunkirk was still in full swing despite Luftwaffe and shell attacks, the armada of 'little ships' now arriving across the Channel had been instructed to make for the beaches of La Panne, Bray-Dunes and Malo-les-Bains to ferry troops to waiting destroyers and the ships out in deep water. But Freddie Hunn could see that the process was slow and time pitifully short.

> There were queues and queues of soldiers on the beach, all lined up, waiting to get into little boats, to take them out to big boats. I remember coming on to the beach at La Panne and I saw my colonel, Herbert Lumsden, walking up the beach with Lord Gort [commander-in-chief, BEF]. And he came back and said to the regiment: 'Right, make three landing places with lorries on the beach.' And so the colonel instructed us to get lorries, drive them into the sea to make jetties in order to get the little boats to come alongside.

Three 'lorry piers' each of 25 lorries, nose to tail and with their tyres slashed so that they wouldn't float away, helped speed up embarkation and the well-disciplined 12th Lancers were put in charge of the operation.

> And we spent almost three days and three nights loading these men into little boats. They would then pull themselves out by rope attached to the shore, out to the big boat in deep water, offload, and then two or three of them would pull it back. And that was going on for certainly three days. Whether it was three nights, I can't say offhand, because time then . . . we didn't know. We didn't sleep, so we didn't know. Time didn't mean a lot.

Although it may have felt like three days and three nights, Freddie's timing is out. The Lancers' war diary records that the regiment was ordered to embark on 30 May but, on reaching La Panne, was 'personally and directly' ordered by the commander-in-chief to reorganise the embarkation beaches there. This, it says, 'continued in perfect order and with unabated zeal throughout the night' and into the following day, with 3,000 men an hour embarked at one stage, despite intermittent shelling: 'Any plane venturing to fly over the beach was met by a veritable tornado of Bofors and machine gun fire.'

The diary records 'good solid morale'. Reports of panic during the evacuation exist but they are rare, particularly among the British. And Freddie, like others handling the embarkation, had orders in the event of indiscipline:

> If anyone panicked or caused any riot or anything that would cause a delay, you would shoot them. But there was nothing like that. Everybody waited their turn, although the bombers were still coming over, and as they came over, people didn't skulk down, they all had their rifles out and shooting up at the bombers as they were coming over. So there was no panic, and they all took turn until, orderly, they could get away. If they'd tried to rush the boats, they would have been shot.

Would Freddie have been prepared to shoot a man desperate to get on a boat?

I doubt very much if I'd have shot any man . . . I might have warned him perhaps. The thing about being in a cavalry regiment, an armoured regiment, is that you shoot people but you don't see them. If you shot somebody, they'd be so far away you'd never identify who you'd shot, which was a big, thankful thing I think, because I should hate to see anybody that I'd actually shot and killed.

After ensuring the orderly embarkation of thousands of men from the improvised jetties, it was more than time for the Lancers to organise their own evacuation.

By then, the big boats weren't coming there any more because they were within shelling range, they'd gone further up [towards Dunkirk]. So we then had to walk from Le Panne to Dunkirk, about eight mile. It was a scorching May day and we were carrying our guns, ammunition, I was still loaded up with all this ammunition. As you were walking along by the sea, dead bodies, all sorts of litter, bodies on the beach. It was all unreal to see it, you can't draw a picture of it. You suddenly see a person shot to pieces and things like that.

Once we looked up and there were three fighters coming towards us at ground level . . . firing their machine guns. So you'd dive under anything. If there was a matchstick there, you'd dive under it. There was three of us, we dived under what we thought was a bit of shelter. You saw the sand being kicked up by the machine gun bullets as it goes by you . . . and that went, and we were all right, we weren't hit. We got up and we were laying under a torpedo. It'd been shot up from a German E-boat, missed the target and skidded up on the beach. And that's what we dived under.

When we got to Malo-les-Bains we found . . . Dunkirk had finished, the main docks and all that were finished. We were lined up on the seashore and the boat was out there and we had to wait there for an hour. And from behind us came three more Messerschmitts. Fortunately they didn't machine-gun us, they were going out to the ships out at sea.

It was well into the evening of 31 May before their turn came.

When we were told to get in the water . . . and of course it's quite high to get in if you're up to your neck, to try to get over into a boat. It's bad enough if you were in a bathing costume, but if you had all that ammunition like I had, and you had your guns and boots, and your battle vest was soaked, it was all heavy, so it was a job to get in. But you had somebody behind you who'd give you a push up, and you'd tip forward into the boat. When the boat was full you'd pull on the rope, which would take you to the boat out at deep water and a couple of you would come back, pull it back and you'd do a shuttle service like that until there was nobody on the shore. And we got on this boat which turned out to be a mud dredger that had come out from the Port of London Authority. You couldn't get anything lower than that, could you?

Humble dredger or naval destroyer, it was an achievement to get on any vessel bound for Britain. In fact, the war diary records that the 12th Lancers were embarked late on 31 May 'chiefly on dredgers belonging to the Tilbury Construction [Contracting] and Dredging Company', welcomed by their 'very charming' hosts.

Shortly before midnight Freddie was still waiting for his dredger to weigh anchor off a town now ablaze.

Everywhere you looked was just explosions, smoke and flame. I took a last look at Dunkirk, and if there was a hell, that was it. I lay down on the iron deck and fell asleep.

Meanwhile, Jim Purcell and his fellow Engineers had marched over 150 miles in four days, scrounging food along the way, to get to the coast. Now, exhausted and thirsty, they had to walk the last seven miles along the sands from Bray-Dunes to Dunkirk. At last they reached the harbour mole, where troops were queuing patiently for rescue.

There was a great big queue, real long queues to go on to the ships. And then the Germans blinking bombed and there were some real tragic things. There was this hospital ship [HMHS *Paris*] and this German bomber come across and dropped the bomb and it went straight down the funnel. Ship's gone. All the wounded, everything, gone. Gradually we walked up and the queue was getting shorter. We climbed down a ladder nearly 50 feet to this little tramp steamer and we got on there. Guess what was in there? Tins of fruits and Carnation Milk! We made ourselves sick, and then we moved off, but the Germans didn't want us to come home, they come in, and the blinking guns were going, we were getting strafed. And you know, you get into a state with things, the bad things become normal.

Homecoming was a bittersweet affair for Freddie Hunn.

Seven o'clock the next morning there was a shout from somebody: 'Blighty!' And there we were, at Margate. So we got off the boat and the people there were fantastic. Tea, sandwiches, cakes, placards – 'Welcome Home' – tears and smiles. 'Welcome home, our brave BEF!' Well, I didn't feel a bit brave. I felt rather ashamed myself, because all these wonderful people there, bringing us out food, and looking on us as some sort of heroes, which I didn't think we were, and relying on us to protect them in the future from the hordes of Germans that I knew were on the other side of the Channel. And what did we have? We didn't have a thing to protect them with. All our materials, our equipment, were on the other side and they seemed oblivious to that. And I felt awful about it.

Jim Purcell had similar mixed feelings on his arrival home three days later to a similar reception.

We got home on the 4th of June. We couldn't understand it when everybody was praising us and cheering us. To us it was a defeat and we couldn't understand it. We got back into Folkestone and we left on a train and ended up in Wales, and we went to one place and people were giving us all sorts of things and as we passed through Reading and everybody was cheering, people were being given all sorts of presents, you know, food, chocolate, and an old lady walked up and gave me a couple of home-made buns.

It was a scene repeated at stations all over Britain. At Woking, 19-year-old bank clerk Eileen Younghusband was volunteering at a mobile canteen serving arriving troops, when from one of the many trains stepped a young Frenchman she'd met two years previously on a school language exchange.

He got out of the carriage almost opposite me in his French Air Force uniform. He came across and said, 'Mon Dieu – Eileen!' And that amazing coincidence and then learning that my own cousin, who was a pre-war RAF pilot, had been killed, and knowing that my father was in the Royal Flying Corps in the First World War, I thought, I'm not just going to help in a canteen. I'm joining up. And that's when I decided to offer my services to the Women's Auxiliary Air Force.

———◆———

The heroic narrative of the Dunkirk evacuation tells of victory snatched from the jaws of defeat, of stoic bravery, little ships and big hearts. It is the story of miraculous deliverance. But there's another, less celebrated, story.

A long way from Dunkirk, David Mowatt was with the rest of the 51st Highland Division, south of the Somme and cut off from the rest of the BEF by the rapid German advance. They too had been shielding the rear of the retreating BEF. Meanwhile the evacuation was happening without them. On 4 June, as Jim Purcell was arriving on English shores, the Highlanders were sent on the offensive and David saw his first real action, shooting German soldiers patrolling the far side of the riverbank.

> They scarpered but I'm pretty sure I got them because I was Dead-Eye Dick. I thought, I've got to get you first, mate! We were taught to shoot first, ask questions later. You were a soldier and your rifle was your best friend. That man over the other side isn't.

As it turned out, this would be the first and last shot he would fire. Soon there were many injuries and fatalities among his comrades in the Seaforth Highlanders, boys he'd signed up with at home. The Highlanders, with heavy casualties and unable to drive the enemy back over the Somme, now attempted to hold the much smaller River Bresle. As company runner, David's job was to maintain contact between three platoons, relaying information about coming attacks. David's platoon were holding a bridge and about to come under shellfire; he had to warn the next platoon in the line of fire to pull back. Under machine gun fire and crawling along a ditch filled with engine oil, he delivered the message to the next platoon. Here he was told the third platoon was already under heavy fire and he'd never reach them, but David felt it was his duty to try. When he finally got there he found a solitary infantryman.

> Lance Corporal Rose was his name. I said, 'Where's your officer?' 'He's dead.' 'Where's your sergeant?' 'He's dead.' 'Where's your corporal?' 'Dead.' I said, 'You're the only one left in charge?' 'Yes,' he said.

There was a plan to evacuate from Le Havre but the route was blocked by the Germans. Orders came direct from Churchill that they were to carry on whilst the French were still fighting alongside them, but the French were demoralised, ill-equipped and slow, holding up the withdrawal. The Highlanders were exhausted, having marched, pulled back and held line after line: 'We were at the end of our tether.'

They started out for Dunkirk, on the way looting whatever food and drink they could find from houses and abandoned military vehicles. In an episode of light relief, David broke into a house one night and 'liberated' three bicycles. 'Let the boys cycle rather than march!' he told his company commander. By this time the officer was past caring: 'Do what you bloody well like, Mowatt!' David took him at his word: soon every man in the company was provided with a looted bike. It was far from the Highlanders' proud image, but they were now intent only on survival, trying to get to the coast through countryside thick with German troops: 'We were under terrible, terrible pressure. We were on our knees.'

Finally, around 10 June, almost a week after the last ship had left Dunkirk for British shores, the remnants of the 51st Highlanders (but still numbering several thousand men) reached the small fishing port of Saint-Valery-en-Caux, west of Dunkirk, with hopes of being taken off by navy destroyers. But the Germans were already occupying gun positions on the cliffs and by the following day the port was surrounded and being heavily shelled. Despite the order to evacuate, no navy vessel was in sight and anyway, the sea was shrouded in fog. Some men tried to escape down the steep cliffs using improvised ropes but 'the Jerries were coming along at the top of the cliffs and cutting them. It was murderous.'

Stuck on the cliffs on the Dunkirk side, the company commander went to check on the likelihood of rescue. David went with him, but it was hopeless. 'We knew we'd had it then.' Their commanding officer, Major General Fortune, surrendered to Field Marshal Rommel, commander of the 7th Panzer Division, at 1000 hours on 12 June.

As we waited for the Germans to walk in, Rommel was on one of the first tanks to arrive. He spoke to all of us: 'I hope you'll be treated fairly and that you won't be a prisoner of war for too long'.

It was no comfort to the exhausted and demoralised Highlanders as they were marched away. Among them was Margaret Rhodes' brother John, an officer with the Black Watch.

Back in Britain, Churchill was clear that 'wars are not won by evacuations'; Dunkirk had been a 'colossal military disaster'. Yet in the public mind as much as in the surrounding press propaganda or Churchill's rousing rhetoric, there was something uniquely heroic about the orderly evacuation of almost 350,000 battle-weary men by such an unlikely rescue flotilla. It was a shock defeat but one that woke Britons up from their Phoney War lethargy. Instead of destroying morale, Dunkirk was the start of a new kind of perverse pride and resolve in adversity. People now had a clearer idea of what they were fighting for. The enemy was real and rather too close for comfort. The war had finally come home to them.

Fred Glover had been sceptical about the war but Dunkirk changed that.

> After Dunkirk, you suddenly realised what we'd got here was enslavement of Europe and all that meant. I suppose I was a pacifist on the grounds that these [wars] are fought for colonial possessions, all these sort of things. But when I saw the implications of what was going on in Europe, it suddenly struck me that we're in a different ball game entirely. I think it was probably at that point that I decided that I would enlist.

A few months short of his seventeenth birthday Fred lied about his age and enlisted in the 70th (Young Soldiers) Battalion of the Royal East Kent Regiment.

Simple things now assumed new significance. In the lean years of the Depression Joy Lofthouse's father had been lucky to get a job as superintendent of the local lido, where he taught people to swim.

There were boys who came back from Dunkirk and thanked him for having taught them to swim. They said you didn't have to swim out to the boats, you were walking up to your chest carrying your arms, but the fact that you were capable, it gave you the confidence to know you weren't afraid of the water. I'll never forget him being so pleased about that.

For the young men bloodied by their first encounters with the unromantic realities of warfare and bewildered by their rapturous reception on their return from France, this was the start of a long haul that would test their physical and emotional strength – and their patriotism – to the limit. They'd be followed into the ranks in due course by many others as keen, and as green. At home, with the threat of attack and even invasion no longer a science fiction nightmare, Britain's young civilians would soon have to shape up smartly too.

5

The Battle of Britain
June–September 1940

When you were working you didn't have feelings. You didn't have time. It was when you came off duty that you thought about it, and you hoped you'd done the best you could.

Eileen Younghusband, WAAF filter plotter, aged 19

The 'miracle of deliverance' at Dunkirk prompted a brief public mood of defiant jubilation. The fact that Britain's allies had all been overrun didn't seem to worry people: ages-old enmity with the French encouraged a popular belief that Britain was probably better off alone. That feeling no doubt helped boost morale but an unshakeable confidence in the country's ability to defend itself from attack was misplaced. A large proportion of the British Expeditionary Force had been delivered from France, but practically all of its equipment lay abandoned in rusting piles along the roads to Dunkirk. Britain's ground forces were severely depleted: 8,000 men had been killed; twice that number were seriously injured; another 40,000 were left behind as prisoners of war. To defend the country a much heavier burden would now fall on the RAF. The Royal Navy and the Merchant Navy would play their part too.

After France capitulated in June and Churchill's Cabinet comprehensively rejected Hitler's invitation to surrender, there could be no doubt that Britain was in the gravest danger of invasion. Churchill's 'on the beaches' speech of 4 June stiffened sinews and prepared the country for the long fight ahead. Behind the stirring rhetoric, practical measures on the ground to prevent – or at best impede – a German invasion were often laughably inadequate. The seeds for *Dad's Army* were sown.

Gunner Fergus Anckorn, like many young men in the army, found himself on invasion duty soon after the Dunkirk evacuation.

> I was on sentry duty on the cliffs outside Bexhill so I was walking up and down there in the night on my own. This didn't bother me because the boys from London were frightened to death of the dark, so I used to do their sentry goes for them for five bob. I loved standing in the middle of the woods and just keeping still and watching the rabbits, so on the cliffs at night I was quite happy. The sergeant who took me there pointed to a box and said, 'There's your telephone exchange.' I said, 'What do you mean?' 'Oh,' he said, 'if you see two red flares and a white, there's an invasion coming and you'll have to turn that, and ring up and you'll be put in touch with the mayor in Eastbourne. Because there's only you between here and Hitler.'
>
> I thought, Well, this is dangerous. And it was pouring with rain. I had an overcoat on that went down to my ankles and it weighed about half a ton within an hour. Round about two in the morning I thought I'd better make sure I know how to work this, so I thought, I'll phone up and say, 'Testing, testing,' just to make sure. So I did this and I did a back somersault on to the ground because it was an induction coil and it was all soaking wet and it was like going to the electric chair. I thought, I don't care how many reds and whites are coming, I'm not touching that thing again. If I see two reds and a white, I'm legging it.

Freddie Hunn and Jim Purcell, hardly recovered from their ordeal at Dunkirk, were soon on invasion duty too. Jim was active as a sapper on the south coast of England.

> We had two days' leave and then we were back. My regiment went all round the south coast to make sure they couldn't get here. My first job with my mates was to blow a blinking big hole

in the middle of Bournemouth Pier so that the Germans couldn't
get through, and then after that we went all along the south coast
building defences, laying mines on beaches, deepening rivers so if
they did invade their tanks couldn't get through.

Freddie Hunn's 12th Lancers used the 'Beaverette', a small
armoured car commissioned by Minister for Aircraft Production
Lord Beaverbrook. Freddie went in this on invasion patrols along
the Kent coast, armed with a Bren gun and a supply of Molotov
cocktails. His job as part of a rapid-response unit was to rush to
where enemy parachutists had been sighted. But the Beaverette
was unlikely to rush anywhere. Encumbered by its steel and oak
armour plating over an ordinary saloon car chassis, its top speed
was 24 miles an hour.

Enemy paratroopers arriving as an advance army of invasion
– variously disguised as priests, nuns and, even more bizarrely, AA
patrolmen – were the bogeymen of those fearful months of 1940.
Paratroops had played a successful, if minor, part in the invasion
of Belgium and stories of ingenious disguises probably started
there. The idea of a pernicious fifth column, enemy spies (whether
arriving by parachute or not) infiltrating and undermining British
society in a softening-up exercise prior to invasion, was another
Continental import, this time from the Spanish Civil War, that
gripped the public imagination but had little substance in fact.

The months following Dunkirk were a time of anxiety fuelled
by uncertainty. German propaganda broadcasts by William Joyce
(Lord Haw-Haw) started wild rumours, inflated fears and contra-
dicted everything official sources were saying. Bill Graves first
heard him on the radio when he was on duty as an ARP messenger
boy in Bristol.

The things that struck me were his peculiar little voice and how
different the things he was saying were to all the other broadcasts
on the radio. Many people treated it as a bit of fun but others
took everything he said very seriously. I switched it off when my
superiors came in. The powers that be didn't allow his propaganda

as it went against their attempts to maintain morale. He was a figure of fun, but I did wonder how this man on the radio seemed to be aware of everything that was going on. Once he talked about 'the poor people of Bristol' who were about to be attacked. It proved to be true.

Haw-Haw and the German propaganda machine fed people's craving for information at a time when the Ministry of Information was being criticised for crass censorship of bad news and patronising poster campaigns. Bill recalls the resentment in Bristol.

Propaganda was everywhere. People were both aware of it and cynical about it. They felt they were being dictated to and they didn't like it. People were glued to the radio and newspapers but even these sent out the messages we were supposed to hear, rather than the truth, but it was the only way to stay informed and people were worried. They needed any information they could get, especially those families with loved ones in the services.

Anything could happen, so it wasn't surprising that every colourful new rumour quickly gained currency and suspicion of anyone with a foreign accent was rife. Barely suppressed xenophobia was now given full rein, stirred up by right-wing newspapers: every non-Briton was a possible fifth columnist, even if they were a recently exiled Czech Jew or a third-generation Italian ice-cream parlour proprietor. Indiscriminate internment following the Fall of France proved the flip side of Britain's pre-war generosity to refugees. By June 1940 tens of thousands of 'enemy aliens' were being rounded up for internment, the vast majority of whom posed absolutely no threat to Britain. Enid Wenban was stationed in a 'hush-hush' establishment on the Isle of Man, home to one of the biggest concentrations of Italian internees in the country.

We were housed in vacated hotels on Douglas seafront, behind a barbed-wire fence, so we were a guarded camp. Just along the promenade was a large internment camp, similarly placed, but with barbed wire to keep them in! We saw the internees behind barbed wire, but they certainly wouldn't have talked to us. They were guarded.

Though many internees were freed after the imminent threat of invasion and its attendant panic had passed, more than 7,000 were deported to far-flung corners of the empire. Some of these entirely innocent deportees perished on the journey when their ships were torpedoed.

———◆———

Fears of invasion by sea or air soon prompted the formation of a new homeland security force. Jimmy Perry, then 16, remembers how it came about.

> After Dunkirk all the papers were full of German troops dropping by parachute. That was the first time we'd ever heard of parachute troops, fifth columnists, quislings . . . Parachutists were landing everywhere! And then it was decided to form a force to guard Britain and on [the radio] came Anthony Eden: 'We want large numbers of men, seventeen to sixty-five, to defend the shores of our beloved land.' And I thought, That's for me, I'll go! But my mother said no.

The new force was to be called the Local Defence Volunteers (LDV), and its job was to watch for possible landings, impede enemy progress and protect 'vulnerable spots, of which there are a great number everywhere'. Within 24 hours nearly 250,000 men – those too old or too young to fight or who were otherwise unfit for military service – had volunteered. What they lacked in fitness, professionalism and equipment they made up for in enthusiasm. Their false alarms and indiscriminate roadblocks infuriated the hard-pressed military and caused havoc; their drills using First World War bayonets wired to broom handles caused hilarity. Uncomplimentary variants of their initials circulated, 'Look, Duck and Vanish' and 'Last-Ditch Venture' among them. At Churchill's insistence the name soon changed to the more professional-sounding Home Guard. With the arrival of arms from America under the Lend-Lease scheme and with leadership from seasoned army veterans, the motley collection of military rejects began to look more like a respectable defence force. Jimmy, now 17, was itching to join.

> I said to my dear mother, 'I'm sorry, I'm going,' and I joined the Home Guard. By the time I joined, we were a fighting force. All the young men waiting to be called up would join and we were a huge number of very young 17- and 18-year-olds. Our commanding officer was an ex-schoolmaster who'd fought in the Spanish Civil War and he used to say to us, 'Kill the bastards! If you see them, shoot the bastards! Dismissed!' None of your la-di-da. Because we were fighting for our lives and we were trained to kill them.

Bill Graves, 17 and in the Home Guard in Bristol, was more sceptical.

> The training was ridiculous. We used this large building in Frenchay. We were told to imagine it was a base for German paratroopers and taught to charge them with fixed bayonets. This was pointless as these skills were never needed and anyway, the building was at the top of a hill and any such advance would have been met with German guns.

The bureaucracy and sometimes inexplicable discipline could be trying: when Bill and some young comrades took the initiative and manned an anti-aircraft gun to try and disable a stray German plane, they were put on a charge. 'I thought all this fuss and red tape was a load of old crap, but I'd been raised to respect my elders and betters.'

If the British Army had suffered a blow at Dunkirk, the RAF was in rather better shape. Fighter Command was by now a tight and well-organised force with modern Hurricanes and Spitfires fast coming on stream. Rapidly developing radar technology provided a vital competitive edge and the code-breakers at Bletchley Park could often give advance warning of German air attacks.

As British aircraft factories worked all hours to turn out fighters and bombers, the RAF needed many more pilots than the regular RAF could provide. From being an elite corps supplied by the public schools, the RAF had to become more meritocratic. Now the young trainee pilots who'd joined up before the war in the Royal Auxiliary Air Force (RAAF) or the RAF Volunteer Reserve would come into their own. But even to get this far, being 'the right sort' still mattered. In 1938, 18-year-old Tony Pickering applied for the Volunteer Reserve.

> The first question they asked me was 'What school did you go to?' I told them Market Harborough Grammar School. Then they asked me what my father did in the first war. I was able to tell them, 'Warrant officer, Royal Navy' – a regular. And then, what sport I played. Now, I must be quite honest with you. I didn't tell them I played soccer because I didn't think the Royal Air Force would welcome a soccer player. I had actually picked up a rugby ball once, so I said, 'Played rugby, sir.' And I got full marks for that, but it wasn't strictly correct.

A grammar school boy from the provinces would do as a sergeant pilot in the Volunteer Reserve. After flying 'Saturday and Sunday afternoons when the weather was suitable', Tony was called up to the RAAF on the outbreak of war and started his full pilot training. By July 1940 he was ready for his baptism of fire.

> After we'd been kicked out of France, I joined 32 Squadron at Biggin Hill. The squadron commander turned to us three sergeant pilots and said, 'How many hours have you done on Hurricanes?' I said, 'Sir, I've never even seen a Hurricane.' 'Well,' he said, 'you'll

see one this afternoon because you'll do three circuits and bumps and tomorrow morning at four o'clock you'll be awoken and you'll join the squadron at dispersal and fly immediately it's light down to Dover and you'll take part in any combat from then on.'

We were pulled out of bed and given a cup of tea and I reported to my flight commander, who a few weeks before had been a sergeant pilot with 501 Squadron, having been promoted very quickly to flight lieutenant. And he said, 'I want you to stick right behind me and you'll put your gun button in the Off position, I don't want you sitting behind me with your gun button on. If there's any firing to be done, I'll do it.' So we took off to defend Dover from attacks by Junkers 87 [Stuka] dive-bombers and I was flying as his number two.

Tom Neil's fascination with aeroplanes started with Amy Johnson's solo flight to Australia. He joined the RAF Volunteer Reserve in Manchester in 1938 but the weather was so bad at his local airfield that it took him till early 1940 to get his flying hours in and complete his training.

I was posted to a fighter squadron, 249(H) Squadron. I deduced 'H' was for Hurricanes, which was a great thrill for me because I'd been trained on biplanes, I'd never been near a low-wing monoplane and it was exciting to think that I was going to be flying Hurricanes. So I turned up on the 15th of May 1940 at Church Fenton as a young pilot officer and nobody had ever heard anything about me, nor indeed had they heard about 249 Squadron, and I thought I'd come to the wrong place. And then a chap turned up with a lot of gold braid, Air Vice-Marshal Richard Saul, and he stood us in line, ten of us. And he said, 'Right, you've got five weeks to get yourselves in trim to take on the might of the German Luftwaffe.' And we looked sideways at each other because we didn't have any aeroplanes for a start and none of us had ever flown a monoplane, much less a Hurricane or a Spitfire.

That was about to change.

We had a Spitfire mounted on trestles in a hangar and each one of us was plonked in the cockpit and the chap said, 'This is the throttle, this is the control column, these are the knobs and the bits and pieces, and now we're going to blindfold you and you're going to sit here for three hours and work out where everything is.' And this I did for a whole morning, then after lunch they sat me in the big Spitfire and said, 'Right, off you go!' I'm sitting in this aeroplane in a Mae West [life jacket], which I'd never worn before, I'd never flown with a radio, I'd never flown with oxygen, with a mask over my face, all these things were new to me. And I remember sitting there and realising I didn't know how to start the engine!

With instructions from his 19-year-old rigger to remember to look right and left to see where he was going and 'not to boil the bloody engine', he got the Spitfire started, took off 'like an electric eel' and flew at 300 miles an hour faster than he'd ever flown before. After a month on Spitfires a consignment of 18 Hurricanes arrived.

We stepped out of Spitfires into Hurricanes. It was dead easy because both aircraft were childishly easy to fly. Then the chap with the gold leaves round his hat came back and said, 'Right, you're operational now, you're fit to fight the enemy.' This was the morning of the 4th of July 1940 and in the afternoon I intercepted my first enemy aircraft.

Tom's log records the auspicious event.

My first flight. Nearly died of shock. North Weald heavily bombed. Me110s very fierce. 2 engagements with EA [enemy aircraft]. Didn't even fire guns. Chased round sky by Me109s.

The Battle of Britain was now officially under way. Throughout July and August the Luftwaffe mounted increasing daytime attacks on Channel shipping and southern coastal ports and airfields. At night they went further north, east and west to attack aircraft factories and RAF installations. From mid August they concentrated their fire on airfields in the south-east, aiming to exhaust RAF fighter defences completely. Tom Neil recalls North Weald airbase in Epping Forest at this time being bombed by '30 or 40 bombers dropping a hundred or more 500-pound bombs, escorted by 50, 60, 70, 80 aircraft'.

The Luftwaffe was making serious inroads into RAF defences and, to a lesser extent, its aircraft factories. It was now imperative for the RAF to put as many German bombers out of action as possible. Tony Pickering was clear about the importance of the task in hand.

> We knew that we had to do something to stop the Germans getting over because had they have crossed the Channel it would have been very, very difficult then to have defeated them. We had to make sure they didn't knock our squadrons out of action, that we had to be there. Our morale was so high that we felt that they could never beat us. There was never any doubt about whether we would be beaten. Occasionally squadrons that were carrying an establishment of twelve, sometimes they were down to eight or nine, we could only get eight or nine in the air: aircraft had been damaged, pilots had been lost, we lost some good friends, but we never doubted our ability to stop them getting over.

Morale may have been high but the battle wasn't necessarily weighted in the RAF's favour. Each side's aircraft had its advantages over the other – and its faults. The Hurricane was slower and more lightly armed than the Messerschmitt Bf 109 fighter so it was unwise to pick a fight. Its target lay elsewhere:

> As Hurricane fighters, our job was to attack the bombers. The Spitfires who were flying above us looked after the Messerschmitt 109 fighters. Our job was to attack bombers but if we could get into the bombers before the 109s came down upon us then we were lucky, but we occasionally got through and we fired our guns

into these massive ranks of German bomber formations of probably a hundred, all tightly knitted together.

Even when they got through, it was a tall order for a Hurricane to cripple a huge bomber with its relatively low-powered guns, when the German fighters had cannon fire at their disposal. Tom Neil had no illusions about his firepower.

In terms of armament we had an inferior set-up. We were flying peashooters really because we were shooting .303 rifle calibre machine guns and we only had 15 seconds of ammunition.

But the Hurricane did have its strong points, as Tony Pickering points out.

We could take a lot of punishment in the Hurricane from the German gunners in their bombers and still fly, whereas I'm afraid that if the Spitfire had taken the same punishment as we took, it would have fallen to pieces. I appreciate the Spitfire was a better fighter aeroplane but it was highly stressed and we could take this punishment, so in we went with the bombers.

All through that hot summer, the battle continued over the south-eastern counties of England. However, 7 September 1940 proved to be a watershed for the RAF, for German air strategy and for London. British air raids on Berlin, ineffective except for their propaganda value, impelled a furious Hitler to redirect his bombers away from military to civilian targets. London was to get the full blitzkrieg treatment.

For the young pilots who'd already spent much of the summer on adrenalin-fuelled sorties, often eating by their aircraft and snatching sleep between flights, this was just another day, or so they thought. During the day, it was pretty much business as usual, attacking raiders as they approached military targets. By then Tony Pickering was based at Gravesend on the Kent side of the Thames estuary.

We got back after our morning combat, which I can remember very little about other than just pressing the button and seeing my bullets tearing into these bombers, but after lunch we were told that we would go on '30 minutes available', which meant we were more or less put on rest with 30 minutes given to get into the air. There were about six of us, mainly sergeant pilots, who decided we'd go to the local cinema. British Movietone News or Gaumont were showing a newsreel with our squadron – unidentified, of course – taking off to repel the enemy, and we wanted to see this. When we got there we reported to the manager and told him that in the event of a call from the CO [commanding officer] he was to get us immediately into our wagon because we only had 30 minutes to get into the air. We'd been sitting there for about an hour watching ourselves on this newsreel and the manager suddenly came dashing in with lights flashing: 'Back to the airfield, you boys!' So we got into our truck and as we were going back we could see the German bombers going to the docks of London, masses of bombers, possibly 2,000 or 3,000 going towards the docks. We were off within 25 minutes but as we were taking off the German bombers had dropped their bombs, the docks were a mass of flames and smoke and there we were climbing up from zero feet up to about 20,000 feet to repel these bombers but by that time they were on their way over the Channel . . . So it was a negative sortie. We just couldn't get to them. We saw them, but we couldn't get to them.

The fact that another dozen fighter squadrons from North Weald, Kenley and Biggin Hill were already up there doing battle was little consolation. Tom Neil was also in action on that day.

The 7th was a day I remember because I flew four times on that day. The first two we may have seen signs but we didn't intercept anything. About 4.30 p.m. we came across a big raid and it really sticks in my mind because we attacked Dorniers and the Heinkels as they were flying towards London and I shot down my first aircraft, a 109 fighter. We climbed up 13,000, 14,000, 15,000 feet over

Maidstone and suddenly I'm going towards a mass of anti-aircraft fire and there in the middle were these enormous formations of German bombers, and behind them the fighters all stepped down like flies and you looked to left and right of you because you were only flying in a single formation, and you think, My God, were do we start?

The 7th is memorable for Tom for another reason. It was the day his squadron lost half a dozen aircraft in as many minutes, when Bf 109s surged in behind them. The Hurricane was particularly vulnerable to catching fire if it was hit, as it had a fuel tank on each wing, left and right of the pilot's feet.

The fire would come up the cockpit straight into the pilot's face and hands and this is why almost all Hurricane pilots who were shot down were hideously burned because the fire used to come up and you had to get out of the cockpit by about three seconds otherwise you were barbecued where you sat. At the end of the day we lost about six, I think, including two of my closest friends.

It had been a particularly traumatic day and Tom returned to base unharmed but exhausted.

If you're very hotly pursued by the enemy and you've escaped with your life, you feel like a piece of chewed string. You get back and you're just worn. You flop on your bed and you sleep.

His log records the day's events.

Me109 vicinity Maidstone 18,000ft. Got him in glycol [fuel tank] & finally made him jump. We lost half the squadron: Boost Fleming killed. Wells, Killingback, Smithson, Granby & Barcly all shot down. I was very very scared. Results negligible.

Losses were a fact of life. Tony Pickering too, lost good friends.

We suffered casualties, of course. One time at Kenley there were four sergeant pilots sharing one room. At the beginning of the week there were four of us, about Tuesday there were three – one fellow had been killed. The next day another one had gone – he was wounded, bowed out. The next day another one went and on that last day I was there by myself. I did lose some good friends, but there again we were trained to do a job and being very young I suppose I hadn't got much imagination, let's put it that way; I was able to erase those sorts of thoughts from my mind and get on with my job and I think the majority of us did that.

Tom Neil shared this dogged determination to just 'get on with it', even if at times this was difficult.

At the end of a day, I felt very worn, and very conscious of the fact that when I was lying on my bed at night there were bombers droning overhead dropping bombs and there were empty beds to the left and right of me, people that I'd known, and they were up there. Normally it wouldn't worry us because sometimes, after a hard day's fighting, your friends would turn up the following day, having come back on the Tube with a parachute under their arm. So it wasn't axiomatic that they'd been killed. Often they weren't. I can't remember ever thinking, Oh my God, all my friends are dead, and I never came across a feeling of 'Oh my God, I can't go on'. It didn't happen that way. You just got on with the fighting. There was no counselling or anything like that. You were just concerned with the matters of the moment. You just got on with it.

Yet some casualties were particularly hard to bear.

The Germans were probably more chivalrous than we were because, at one time during the Battle of Britain, word went round that they were shooting at our chaps coming down by parachute. It was never true, they never did. The only people who shot us in our parachutes were our own people – army oiks, I call them. LDVs, the forerunner of the Home Guard. They couldn't recognise the difference between enemy and friend. The chap from 249 Squadron who got his VC [Victoria Cross] was crippled, shot by an army fellow on the ground just as he was about to land. And a friend of mine came down by parachute having been set on fire, but the army did a better job on him. They killed him, in the air.

◆

RAF aircraft losses were great, but not as great as those of the Luftwaffe, who suffered half as many again. A critical factor too was that German production was not keeping up with its losses, and neither was its supply of trained air crew. On both these counts, forward planning, the contribution of Polish, Czech and empire pilots, and an all-stops-out push by Lord Beaverbrook on aircraft production gave Britain a decisive edge as the Battle of Britain reached its zenith in September, as Tom Neil acknowledges.

A point very seldom mentioned when you talk about the Battle of Britain is the efficiency of our supply chain, because very often we were down to five, six, seven aircraft at the end of a day, but by lunchtime the following day we'd be back to full strength. We were never short of aircraft.

Women kept that supply chain moving. Young Gladys Parry from Hulme was one of them at Avro's Woodford factory.

I got drafted into war work in a Lancaster [bomber] factory and it was the noisiest factory, very big and noisy. And first of all I went doing itemising, like putting a number on a piece of metal. Well, I thought that was rubbish. But then they found out I could use a sewing machine and I was doing the parts for the inside, the seats – very fine leather it was. And I used to put little notes in when I was doing it, 'God bless you, and hope you're safe' and all that, you know. I'd sew them together, these pieces of leather to make the parts to go in the cockpit, for them to sit on because there was no such thing as plastic in them days and material would never have done. I used to make a spliced loop on the end of a wire for quick release, to allow the pilot once he pulled it to get up out of it. And I was hoping that maybe, if he got back, he'd find these little notes saying 'God bless you, hope you come back safe' and 'My name's Gladys and I worked on making this seat for you'. Oh, it was very emotional, it really was.

Gladys's emotional involvement was total: she had her own airman boyfriend until he was shot down over Germany, missing presumed dead.

I was heartbroke. I still hoped they were wrong and he would come back but he never did. He used to say don't get too friendly because they might not come back, so this is how you tried to keep a relationship a little bit . . . not too loving, you know?

But being heartbroken or even unwell was insufficient reason for staying off work, and the hours were often long and arduous. Soon she was moved from making seats to splicing wire.

You just couldn't let the blokes down. It didn't stop you from carrying on and it were a bit more patriotic that you were doing something for them, you know. My work was not hard, because it's not hard to splice fine wire. The hard work came when you were carrying the cable. That was hard, to carry it outside and run it up and down, and carry it to the place where they burn the ends so they don't fly up. But the long hours . . . It was tiredness more than anything. We used to get there seven in the morning and if we were lucky we could get home at five but most nights we were asked to work till seven o'clock and it was eight and half past before you got home of a night. But those Lancaster bombers, they've got a heart in them as big as a bucket. We were all very proud of them. The whole factory was a unit. We were very proud of helping the country, building aeroplanes that were going to stand up to anything. We did the best we could. Even though we were knackered!

By the end of the Battle of Britain, British aircraft factories had more than doubled the output of their German counterparts. Aeroplanes were ferried from factory to airfield by the Air Transport Auxiliary (ATA), who employed qualified pilots who weren't suitable for combat flying: overage men and those with disabilities – and women. One in eight ATA pilots were women. One of the first to offer her services was Amy Johnson, who died in January 1941 after her ferry flight crashed into the freezing waters of the Thames in mysterious circumstances.

The Battle of Britain had a great influence on tomboy Joy Lofthouse. She grew up surrounded by RAF stations in Gloucestershire and by 1940 she'd left her grammar school and was working in a bank. Making friends with locally stationed airmen and wanting to learn more about their world, she bought a monthly magazine, *The Aeroplane*, and gradually became absorbed by the magic of flying. She was too young to contribute to the Battle of Britain, but then she saw a news item in *The Aeroplane*:

> It said the ATA had run out of qualified pilots and were training up a new issue. I thought, Well, I'd planned to join the services anyway and this sounds much more fun than going in the ordinary WAAFs [Women's Auxiliary Air Force]. And so I applied. So did my sister, she saw it too. Of course everyone said, 'You must have had influence.' Rubbish. We were just hicks from the sticks.

It was the start of a magnificent adventure for Joy and her sister, and a singular contribution to the war effort.

Women were a vital asset too in operations rooms in every RAF base. Eileen Younghusband was determined to join the WAAF after her cousin was killed in action. Before her interview she was tipped the wink by a school friend already in the service.

> She said, 'They're sure to ask you whether you want to be a cook or a driver. And you've got to say, "Neither. I want to be a clerk (special duties)."' So I said, 'What's that?' And she said, 'I can't tell

you, but just tell them you're good at mathematics,' which was my best subject. And that's exactly what happened. I was enrolled as a clerk (special duties), not having a clue what I was going to do.

In training she found herself part of a very mixed bunch.

We had vicars' daughters and office people. We had prostitutes. We were all there mixed up. And before I knew anything, I had to sign the Official Secrets Act. This would keep me silent for 30 years, even when the war was finished. Even later on when I was married and had a son, neither of them ever knew what I did in the filter room of the Royal Air Force.

At barely 19 Eileen became a filter plotter, part of the RAF's most secret radar operations, making complex mathematical calculations to identify and track incoming enemy aircraft so that within minutes fighter squadrons could be scrambled to intercept them. Seconds counted and able young women like Eileen were quick. And, like Gladys Parry in the Lancaster factory, they had a compelling emotional attachment to their work.

We were 19, 20, 21. Girls still, really, and all of us had got brothers or husbands or boyfriends in the air force and we knew the squadrons that were operating and we had that responsibility of tracking in German bombers that were going to bomb our families. This great responsibility weighed on us but it made us even more determined to do the job properly.

The work was intense and the eight-hour watches took their toll.

You had to keep going and the pressure was enormous. You had to make the right decision, because air-raid warnings were being given on what we were saying, aircraft were being shot down if we didn't identify them correctly. When we came off watch we were absolutely drained. We'd have a meal and we'd be semi-hysterical, we'd laugh and giggle because it was letting the emotions out that had all been bottled up during those hours.

But there were compensations:

Quite often when you'd go back on watch, the controller would say, 'By the way, you'll be happy to know that we managed to shoot down so many aircraft on that last watch because of your information.' And that's when you felt good about it.

The Battle of Britain officially started on 10 July with the first concerted raids on ports and shipping, and ended on 15 September in a huge and decisive battle involving 17 RAF squadrons and heavy German losses. Goering was forced to concede that his campaign to defeat the RAF was failing. As a result, Hitler postponed his invasion plans indefinitely, turning his attentions east towards the greater enemy: Russia. During those critical 16 weeks Tom Neil flew 141 operations. Like Tony Pickering, he was still only 19. Did he ever doubt that Britain would win the battle – or the war?

To me the Royal Air Force was indestructible and Great Britain would never lose a war. It could lose a battle from time to time, but even during the retreat from Dunkirk, it never occurred to me for a moment that we would lose. I never knew anybody in the RAF, right or left of me, who thought we would lose. We were going to win. That's all there was to it. We were better than them. It hadn't occurred to me otherwise.

For Tom, the real turning point in the battle, and the war, was not 15 September but 7 September, when Hitler instructed the Luftwaffe to bomb London.

The first principle of war is 'maintain the aim'. On the 7th they changed the aim and they lost the Battle of Britain because they ceased trying to destroy us in the air, our 650 fighters. They ceased bombing our airfields, they ceased bombing our factories and now they went for London.

The air war didn't end with the Battle of Britain and depended on many more men and women than the brave few in the front line. But this first decisive engagement inspired confidence after the debacle of Dunkirk and proved the mettle of those determined to see it through the dark days ahead.

The First World War was a character-forming event for the children born before 1914. *Above*: Gus Bialick poses proudly with his father (left) and uncle, *c*.1918. *Below left*: Armistice Day celebrations on 11 November 1918 are still clear in the memory of the oldest members of this generation. *Below right*: aged seven, Donald Overall was among the crowd in Whitehall to witness the unveiling of the Cenotaph in November 1920.

The home lives of children growing up in the 1920s and 1930s were sharply differentiated by class: (*above left*) Jim Purcell's childhood in Jarrow was marked by illness and poverty; (*above right*) Diana Athill grew up in a comfortable upper-middle-class family on a country estate; (*left*) home for young Margaret Rhodes (centre, between her father and mother), the daughter of Lord Elphinstone, was a spartan Scottish castle.

The East End housed many of London's immigrant communities. Connie Hoe grew up in Limehouse, the original Chinese settlement.

Almost every family was affected by the Spanish influenza epidemic of 1918–20.

Empire Day on 24 May was one of the most important dates in the calendar for British schoolchildren. They celebrated with street parades, pageants and patriotic songs.

Three events in the autumn of 1936 illustrated the seismic social and political shifts of the times: the Battle of Cable Street between Mosley's Blackshirts and immigrant communities (*above*); the Jarrow March of unemployed men to London (*below left*); and the abdication of King Edward VIII (*below right*). They were the background to our generation's adolescence and young adulthood.

At eighteen Fergus Anckorn was already performing professionally and was, in his day, the youngest ever member of the Magic Circle.

Above left: the Scout Movement gave boys the opportunity for outdoor fun – and inculcated initiative, obedience and patriotism. *Above right*: George Montague, choirboy and enthusiastic Boy Scout, *c*.1936.

In the run-up to the declaration of war in September 1939 Britons were drilled in Air Raid Precautions (ARP, *above left*) and numerous ARP wardens recruited – many of them young people like Dorothy Hughes (*above right*).

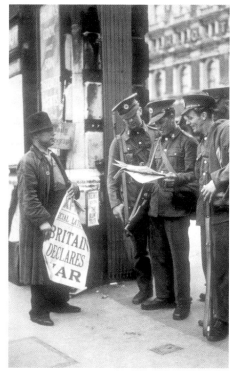

Dorothy Bohm (*above left*) was one of thousands of European Jews who were given refuge in Britain between 1938 and the outbreak of war (*above right*).

Local Defence Volunteers (later called the Home Guard) depended
on old soldiers and teenagers like Jimmy Perry and Bill Graves
to defend their homeland.

The shock evacuation of the British Expeditionary Force at Dunkirk in
May–June 1940 was a watershed in Britons' attitudes to the war. Freddie
Hunn of the 12th Royal Lancers (*above left*, shown here on the BEF's
'fighting retreat') was one of the nearly 340,000 troops rescued from
Dunkirk's beaches by the Royal Navy and the 'little ships' (*above right*).

Young people played a key part in the Battle of Britain (*above right*) in the summer of 1940 and the Blitz that followed in London and Britain's ports and cities. Eighteen-year-old Tom Neil of the RAF Volunteer Reserve (*above left*) was a Hurricane pilot in Fighter Command; nineteen-year-old WAAF Eileen Younghusband (*below right*) was a Filter Plotter tracking incoming enemy aircraft; seventeen-year-old Richard Holsgrove helped save St Paul's from the flames during the 'Second Great Fire of London' in December 1940 as a Junior Fireman in the Auxiliary Fire Service (*below left*).

6

The Blitz

September 1940–May 1941

The whistle of the bombs, the drone of the aircraft and the smell
. . . the awful smell of burning flesh and burning buildings.
Dorothy Hughes, ATS anti-aircraft battery

The first phase of the battle for Britain – the battle for air supremacy – had been won. The threat of invasion, if not vanquished entirely, was at least now more remote. The RAF's job was by no means done, but a different kind of battle would now have to be fought on the ground by those who lived in the capital and the big cities. Unable to cripple her air power, Hitler now sought to destroy her morale by bombing Britain into submission.

On Saturday 7 September 250 German planes dropped 625 tons of high explosive and 800 incendiary canisters on the East End in an eight-hour raid. While Tom Neil and Tony Pickering could only watch the docks burn from the air, 17-year-old Junior Fireman Richard Holsgrove and his crew had been called out from Tottenham fire station to attend the massive fires burning out of control in the riverside warehouses and streets around the Pool of London. It was Richard's first big 'shout'.

The term was 'the bells go down', and when the bells went down we jumped into our boots and our fire gear, ran out to the engines and off we went. We wasn't allowed to stop on the way, even if a place was on fire, our duty was to go where we were ordered to go. So we went to the Surrey Commercial Docks and when we got there of course I had my first sight of what a fire was really like. There was wood burning from the woodyards and flames going up . . . We got to the point of the fire, the fireman who I was with, he held the hose and I had to stand behind him and help hold the hose because you had something like 40 to 60 pounds of pressure coming through that nozzle and if you was to let that go, the hose would have been whizzing round like a serpent. If it hit you it could kill you, it could break your limbs. So our job was to hold on to that hose and not let go. The older fireman, he helped me by saying, 'It's all right, lad, don't worry, just stand by me but whatever you do, just hold on to that hose.' As we stood there playing water on the woodyards, bits of timber were flying in the air, bits of red were falling on our uniforms and we was getting wet of course with the water coming back and our uniforms were steaming.

There was soon a new call on Richard's fire training.

There was a building where the men had their lunch and we could hear someone calling out, 'Help! I can't get down the stairs.' It was all alight up there. So what we done, it was three storeys up, we used what we call a hook ladder. I'd done hook ladder drill and [the senior fireman] said to me, 'Can you do it? I can't let go of the hose.' So I done the ladder, got up there to where this chap was and the room was all starting to catch alight, so I leant over the windowsill, got the chap. I said, 'Look, get your legs on the ladder and I'll go down with you, right? I'll hold you, don't worry.' I got behind him and helped him because he was all shaking. So we climbed down to the next floor and the next till we got down the bottom. He was so shaken, he was trembling, shaking all over. We got a blanket and gave him a little tot to warm him up and he gradually came to. But that was a life saved and I was really proud because I was part of it. As a young man of 17, I felt I was doing a real job of work there and I was very proud, pleased as Punch to be there.

Richard was in good company. Trying to control the raging furnace at the docks that night were over a thousand firemen, in crews from as far away as Brighton. Among the 650 people dead on this first night of the Blitz were 25 firemen.

For civilians it was their first shocking taste of what was to come. Eighteen-year-old Connie Hoe was working in Woolworths that first Saturday of the Blitz.

> The manager made us close the store and go into the shelter. It was about three or four in the afternoon and as we walked to the shelter we saw all these planes in the sky, German planes, though we didn't know that at the time. We stayed in the shelter till the all-clear went, then I had to walk home because there was no transport. As I approached where we lived I saw that a bomb had dropped and all the houses were blitzed.

In particular, her Chinese boyfriend Leslie's home was 'just ruins' and his mother and sister were wandering about in the street. After checking with his commanding officer, Connie was relieved to discover that Leslie was on duty on HMS *Chrysanthemum*, moored on the Thames. He was covered in mud after a bomb had dropped on the Embankment, but otherwise unharmed.

The raid on the 7th was just the first of 57 consecutive nights of bombing in London, initially concentrated on the East End, though bombs also fell elsewhere in the capital. On 13 September Buckingham Palace had a direct hit. No one was seriously injured but the bombing released a great many rats into the palace grounds. Margaret Rhodes recalls that Queen Elizabeth used them as target practice.

> Queen Elizabeth did learn how to shoot a pistol in the gardens at Buckingham Palace. I suppose, quite rightly, she thought if parachutists came down and whisked them away somewhere, she could at least take a parachutist or two with her.

The press, no doubt with firm guidance from the Ministry of Information, played down the damage and played up the strong

morale and determination of the cheerful cockneys to carry on
regardless. The reports of Mass Observation, an independent
research organisation set up in 1937 to monitor public attitudes,
were more realistic. By October, they were reporting 'grim resignation' at the continuous nightly raids. In London at least, local
authority and voluntary services for the injured and the many
thousands made homeless were starting to be better coordinated;
the situation in some other bombed cities remained chaotic for
months to come.

Life in London went on, if not as usual, then as close to usual
as its workers, residents and authorities could make it. Enid
Wenban was still going up to His Majesty's Stationery Office
(HMSO) every day.

> I remember seeing people being dug out when I got to London
> Bridge, the rescue workers digging in bombed houses. In the road
> where the office was was a great big building. I suppose it might
> have been an old workhouse, but it was an old people's home of
> some kind. It had obviously been hit and all the beds were hanging
> out . . . But you just got on with your job, you just got on with
> things. And in the evenings when you went home, all the people
> gathering on the platforms with their bedding, ready to spend the
> night.

In Croydon, 17-year-old Joan Wilson was fire-watching with a
group of neighbours. She noticed how the Blitz was changing
people's attitudes and behaviour.

> It opened the door, to know what was happening to other people.
> In these suburban houses you didn't really know much about your
> neighbours. Your neighbour might be unwell, but too bad. But
> this was a people's war, people started speaking to each other. You
> had to go round with a warden and see everybody was all right
> up and down the street. People would open their doors and say,
> 'What's happening?' It was a way of communicating with people.

German-Jewish refugee Dorothy Bohm had just left school in Sussex and had been in London a week when the Blitz started. She wasn't there long but that time cemented a lifelong love affair with the capital.

> My love for London and my admiration is because in those two weeks I was there people were remarkably good to each other and kind. If somebody had been bombed they would help them and there was no feeling of people being afraid. I've talked to people who've been on the Continent and cities being bombed. There was panic, but not in London.

Young people were now being asked – and being inspired – to take on more responsibility. Bob Frost, now 17, had had only mundane tasks to do during the Phoney War as a messenger boy with the Auxiliary Fire Service, like guiding bewildered customers to their local pub in the blackout.

> But when the London Blitz started we had work aplenty to do taking messages, and if an incendiary stick landed you got a sandbag – there were sandbags everywhere – you'd put them over the stick to extinguish the flames, trying to help in any way you could. Because there was lots of broken glass in the streets and you couldn't buy bicycle tyres for love nor money, you very often had to pick up your bicycle and carry it.

Bob was frightened sick at times by what he saw, but one incident made him reconsider his modest role as a messenger boy.

> I was going home off watch and I saw this man near Mornington Crescent after a raid, digging at what had been his house. His mother was buried inside and he was digging with his bare hands. I said to myself, 'Frosty boy, helping to put fires out isn't going to stop them happening. So join up!'

He joined the RAF as soon as he was 18 on 1 January 1941 and started his training as a rear gunner.

At Broadcasting House, where 600 mattresses had been installed in the Radio Theatre for staff unable to get home during night raids, Charles Chilton was gaining a reputation with his jazz programme, *Radio Rhythm Club*. In October 1940 he was fire-watching on the roof of Broadcasting House, when the BBC took its first hit of the Blitz.

> We were up there with shovels and buckets of sand. If firebombs fell on the roof we could put them out, and we were on the lookout for bombs dropping and report to BBC Security for possible evacuation. Suddenly I heard coming towards us what I thought was an express train – a bomb. It hit Broadcasting House about two floors below us on the seventh floor, through a window, through an office, through the door and into the internal part of the building, an unexploded bomb where there were lots of people working. I was told to go down to every floor and tell everyone to go down to the basement because this bomb was liable to go off. So people started rushing down to the basement. The bloke in charge decided – it was ridiculous, really – to deal with the bomb by putting a rope round it and dragging it to somewhere it could do least damage. And of course the minute he started dragging it, the bomb went off. He was killed, seven fire-watchers were killed and the whole of the middle of Broadcasting House collapsed in itself and dozens of people were trapped. Then the ARP people came in and started the rescue and we were at it all night. And what a night it was, taking dead people out of the rubble. I was grateful when morning came and I could get to the canteen and get myself a cup of coffee. I was in a terrible state.

At the moment the bomb went off, newsreader Bruce Belfrage had just started a bulletin. With BBC sangfroid he carried on, covered in dust and debris.

Singer Vera Lynn had a regular BBC radio programme and was performing in the West End throughout the Blitz. She went about

London in her little Austin Ten tourer with its canvas roof – not the best protection in a raid.

> I always carried a tin hat beside me in the car. If you got caught in a raid you went down into a shelter or they told you to lie in the road, in the kerb. What good that was doing, I don't know!

The Underground was a ready-made deep shelter, used by thousands as soon as the Blitz started. Conditions were squalid until things were properly organised later in the war, and Vera avoided it if she could.

> The Underground was terrible, horrible: crammed up with people, no toilets, no facilities. But you took a chance if you stayed up top. We were pretty lucky. In East Ham where I lived with Mum and Dad, we had a friend next door with a shelter under his garage. So if I was at home, if I wasn't in London, we'd go down there. They'd rigged it up with a kettle and water – anything for an emergency – and we'd stay there till the raid was over. And then we'd come up, you know, and find the street next door had been bombed . . . but everyone dug in and helped everybody else.

At the time of the Blitz, Gus Bialick was stationed in the countryside near Bath and unaware of what was happening in London.

> The sergeant came to me one day and he said, 'Bialick' – that was the way they talked to you – 'Bialick, you've got a pass for London. Your house has been bombed.' So I went up to London and I got as far as London Bridge, I couldn't get to Aldgate, I'd arrived in the middle of an air raid. I was walking across London Bridge, bombers were all over the East End and other parts of London dropping their bombs, as I was walking towards my home. I looked over my shoulder and found I was the only one walking across the bridge . . . A policeman was in an alcove and he shouted across at me. He swore at me in fact. He said, 'Where the f*** are you going?' So I shouted back at him, 'I've come from the countryside,

I've never been in an air raid before.' So he said, 'Come over here, you silly bugger.' So I stood with him in the alcove till five o'clock the next morning, when I walked through the City, past Tower Bridge, and I got to my home in Newnham Street and found the roof on the ground. It was a shock. They'd lost everything. But I couldn't help them because I only had a 24-hour pass and I had to go back.

To the west of London in Barnes, teenager and recent Home Guard recruit Jimmy Perry was sheltering under the stairs with his mother during a raid when she said something that left a lasting and emotional impression.

She said, 'You know, if the Germans come, they'll put your dad in a concentration camp?' See, my dad was Jewish. He was a very smart, wonderful man, a wonderful father. That was it. That's why we fought.

———◆———

While the bombing continued unabated in London, other cities were getting the same treatment, starting with a shocking raid on Coventry on 14 November in which the medieval heart of the city, including its ancient cathedral, was completely destroyed. Charles Chilton, by now evacuated with his BBC department and new sweetheart Penny to Evesham, remembers that night well.

We were standing on a bridge and we could see on the horizon Coventry burning. It was like Guy Fawkes Night and I remember saying to her, 'We're standing here and where those flames are, people are dying.' And it was at that time that I told Pen how I felt about her, and she said she felt the same about me. Quite a dramatic time to find out you were in love with someone.

Attacks on other cities soon followed where, by the end of the war, four million Anderson shelters had been distributed to households. These small corrugated iron shelters, partly buried in the ground and with a covering of earth on top, were notoriously damp and uncomfortable, but properly installed they gave effective protection, even from a direct hit. In Manchester, Mabel McCoy was still at home with her family.

> We had an Anderson shelter in the back garden, fitted by the council, very small for four people, quite squashed. Manchester, unfortunately, had not only their own air raids, they had the bombers going over to Liverpool for the docks and then to Belfast for the docks there. So we had warning after warning, but my father would never go in the shelter however much my brother and I tried to persuade him. We could never understand why my mother never tried. Even though the ack-ack guns were going and the searchlights were going, he'd be walking the streets because he could not face being in the small shelter, which no doubt reminded him of the problems he had in the First World War.

In inner-city gardenless Hulme, Gladys Parry had her own sheltering problems.

> Well, I used to have to carry my stepmother down the cellar steps on my back, the best way I could, and get her sat down. And I used to stand by the window of the grid, down in the cellar, and look up at the sky. Because you could see the incendiaries, where they were going, and you could hear the thump. But it got a natural thing that we were going to get bombed every night and you walked along, you never thought about being killed. It never struck you, because now it had become normal. I can remember one time, if I'd have been one more step forward this piece of shrapnel would probably have hit me one. That's when you realised that it was daft to walk about because there's shrapnel all over the place. The kids used to go looking for it the next day and pick it up . . . But I can't never remember being frightened to death, only that time when we thought the Germans were going to invade.

By the early months of 1941 coastal and port cities were also targets. In Swansea Dorothy Hughes, born in 1923 into a strict Welsh Baptist family, had just left her grammar school and now found herself on the front line.

> Swansea was a port and a coal-exporting port. We had a steelworks, we had an oil refinery. And oftentimes planes used to come up the Bristol Channel and drop bombs. In January 1941 we had three days of heavy blitz. Night and day, the bombers just kept coming over. The first day it was incendiary bombs and we were fighting them with a bucket of water and a stirrup pump . . . We got a badly damaged roof and a tarpaulin was put over it. The second day we had the heavy bombs and the mines. They used to float down and it was really, really frightening. The noise was horrendous and the smell and the shrapnel – everything around you seemed to disappear. And on the third day we had an unexploded bomb that had been dropped under our air-raid shelter on the first night. My mother was in the house by herself when the bomb went off. We came home to find a ruined house and the police saying, 'Keep back, keep back!' . . . It took them six hours to dig her out. Fortunately she was in the larder under the stairs and a marble shelf had fallen and stopped the ceiling coming in on her. The neighbours were absolutely fantastic, they took us in and sheltered us and when my mother was dug out, she had a few bruises and scrapes, but that was all. But that six hours it took, it was the longest day of my life. I'll never forget it. You were terrified. You desperately wanted to help. Nothing you could do.

In Bristol, Jim Purcell was busy with the Royal Engineers clearing up after raids.

> We worked night after night in Bristol, pulling down walls that were dangerous from bomb damage. We pulled them down, we blew them up, and we had some fun, we were a great crowd of

Geordies. Some of the safes couldn't be opened because of fire damage, so we became safe-breakers, using explosives to blow them open, and if there was any money in them, they'd give it to us. And our lads were good lads, we started a fund and any person or family that was bombed out, no shoes or clothes, the lads gave them the money. We done it as a group. We were all mates, we were a family, a family of boys. We used to drive street to street and have a little sing-song together, '[Kiss Me] Goodnight, Sergeant Major', all the war songs. While I was away, though, I got word that we'd been bombed out in Jarrow. No one got hurt but we lost a lot of stuff, all my stuff from a boy. I had three days' leave and they had to meet me at the station because there was no home to go to.

Bill Graves was in the navy by this time, but he returned to Bristol on leave and has clear memories of people's reaction to the bombing, and of Churchill's visit to the city.

Churchill had a rough reception. He drove around in a car with the mayor before arriving in Easton. There were crowds of people there but they heckled and jeered him. Churchill wasn't popular with the working classes. People remembered the 1926 General Strike and how Churchill used the army to end it at the expense of the working man. I grew up thinking his name was 'Bloody Churchill' – my father and grandfather detested him.

People were very aware of press tactics in downplaying the attacks on Britain. They were cynical and didn't like being deceived. When a city was bombed the press would often refuse to name it, calling a city 'a town in the north', or 'the west', which was ridiculous as everyone knew about the bombings within half an hour: 'Looks like Plymouth's had it tonight'; 'Coventry's got it rough today then.' My father was a railwayman and saw much of the damage first-hand. It was bloody daft that they would try and cover it up and it bred suspicion: if they're hiding that, what else are they hiding?

The Blitz morale of popular myth was by no means universal. Raids, blackouts and rationing opened new opportunities for black-market dealing, crime, looting, illicit sexual encounters and children running wild. Bill saw looting whilst he was with the Home Guard in Bristol.

> There was a bombing near Old Market Street which heavily damaged a big department store. Two of us were sent over to prevent looting. We were too late. By the time we'd got there and fixed bayonets, most of the stuff had gone. After a while a man stumbled out carrying a large box of tea. Instead of being ashamed or embarrassed, he threw a packet at me and said, 'There you go, son. Have that and shut your eyes,' before wandering off. We didn't know what to do so we let him go. I'm pretty sure our sergeant kept the tea.

After the Swansea raid in which her mother had a narrow escape, Dorothy Hughes decided there was something she could do for the war effort: she would enlist. She was only 18 and had to have her father's permission, but despite family opposition she joined the Auxiliary Territorial Service (ATS) and was posted to the Royal Artillery. She soon found herself training on anti-aircraft guns, where she suffered racial taunts ('Oh, you come from Wales! Do they paint their faces with woad?'). There was more discrimination to come: once her unit was operational at a battery in London, the ATS women faced open hostility from the male gunners.

> The men absolutely hated this, simply because they were regular soldiers. Women should be in the home. They hated the idea that we were stepping into their territory. The shells weighed 28 pounds and they'd deliberately have us unloading the shells and stacking them up, thinking we couldn't do it, but we did. And of course operating the equipment was a cinch because women are much better with their hands at operating small dials, so they had to give in in the end, but it was hard going. It took them well over

six months to accept that we could do the job as well as they could.

She soon realised that, despite their efforts, London and Britain's cities were ill-equipped to tackle the German bombers.

During the Blitz 30,000 bombs were dropped on London and we had very few guns. The number of guns in the whole of the United Kingdom was only half of what was needed for London, and the guns were old. A lot of them were from the First World War and their ceiling height was 15,000 feet. The bombers were flying at 20,000 feet. If they were flying too high, we were told to try and split the formations up so that fighters could get through. And we had to keep the noise up for the civilians to realise that we were fighting back. I felt sorry for the civilians because they had to sit and listen to it.

There were some terrible times:

I think one of my worst moments was on one of the gun-sites. The fuses were Swiss and very reliable but of course our Engineers hadn't a clue how to make them properly and as the shell rotated it went off in the gun and blew the gun to pieces. The guns opened up like bananas and of course the six operators were instantly killed. We'd had breakfast with these gunners that morning and we knew they'd be in pieces. We were asked, please, would anyone volunteer to help clear the place up? We were given black bags and we volunteered to go in and try and rescue as much as possible of these men to keep their bits and pieces separate so they could go in a coffin. And that was really ghastly because you actually knew the people.

Dealing with death became an everyday desensitising necessity.

In other raids you'd walk past and see people digging out dead bodies but they weren't known to you, so you sort of put it to one side. But you couldn't face up to the fact that you might have been one of those people who . . . who were killed. You honestly felt: It's not going to happen to me, but knowing deep down, it probably would. You learned to live with death. You had to.

———◆———

Southampton, Birmingham, Liverpool, Manchester, Sheffield, Clydeside, Bristol, Swansea, Plymouth, Coventry, Portsmouth, Belfast and Hull: they all suffered their own Blitz horrors between September 1940 and May 1941. Though the raids didn't stop after that, they were no longer as intense or as continuous. But one raid in the dying days of 1940 came to crystallise what the Blitz meant to the people of Britain. At 6 p.m. on 29 December, after a brief Christmas respite, German bombers started dropping 300 incendiaries a minute around the area of St Paul's Cathedral. Within half an hour over 50 fires were ablaze, threatening to consume the medieval heart of the old City. The Second Great Fire of London had begun.

Junior Fireman Richard Holsgrove was called out with his crew to Newgate Street, close by St Paul's.

Our job was to spray water on the buildings to stop the brickwork cracking and tumbling down, because a building next to us did fall down. Lucky for us it fell to our left, but unlucky for the West Ham crew, there were three there; they died. The building went down and fell on top of them.

At the height of the raid they were told to leave surrounding buildings to burn and play their hoses on the one that wasn't yet ablaze. On direct instruction from Churchill, every available fire crew was to save the most potent symbol of London's power and Britain's defiance. Richard could understand why.

Hitler's objective was St Paul's. He felt that if he got St Paul's he would break the spirit of the London people and the rest of the country. It was a place of worship, a place of trust, confidence, people were sheltering, sleeping in there. God was there. If we protect His place, He'll protect us.

Such was the terrific heat coming from the burning buildings all round the cathedral, there was a danger its masonry and brickwork would become so hot that the internal woodwork holding up the dome of St Paul's would ignite and the dome itself would collapse.

We were standing there and the steam was going from us as if we was in a steam bath, but the heat was so terrific that our job was to keep that brickwork on St Paul's as cool as we could. We was working on that, and we was up there four nights.

When all these fires were raging up there, I looked up and in the glow of the fire I seen this cross still there at St Paul's. I realised then, I was only 17, but I said, 'There's got to be somebody there' . . . I felt yes, I believe in this. I really believe. Before that, I hadn't give it a thought. I'd been a Boy Scout and been to church and that but I hadn't give it a thought. But that time of looking up and seeing the glow of the fire and seeing that church up there . . . that's when I woke up to it.

With the superhuman efforts of firefighters and the fire-watchers who threw live incendiaries from its roof, St Paul's was saved. The cost elsewhere was great: hundreds of civilian casualties, 14 firemen dead and 250 injured. By the first day of 1941 it was clear that more of the old City had been destroyed than in the Great Fire of 1666.

Raids continued throughout the early months of 1941, culminating in a last-ditch attempt to bomb the capital into submission in May. Earl Cameron, a young seaman recently arrived from Bermuda, was there.

The worst of the air raids I experienced was the 10th of May 1941. I was working at the Savoy Hotel as a dishwasher. I had to get up early every morning so I went to bed about ten o'clock. I was in bed reading the paper. It was Double Summer Time so it didn't get dark till about a quarter to eleven. Suddenly I heard *ba-boom! bbbbbboom!* – the guns going. Always a bad sign when the guns go before the alarm . . . and within a couple of minutes the bombs were dropping. Then I heard this diesel engine dive-bombing, then suddenly *whumph!* and the place shook. There was a second one, the sound getting closer and the second bomb shook the whole area. I got out of bed, my whole body was shaking. I kneeled down: 'God, God, please help me, please help me.' For the first time I was really scared.

I put my trousers and jacket over my pyjamas and rushed to Goodge Street [Underground] station. Tottenham Court Road was alight with fire, everything was like a big Bonfire Night, fires everywhere. Stayed down there a couple of hours, became rather claustrophobic – it was packed with people. I thought, I can't stand this heat, all these people, so I came up. The warden said, 'I wouldn't advise you to go out' . . . He couldn't stop me.

Earl made for a Lyons Corner House where he used to hang out with mates, hoping for 'a nice cup of hot chocolate'.

Walking down Tottenham Court Road and suddenly the guns started to go, heavy guns, and the bombs dropping, and I started to run. The shrapnel was hitting the road, the whole thing was a madness, crazy, and I was thinking, Why did I do this? And I was running like mad, with all the sounds of the bombs dropping, the guns going, and the shrapnel hitting the road. I was very lucky I didn't get killed by all the shrapnel. Eventually I got to the entrance of Goodge Street station and the warden said, 'I told you not to go out. Get down below.' I stayed down there till daylight.

The next morning I went to work, there was a different look on the people's faces. It was a look of defeat. For the first time I saw in most people that they were really scared. The Luftwaffe had hit London the worst they could. The average person in London really felt that if the Luftwaffe would keep this up every night, that would be it, they couldn't take it. But I might say, in spite of that, most buses seemed to run on time, things got back to normal more or less, the people went to work . . . Life went on.

The Blitz had been a critical test of civilian morale and people's ability to withstand all the privations that constant bombardment entailed. Morale did not break, though it didn't always take the upbeat, all-in-it-together character of 'the Blitz spirit' the government sought to portray at home and abroad. The first 20 months of war had planted the seeds of change in British society: people believed in victory and were prepared to make many sacrifices 'for the duration' to achieve it, but they wanted also to believe that, in return, a better, more equitable life in peacetime would be theirs. For the first time, those in positions of power were obliged to listen.

During the battle for Britain young people, whether in the voluntary services, civil defence, the military or in war work on the home front, were shouldering more and more of the burden of war. For many, privation, physical danger and the stiffest tests of morale were yet to come.

7

The War at Sea

1939–1944

A saying of mine is, if blood were the price of freedom, the merchant ship sailors paid it in full.

Austin Byrne, Merchant Navy 1941–46

While the air battle raged and civilians suffered bombardment on the ground, another no-less-costly war of attrition was being waged on the world's oceans far from press and public view. As the 'Senior Service', the Royal Navy had an unassailable reputation as protector of the British Empire, honed over centuries of battle honours and reinforced at home through slick public relations and decades of positive propaganda in schoolboy comics.

Less feted was the Merchant Navy, a civilian force of 185,000 seamen employed by British mercantile companies but thrust into the front line for the entire duration of the war. Its job was to ensure the two-way supply of vital munitions, fuel, food and raw materials between Britain and her empire, allies and overseas theatres of war. Unless these supply lines were kept open, the Allied war effort would founder and its peoples would starve.

In addition to the peacetime hazards of long sea voyages, the Merchant Navy now had a determined blockade to deal with: packs of U-boats firing torpedoes unseen from the depths, floating mines and surface shelling from warships, and bombing raids from the air. As early as September 1939, U-boats had sunk more than 40 merchant ships and over the course of the war up to a hundred ships a month and their precious tonnage were being lost through enemy action.

To offer protection from attack, merchant ships sailed in convoys escorted by as many as 30 – or as few as one – Royal Navy vessels. On board they were equipped with anti-aircraft guns and, if they were lucky, army and Royal Navy gunners. Convoys sailed every ocean but the principal action was focused in the North Atlantic, with ships bringing much-needed supplies from North America and, from June 1941, the Arctic, supplying the northern Russian ports of Archangel and Murmansk with war materials for the fight against Hitler on the Eastern Front.

Convoy crews were made up of old salts and young volunteers in search of adventure, with Chinese and Indian seamen traditionally forming about a fifth of the merchant force. For the young sailors adventure would come hand in hand with hardship and the most extreme tests of endurance.

For the men on the convoys, these tests weren't always associated with the heat of battle or the struggle for survival afterwards. Being away at sea for weeks, sometimes months at a time brought more prosaic trials but they were no less difficult to bear. Physical hardship went with the job: seasickness, primitive living conditions, restricted diet, extreme cold and having to maintain the ship in heavy seas, ice and storms lasting days on end were all part of the deal.

Keen swimmer John Harrison joined the navy 'for the simple reason that I liked the water'. He had plenty of it as an ordnance artificer escorting tankers across the Atlantic on HMS *Belfast*.

If you're on a small destroyer or escort vessel you're about ten foot out of the water, and when you get big swells like 50 foot, they look awfully big alongside of you. That's fine when you're going [straight], but when you've got to turn . . . you see this mass of water up there, waiting to go somewhere. You hope it goes under. Well, sometimes it didn't; it crashed on the top, but you never went on the upper deck in rough weather like that without a rope round you. The next thing you know is, a bloody great wave comes and takes you over the side. If you've got the rope on, you just swing up and come back on deck!

David Craig was born in 1925 in the north-west Highlands of Scotland, close to the arctic convoy base at Loch Ewe. By 1943 he was a young Merchant Navy radio officer. For David, the cold on 'the Russia run' was the worst of it.

> When you were up on the bridge – they were open bridges in those days – you had your sea boots and your sou'westers on, and heavy duffel coats, they were canvas on the outside and fur on the inside. You'd have a hood up and an ordinary knitted cap to keep your ears warm. And when you were standing the wind would be coming against you. The side of your face used to get coated with ice. Whenever you went out of the door of your cabin out into the cold, the hairs in your nose froze and it was a strange feeling because you felt you had chips of wood or something up your nose. You just had to get used to that!

Though they weren't popular with seamen, David understood the rationale for the 1,500-mile, eight-day voyage to Russian ports inside the Arctic Circle.

> It was a decision taken by Churchill after Hitler invaded Russia that we should help the Russians as much as we could and it was the correct decision. At that time Europe was overrun by Germans, there was nobody fighting against them, the Russians were the only people left that could fight against them so Churchill decided it would be wise to send supplies, guns, tanks, aircraft – anything we could spare so that they could use that against the Germans and help use up some of their divisions.
>
> We knew about it to a degree but we didn't know about the losses on the run . . . We knew it was dangerous, no question about that, because anyone that had been there would have gone 100 miles not to go back, but if you were sent there you had to go back. When we joined a ship, we took the ship wherever she was going and that was the way it was. And apart from that we were young and it makes a big difference when you're young because you're a wee bit daft into the bargain. But the thing is,

you took life as it took you and that made it easier for us.

Bradford-born Austin Byrne was called up to the navy and told he was to be trained as a gunner on merchant ships. At 19 he was a novice sailor but, like all merchant seamen, he had no idea where his ship was bound.

It were exciting for me, a first-tripper, first out to sea . . . I'd never been to sea before. I'd only ever seen sea at Redcar or New Brighton when we'd been on us holidays. They sent us down to Greenock and I was told I was going on a ship called the *Induna*. We climbed up a ladder. It were difficult getting over the railings because the petrol barrels were level with the railings. And then we found out she was going to Russia. The gun-layer said to me, 'In eight days' time, Titch, it'll be colder than you've ever thought' . . . I didn't know anything about the Arctic convoys, I didn't know it'd be like it was.

He got an inkling of what was in store when they were issued with Arctic gear ashore in Iceland.

It were big leather sea boots. I take a 6. They only had 10s, 11s, 12s, very thick long johns, like hand-knitted, a sheepskin-and-leather jacket, no sleeves. And an Arctic duffel coat, which was fantastic. And some Arctic gloves. They only had big sizes and I'm small so the duffel coat came halfway down my legs and the underwear was miles too big for me. I put my ordinary socks on, then some black tropical socks and rolled them above my knees, put my knitted long johns on, then my trousers and I had two jumpers, my leather jacket and then my duffel coat and two pair of gloves and my Arctic gloves, two scarves, a beret and a balaclava. And then my hood up.

As they were leaving Iceland, he soon realised the sea was very different from the one he'd paddled in at Redcar.

The seas were very heavy. She's going up, up, up and the waves are coming and half of the ship's out of the water then she dips and the other half's out of the water. And then we were on watch and there was one of the crew on lookout and she were going down, down, down and water were coming over the bows and up to amidships and he said, 'Lift, you ****!' four-letter horrible word. And the mate said, 'Don't you dare swear like that at the old lady. Your life depends on her.' That storm was three, four days. It's dark and the wind is bitterly cold and the rain is cold. You're tired and you're hungry and you eat what you can and you're seasick . . . You slept in your clothes and you slept in your lifebelt. I never had my clothes off from leaving Loch Ewe.

There were lighter moments.

We all listened to the radio and we all liked the songs, but Vera Lynn was the one. Oh yes, the Vera Lynn songs were great. You used to stand in gun pit and sing them, you know, as if you had a bird with yer. 'Yours till the stars lose their glory' – that was always my favourite.

In March 1942 SS *Induna* left Iceland with a cargo of war materials and gasoline as part of convoy PQ-13 to Murmansk. The weather was squally with snow showers. When it worsened to storm conditions on the night of the 25th/26th, the convoy was scattered. The following day the weather cleared and some ships regrouped but they found themselves under attack by a Messerschmitt Bf 110. Austin was at his Hotchkiss gun.

You wait for it to come and you balance and – there's nothing else in your mind. Your mind's clear: I've got to hit this. And then he's in range. You think he is. I'd never done it before. You see your tracers going in and you follow him as he's coming down . . . As he came amidships, I could see the bullets going into the cockpit. You know that you're hitting somebody, and it's a good feeling. You're doing what you have to do.

Four bombs damaged two nearby ships, the SS *Ballot* and the SS *Mana*, then the Bf 110 limped off.

> The captain said, 'You've hurt him. You've got him, boy!' When I got out the gun pit on to the bridge, the captain give me a big hug and said, 'You done really well, boy!' He were a wonderful man. I felt as if I could do it. I felt as good as anybody else.

Now steering north through ice floes in poor weather conditions, *Induna* and the remains of the convoy picked their tortuous route towards Murmansk. Temporarily stuck in 4-foot-thick ice, *Induna* got separated from the others and had to steam as fast as she dared to catch up. On the morning of the 30th, in snow squalls and a heavy swell, Austin was on watch in the gun pit.

> We were chugging on and she was shuddering, *donky-donk, donky-donk*. And we thought, Tonight we'll be there, we'll make it. And then all of a sudden, *bang!* And she shudders and everything goes on fire, aft. Nobody has to tell you what's happened. You know it. You're brand new, but you know we've been hit and the aviation spirit were exploding and the sea were on fire.

At 7.20 a.m. an unseen torpedo had gone straight into the hold containing gasoline drums.

> The mate saluted the captain and he said, 'Sir, she's been torpedoed in number five hold. She's on fire aft and sinking fast.' And the captain just said, 'Very good, Mr Mate. Abandon ship.' The captain said to me, 'Go to your lifeboat station, boy, and good luck to you.' . . . I'd never seen a lifeboat launched, I were just a blank mind. I didn't know what were going to happen.

The bosun maintained discipline and made them line up and get in the lifeboat in an orderly fashion. Austin got in with another gunner, Robinson, and seven others.

We were in the boat, and we saw this fella coming through the fire. He'd no shoes on and he were absolutely burning all over and you could see his footprints, red, red blood. Mate said, 'Get him in the boat, pull him in.' And me and Robinson beat the hell out of him to get the fire out. By then she were really going down.

The bosun lowered the lifeboat and they managed to cast off, away from the sinking ship, leaving the mate on board with instructions to pick them up from the opposite side of the stern. They rowed round the stern, just short of the burning ship.

I could see the mate lowering a rope ladder. And the bosun said, 'Row, row, come on, let's get 'em off!' And we started rowing and we weren't far from the ladder when *bang!* He put another torpedo in it and she just went down by the stern, and you could see the captain trying to launch the smaller lifeboat, and the mate putting this ladder down. And then she just tipped up and went down and you thought, Oh, oh, oh, they're all gone! That's the thing that I remember every day – looking up and seeing them . . . You'd never forget their faces, and it hurts.

The weather worsened and the lifeboat started to let in water. Austin and Robinson bailed with buckets whilst the others tried to keep out the cold with cigarettes and rum.

When the wave hit the side of the boat and the spray came up from a good yard, it weren't water that hit you, it were ice. And when you were in the boat, bailing, you kept your back to the weather and every now and again you moved your back and the ice cracked that had formed on your coat. That's how cold it was . . . The Yank that were badly burned said, 'Can I have a cig?' So I give him one. His hands were burned. His face were burned. His hair was gone. I lit him a cig and he couldn't hold it so I did it for him and when I put it in his mouth and when he wanted it out, I did it. Robinson and me kept bailing and we did that for the rest of the four days.

Austin, the 19-year-old, found himself comforting Anderson, a 16-year-old cabin boy.

> On the first day he said, 'Oh, I'm frightened. I want my mum.' And he got his wallet out to look at a picture of his mum and £3 10s fell out and in the water. I said, 'Pick your money up.' 'Oh, it's no good now, we're finished, I want my mum.' So I said, 'Say your prayers, say the Our Father. If you don't know any prayers, just talk to God in your mind and tell Him how you want His help. Just talk to Him and that'll help you.' I found that I could put bucket in the water, lift it up, say 'Hail Mary, full of grace' and I could get three buckets out to a Hail Mary and four buckets out to the Our Father.

Their fresh water supply had frozen and there was little food.

> We were hungry. We found some ship's biscuits and some little boxes of pemmican – like solid Bovril – and I ended up with breaking two teeth. You were hungry but you'd to live with it. And all you did were bail and pray . . . I always thought I could make it. You've got to have a purpose to live. Those that thought they were going to die, died. Once you give up hope, you die.

After four days alone in the freezing Barents Sea, they found themselves surrounded by three small ships.

> They came at us in three angles. And when we were there with our hands up you could see them with their machine guns, pointing at you. I thought, Oh hell! As they turned we saw the Russian Red Star. 'Hooray! Hooray! English! English!' I put my hands up to pull myself up the wire ropes but there were no pull left. Two of them put their hands over, got hold of my shoulders and my arms and pulled me up. I felt wonderful. You knew then that you were saved.

In a cabin below, after large measures of vodka, they were tended by women sailors. Austin helped one of them cut the clothes off Anderson the cabin boy, who was frozen solid. When they removed his clothes they saw that his body was black with frostbite. Here too the badly burned American managed to hold out a swollen hand to Austin and say, 'We made it, kid.'

When Austin woke up from the vodka, they were in Murmansk and on their way to hospital, where they found other *Induna* survivors. Starved of supplies, conditions in the hospital were primitive: seven of the survivors had to have frostbitten limbs amputated without anaesthetic. Austin went straight to sleep and woke to the news that Anderson and the American had both died.

After two weeks in hospital he and other *Induna* survivors fit enough to travel got a passage home on the cruiser HMS *Liverpool*. Some complained that the Russians had taken all their warm Arctic clothes and what equipment they'd managed to take with them. Austin recalls that when they were rescued they took everything out of their lifeboat, including a compass that he'd wanted to keep as a souvenir, but he will have no ill spoken of his rescuers:

> The Russians saved my life. They gave me my life back. I wouldn't have been here. I would have been dead at 19, 20 year old. I'd have been gone 70 year ago.

Of the 19 ships in Convoy PQ-13, a third were lost, together with nearly 30,000 tons of war materials. Of the *Induna* crew of 50 and the 16 men she picked up from the *Ballot*, 44 perished: drowned, burned or frozen to death. Undaunted, Austin served on another Russian convoy before the end of his war service.

———◆———

Stoker Sid Graham, 21, from Canning Town, found himself in warmer but no less dangerous waters early in 1942. His supply ship, the *Scottish Star*, was crossing the Atlantic on a special operation. He had no idea where they were bound or what they carried.

Of course we were the lowest of the low, the stokers. They used to lock us in when an attack began . . . You're working your nuts off down there with them fires all the time. You think to yourself, Jesus, I wonder if we're going to make it or not. All sorts of silly things run through your head. You look and say, What's the best way if you can escape? You're looking for the best way for yourself. Every man for himself.

The night we got torpedoed I was caught in the bathroom with a fellow named Chang. Tough Chinese boy, born in Jamaica. In them days we had to bathe in a bucket and when we got torpedoed I went up in the air and hit my ribs on the washbasin . . . busted 'em. Then the door slammed and this Chang was such a strong fellow, he broke the door open. And as we were going out the men were running and one fellow said, 'What's happened, sir?' I said, 'We've been tin-fished.' I got up on the companionway and that's when the submarine started to shell us. We wasn't going down quick enough for him.

Sid had broken ribs and a badly injured arm but he managed to get in a lifeboat with 20 others as they watched the *Scottish Star* go down: 'She started to explode . . . she went down *whoof!*, went down backwards.' They drifted in the lifeboat for nine days, surviving on a tenth of a litre of water a day and ship's biscuits: 'It's not the hunger, it's the thirst that gets hold of you.'

They didn't have the Arctic cold to contend with, but there were sharks.

Being seamen, we always called them 'Nobbys' [rhyming slang: Nobby Clark/shark]. They used to come and float around, come on at the boat, give you a look and try and knock it. And you'd make a noise and beat the sides of the boat with the oar – and they'd float away. They can't stand the noise, we was told, so that's what we done. Happily it worked.

Drifting south into the Caribbean, they were finally rescued by a fishing boat and towed into Barbados, the island of Sid's father's birth. The Seamen's Mission gave them clothes but they had no money and no immediate prospect of returning home.

> Well, we felt devastated because you didn't think they'd ever treat you like that. They treated you like you were an underrated citizen although you were doing your bit for your country.

Sid was more fortunate than his shipmates. He managed to track down one of his father's relatives on the island and she took him in for six months until a ship arrived to take them back to Britain. With no word of him during this time, his family thought he'd been lost at sea. After an emotional reunion with his parents and five siblings in Canning Town, Sid was soon off again on more seaborne adventures.

———◆———

David Craig had already done half a dozen Atlantic runs as a navigator before joining the SS *Dover Hill* at Gourock on the Clyde as third radio officer. Here he discovered he was on Convoy JW-53 – the 'Russia run'.

> We had quite a dangerous cargo, we had cordite and TNT and aircraft and tanks on deck and anti-tank guns and shells and all the stuff that goes with it, as well as food and general cargo. There was 28 of us merchant ships set out with a colossal naval escort. We had cruisers, we had aircraft carriers, we had about 15 destroyers. When we saw the escort, we thought, Boy, we're going to have to fight our way through here, because you didn't usually get as good an escort as that . . . I wouldn't say it worried me. You couldn't spend your time worrying because what difference did it make? You were sailing the ship and you had to sail it. It was as simple as that.

When David joined the *Dover Hill* in early 1943, Britain was losing the Battle of the Atlantic and losses were heavy. Even old ships

were being pressed into service. SS *Dover Hill*, built at the end of
the 1914–18 war, was one of them. They left Loch Ewe in a 'howling
north-westerly' and as they approached the Arctic Ocean 'the gale
turned into a hurricane'.

> We were very happy because all the deck cargo, the drums of oil
> and everything went over the side, we were quite happy to see
> that going, because they were silly things to be above a load of
> ammunition. Tracer bullets could set fire to the oil and if you've
> got barrels of oil burning on deck and you've got cordite and TNT
> stacked up in the hold down below, there's going to be an almighty
> bang and you're going to be needing a parachute instead of a life
> jacket.
>
> But the thing was, we had lorries and crates and she would go
> down the side of one huge wave and she'd put her bow right
> under and when she came up the crates would be smashed and
> there'd be a nice lorry sitting on the deck, an armoured truck
> sitting on the deck. You go down the next wave and up she'd come
> and the truck would be gone, so we lost all our deck cargo apart
> from the tanks because they were tied down with wire ropes and
> chained to the deck and they were absolutely solid . . . You don't
> realise the power of the sea until you've really experienced it.

The horrendous weather damaged six of the merchant ships
and they had to turn back for repair. The cruiser HMS *Sheffield*
lost her main fore gun turret and she too had to turn back. The
flight deck of the aircraft carrier HMS *Dasher* started to break up
and forced her return, leaving the convoy with no air cover. Bear
Island, north of Norway at the western end of the Barents Sea,
was a danger zone for the Arctic convoys. Just south of the island,
JW-53's cruiser escort flagged the presence of approaching aircraft.

> I was at action stations and I could see them coming. Three
> formations of seven planes: 21 planes and 22 ships. They picked a
> ship each and a Junkers 88 came straight for us. We knew that in
> the next few seconds we'd live or die. There's always this fear and

tension at action stations. You could usually try and control it, but on this occasion everything told me to run like hell! If you're a wise man you say a quick prayer – 'Dear God, make it miss!' – and duck . . . The bombs missed us, but the gun-layer had blood coming out of his mouth, he'd been hit by shrapnel. The Junkers came in again and the attack went on but we had no serious damage. I was glad to be up in the open – at least I could see what was going on. The poor lads in the engine room could hear the explosions but they'd no idea whether they were in real danger or not.

There was no doctor on board; to cope with shrapnel injuries they had to stitch each other up. Gunners were most prone to shrapnel wounds but once stitched up, they'd be back in their gun pit, firing. They had to be tough. At times of crisis the men depended on each other and divisions of class, culture or rank had to be put aside.

Our officers were mostly Scottish and the deck crew were mainly Londoners. The Londoners would always break moments of tension with a joke. Shipmates are a funny thing. Different departments may rib each other, but in a crisis all hands are together.

After coming through horrendous weather, losing half their cargo, dodging U-boats and surviving air attacks, Convoy JW-53 was in sight of Murmansk and safe haven. In fact, the German lines were only six miles away: shelling and gunfire were a constant backdrop. They were looking forward to a rest but soon discovered that Murmansk was a city under siege from bombing. The raids started the night they arrived and they were bombed as they tried to discharge their cargo. David was in the mess when action stations sounded and they saw two Junkers Ju 88s come over. He went out on deck when four bombs came down and he was blown off his feet. One bomb went right through the deck yards from him and landed, unexploded, in a coal bunker.

The Russians said, 'Well, if you can get it up on deck we'll send a bomb-disposal officer to take the fuse out,' because we didn't know anything about fuses. The captain decided he'd call all hands aft and he said, 'As you know, boys, we've got a bomb on board that hasn't gone off. We think it's a 500-pound bomb but we don't know. We're going to have to take it out. I want some of you to volunteer with me. I'm going to get that bomb out of the bunker somehow.' Well, I would happily have been about a thousand miles away but the officer next to me was a man with a wife and two children and he stepped forward and I thought, I can't very well refuse, I've got no wife, no kids. So I volunteered.

After two days' and two nights' hard digging we managed to get a rope round it and get it up to the deck. The Russian officer was getting ready to take the detonator out and we decided, we were Merchant Navy officers but we were British Merchant Navy officers and we weren't leaving this chap on his own, so three of us went down beside him. It was crazy in a way. The detonator stuck and he was pulling at it and it won't come, so he reaches into his pocket and brings out a punch and a hammer and he starts punching it to get it to move. This is normal engineering practice, but every time he punched it the hairs on the back of my neck stood up against my duffel coat hood. It wasn't a healthy position to be in. But he got it going.

It was November 1943 before David and the crew of the *Dover Hill* were finally able to leave the Arctic Circle for home.

We thought we'd be away about three weeks but it was ten or eleven months before we left Russia. But it was our job. We were sailors. We had to get the stuff to Russia from Britain, and we succeeded.

Despite heavy losses of ships, materials and men, the Russian convoys continued – with only two short breaks – for the duration of the war. This lifeline, though painfully fragile at times, undoubtedly made a difference to the Russian war effort against Hitler. Russia showed her appreciation in the form of medals for the men who braved the perilous journey, but British recognition of their achievement was more muted once the war ended, and silenced altogether with the advent of the cold war.

After their brave action with the unexploded bomb at Murmansk, David Craig and his Merchant Navy colleagues were awarded a King's Commendation 'for dangerous work in hazardous circumstances'. The army gunners on Convoy PQ-13 got a special mention in the second mate's official report, but Austin Byrne and the navy gunners who fought alongside them went unrecognised. There were no service medals for the men on the Russian convoys.

———◆———

Naval Petty Officer John Harrison survived his convoy experience but suffered a serious accident on HMS *Belfast* in much calmer waters.

> We were going on active service from Rosyth out to the North Sea. We'd gone a little way down [the Firth of Forth] and it was a lovely sunny day. I was in charge of A Turret as an ordnance artificer and I was charging these air bottles to 3,000 p.s.i. and suddenly the lights went out. There was a hell of a bang and I thought one of these bottles had exploded. And then the deck bounced. Well, you don't have a cruiser that size bouncing, but we did, about a foot.

They'd hit a German magnetic mine in shallow water and the keel was blown clean off. In the gun turret John, dazed, thought he was uninjured.

> But the following morning I could hardly move my shoulders or my neck. I went down to the medical department: 'Oh, tough luck, chief. Three aspirins. Report in the morning.' Nowadays

you'd be on a stretcher and God knows what. But that was the routine. But it wasn't finished because there was a lot going on inside my head, and I didn't finish in a very good condition.

In fact, John had sustained a head injury that was to give him problems for the rest of his life. But this also turned out to be the most tremendous piece of luck. While *Belfast* spent the next two years undergoing repairs, all but 16 of the crew were transferred to HMS *Hood*. John was among the 16, kept back to inspect the damage to his turret. In May 1941 the *Hood* was sunk by the German battleship *Bismarck* in the Battle of the Denmark Strait, one of the worst naval disasters of the war. There were 1,415 lives lost and only 3 survivors.

The venerable *Belfast*, having seen further action on convoy duty, in the Normandy landings and in the Far East, survives as an Imperial War Museum ship permanently moored on the Thames by Tower Bridge. John, in his 101st year and emotional about his experience still after more than 70 years, feels he owes her a debt of gratitude.

That's why I always go up to the *Belfast*, walk along to A Turret and say, 'Thank you very much indeed.' Saved my life. Was I responsible? Not on your nelly. Luck. But it did. Otherwise I'd have been with the other OAs [ordnance artificers] on the *Hood*.

About 25,000 Royal Navy escort personnel died as a result of enemy action during the war. But more than double that number of merchant seamen perished, the majority through drowning. The young men who survived everything nature and the enemy could throw at them now talk easily, even lightly, of their experiences. There was a job to be done and they did it. There's sadness at the loss of shipmates and respect for the men who led them. There is also hurt bordering on bitterness that some of them failed to receive due recognition at the time, especially those on the 'Russia run'. Whatever got them through – religious faith, patriotism, youthful innocence or blind ignorance – they are proud of their contribution to keeping vital wartime supply lines open. Typical of the straightforward merchant seaman, Austin Byrne, now 92, says:

> I just feel very proud that I've done it. I did what a lot of other people did and I did what were expected of me. And there's nothing much more you can say about that.

8

The Home Front

1941–1945

No one's going to spoil our show . . . Carry on. And we did.

Fergus Anckorn

If combatants' experience of war was long periods of boredom interrupted by short bursts of sheer terror, then civilians had a rather different time of it between 1941 and 1945. There were certainly terrifying moments, especially for those under bombardment in the cities, but life on the home front was more likely to feel like a sustained period of physical and emotional privation punctuated by brief intervals of release. Every day presented the same challenges: where to shelter; what to eat; how to live without breadwinners and loved ones; and how to cope with the exhaustion of long working hours and the effort of maintaining some semblance of normality in the most abnormal of circumstances.

But there were unexpected and unprecedented opportunities too for women in the workplace and for young people in exciting new forms of war work. And there were all the temptations associated with major fissures in the established order: people and troops on the move; American GIs with their 'Hollywood attitudes' on the loose; social classes, so rigidly segregated before the war, now thrown together in adversity; and husbands absent and women moving beyond hearth and home to mix in wider circles. For the generation now caught up in the upheavals of war, this was a time of hardship but also of adventure, delicious discovery and the glimpsing of new horizons.

For the first time resilience at home was as vital as success in theatres of war. Robust civilian morale was recognised as a precious strategic asset: without it, war production and the essential services that kept everything together would collapse. Apathy, revolt or the dreaded 'defeatism' were the enemies of victory. Public morale was closely monitored, documented and discussed in the Home Intelligence division of the Ministry of Information. Mass Observation, the independent research organisation set up in 1937, contributed its own extensive reports on public response to events at home and abroad as the war progressed, sometimes presenting a startlingly contrary picture to the impression given by the upbeat press stories and official versions of the time.

Looking back, personal memories of wartime morale tend to be positive, even rosy. Fergus Anckorn perhaps saw people at their most relaxed when he was performing his magic in concert parties around the country.

> Oh, the morale was fantastic in this country at that time. You never saw despondency at all. Even when people were blown out of their houses they would come out and say, 'Anyone seen the milkman? I haven't had my milk today.' It was just, 'Carry on.' I remember I was up in London once or twice when I was on leave, seeing businessmen with their homburg hats, their briefcase, pinstripe trousers and black jacket, going to work and no means of transport. There'd be a man going along with a horse and cart and they would all get on the back of it, very much the businessman but nothing was thought to be out of place. So everybody helped everybody.
>
> And at the concert parties, when we would turn up in a town, everywhere, Scotland, all over the place, they would always fill the theatre and it was a wonderful audience, laughter and gaiety the whole time. Even when an air-raid siren went off in the middle of the show they would stop and announce, 'The air-raid warning has gone off and there are aircraft overhead. If you wish to go down to the cellar the stairs are that way. If you wish to stay, the show will go on.' And then we'd carry on with the show and no

one in the audience moved. It was a bit frightening because you could hear the bombs falling . . . but when you're interrupted by bombs or anything like that, it was just a nuisance. No one's going to spoil our show, you know. You don't think that you're going to get the roof come in and kill you, you just do the show. Carry on. And we did.

Of course in reality morale could be neither homogeneous nor constant: it varied by region, class and individual and swung in tune to personal mood as well as national triumph or disaster. Just as the ever-cheerful cockney raising his cuppa outside the ruin of his bombed-out home was a myth, so too was the moaning Minnie who delighted in sapping everyone's morale. People generally got on with the job in hand, often making light of their troubles, sometimes grumbling, but quietly determined not to contemplate defeat.

As Britain emerged from the horrors of the Blitz, there were mixed feelings of relief that the worst of it was over for the time being, and resignation that life would now be a long, difficult slog for the duration. The costs had been great: 43,000 killed and 150,000 injured. Pre-war planners had vastly overestimated the number of civilian deaths and disastrously underestimated the extent of damage to homes: two million people were homeless, some permanently, the majority of them in and around London. But now Hitler had turned his attentions to Russia, Britain had breathing space to repair and regroup. The immediate threat of invasion was past and America joining the war at the end of 1941 raised spirits. Nevertheless, no one doubted that the road ahead would be long and arduous.

There were still sporadic raids, the blackout was still strictly enforced and rationing of food and clothing restricted supply and choice. The lessons of the 1914–18 war had been learned and food was rationed from the start of the war, a measure that many welcomed because, in theory at least, it helped ensure fair shares for all. Enid Wenban, whose mother remembered the privations of 1917–18, was an enthusiast.

There was rationing almost straight away and I thought this was brilliant. I happen to think that rationing worked really well. People seem to think that we were half starved but we weren't. It was adequate. My mother had a frugal upbringing and she certainly didn't waste anything at all.

On the whole rationing did work well, though a black market operated in every town and village, even in the most unlikely places. Margaret Rhodes, mostly in London during the war but visiting her family's Scottish estate, discovered a useful source of black-market underwear.

One had clothing coupons which were never adequate for buying anything. We had a shooting lodge in Inverness-shire, which had a very nice keeper who was exempt from war service for some reason, and he was head of the Inverness-shire black market and he managed to find a factory that had been bombed or something and there were a lot of spare things going around. And I had a large contingent of grey knickers – grey lock-knit knickers – and I wore them for years.

Though many families managed to sustain a reasonable living standard on rations supplemented with the occasional black-market indulgence, in poorer areas of Britain's cities, living conditions had changed little since the last war, or even the last century. Gladys Parry's family home in Manchester was a typical early-Victorian back-to-back with few facilities and many unwelcome guests.

You kept the front room in case anybody ever came round, posh. But quite honestly, there wasn't much in it to be posh about. Now the living room was always dark because it looked out on to the yard and a big wall. The outside toilet was there. And the scullery was a little tiny thing. It had a sink and an old iron stove. Now, if you put your washing up, we used to have it on a rack and you'd put the washing up and nine times out of ten you were walking into it – it was the only way you could dry it in winter. There was a little bulb in there, no light anywhere else. You used to go up the stairs with a candle and my job was to get brown paper and a flat iron that we used to heat on the stove and iron the wax off the carpet – all threadbare but it was still waxed, otherwise it would get very slippy with the wax. That was an everyday thing, people did that all the time.

These old houses – talk about bugs upstairs, cockroaches downstairs. The cockroaches used to run along the floor . . . And that was an average thing in houses in Hulme. No matter how clean you was, you'd get these bugs in the bedroom. Because they were eating into the plaster, and no matter how much you plastered it, there'd be a way that bugs would arrive, and you'd find out one had been in the bed, you woke up next morning and one had bit you. Horrible. It was horrible.

Rationing meant that Gladys, like many women in Britain, had to be more careful than ever with food.

If we were lucky we could get rabbits and they used to be sixpence in them days. You could get a good meal, stuff its belly, sew it up and roast it, it was good. This particular day I'd done the rabbit and I'd left it in the kitchen. All of a sudden I saw the cat, Tiger, with the rabbit in its mouth, running through the living room, down the lobby. Well, I was after him that fast, because there was no way that cat was going to eat my rabbit. It had gone down the grid to the cellar. I tell you, super-strength: I pulled up the grid, got down there, had the cat by the back of its head, his eyeballs were nearly coming out, but he wouldn't let go of my rabbit, and I'm saying, 'You let go of that rabbit or I'm going to punch you right in the ear.' And I got the rabbit off him. I give it a real good washing and we had it that night for tea. I would rather have cooked the bloody cat than not have my rabbit.

At the start of the war Margaret Rhodes was still living on her parents' country estate. But even in Scottish castles wartime rationing and the threat of air attack called for grit and ingenuity.

Because of lack of food – in that we were rationed – I used to go about the estate all the time with a little .22 rifle trying to shoot pigeons and rabbits, anything that was edible. I was in the garden one afternoon when I heard an aeroplane coming and it came over very, very low over the tops of the trees and I could see the swastika on its body. And I had real fun. I emptied the bullets at this enormous flying thing overhead, and I thought it might just hit the petrol tank and explode. Needless to say, it was unscathed and it flew on happily. But I did fire at the enemy!

When she was 16 in 1941 she went to a finishing school in Oxford and from there to secretarial college, evacuated from London to Egham in Surrey. Her 'billet' was nearby Windsor Castle, where she lived with her cousins, the Princesses Elizabeth and Margaret.

I did live quite a long time at Windsor and it was lovely. The King and Queen were being marvellous and really working like slaves. Every day they'd go off to tour different parts of the country which had been bombed and they came back to spend the weekend with the girls, who were permanently at Windsor.

Conditions were fairly spartan at the castle. Margaret remembers it being 'permanent twilight' with the heavy blackout curtains and furniture covered in dust sheets. The King insisted on the same privations as his subjects so their food was rationed – though supplemented by game from the Windsor estate – and bathwater was limited to three inches. Though it was safer than central London, there were still occasional raids.

The head page would come in and say, 'Purple warning, Your Majesty,' or some other colour which meant how near the bombers were. I do remember one night we three girls were woken up and taken to the King and Queen's rooms, where I remember the King opening a bedside cabinet and taking out a revolver. And then we all processed very slowly, because Queen Elizabeth refused to be hurried, and we went down in subterranean corridors for what seemed like miles and eventually got to the shelter which was somewhere in the subterranean regions of Windsor Castle. I can't remember what it was like but I think it was quite comfortable.

In April 1941 Princess Elizabeth celebrated her sixteenth birthday at the castle. Radio and recording star Vera Lynn was there and remembers it well.

> I was invited to Windsor as there was going to be an entertainment. So I was thrilled to go along and sing, because [the Princess] used to listen to the radio and she was young and she knew my songs and knew all about me. It was lovely sitting there, looking out over the gardens and all the marching guardsmen outside. The *ITMA* [*It's That Man Again*] people were there too, performing, so it was all very friendly and nice.

Was it important for public morale that the royal family stayed in or near London? Margaret has no doubts.

> I think it made a huge difference to the ordinary people of England that the King and Queen didn't even consider sending their children to safety because they would not be divided as a family. [Queen Elizabeth] said, 'I would not send the children away without me, and I cannot ever leave the King.' So that's the way she played it, and quite right too.

The royal family were fortunate in being able to stay together as a family unit. Separation was a fact of life for millions of others. Many children were evacuated and didn't see their parents till the end of the war. Mothers with babies and young children were also sent out of the cities. As bombing made life in the East End increasingly untenable, Connie Hoe had evacuated together with others from her community to Wolvercote, outside Oxford. It couldn't have been further from crowded, working-class Limehouse, but they were welcomed: 'They accepted all these half-Chinese children with their funny names and just took them in.'

For mothers separated from their children, things were potentially more difficult. Hetty Bower now had two young children,
Celia and Margaret. Their progressive kindergarten in north
London was evacuated to a large house in Bedfordshire. Hetty
stayed in London with Reg, who had yet to be called up. She
carried on working and volunteering at the local Czech refugee
centre. She was a pacifist and ideologically opposed to the war.
How did she feel about being separated from her children,
especially as Margaret was then only a toddler? 'I was more
concerned for her safety than what I felt. Her safety was more
important than my feelings.' What were her feelings? 'That war
is mad.'

———————◆———————

Able-bodied adults, unless they were elderly or were looking after
children at home, had war work to do, paid or voluntary. Dirty,
noisy, often monotonous factory work over long hours was made
bearable by 'good spirit', music and comradeship, as Gladys Parry
remembers of her time at the Avro factory making Lancaster
bombers.

> We weren't told to work hard. We just did. It was how many, and
> how much you could get through in a day. We were very patriotic
> and there was a lot of camaraderie there. Everybody helped
> everybody else. Didn't matter who it was, they'd get on and work.
> If someone was getting a bit behind you'd help them. One of the
> girls on our team of four, she couldn't work as quick as what we
> could but we'd help her get her quotas out, make sure we made
> the day's amount that was needed. There was a lot of good spirit
> like that.
>
> There was a bloke had this shop up Oxford Road in Manchester,
> and he used to come in the canteen at dinnertime and we'd all
> sing together. 'Roll Out the Barrel', we used to have that, and the
> 'Siegfried Line', that one. The songs we had then, you could always
> remember the words so it meant all of us could sing in whatever

voice you'd got. It were good the lunchtime breaks were, because you'd got something to talk about when you got back to work.

Joy Lofthouse actually got to fly the planes Gladys was making. Having applied to be a trainee pilot for the Air Transport Auxiliary, there was a stiff academic test and she was questioned about sports that demanded quick thinking and fine coordination skills.

> I do very well remember at my interview they asked me did I ski, and did I horse-ride? Which of course were way out of my league. But I said, 'Well, no, I don't, but I do everything else. I'm a good swimmer, I got in all the teams and I was captain of netball and hockey and tennis.'

Once accepted, Joy found herself at the ATA's training school in Thame. Unlike RAF pilots, the ATA women weren't taught 'blind flying' and had no radio contact with the ground, so they had to fly in clear skies where they could see the horizon. They didn't navigate from instruments, they map-read, often following railway lines and looking for landmarks on the ground.

> We were taught to try not to get into bad weather, but if you did, land and wait for it to clear, which was what we did. And if we knew where the nearest American station was, we'd opt for that, because the food was good and they took you to the PX [American equivalent of the NAAFI] and you could buy lipsticks and things like that.

At the end of her training, Joy was finally trusted with a Spitfire.

> There, what you'd been waiting for your whole time, was the school Spit in the corner. Once you'd flown the Spit you were qualified to go to a pool and do ferrying. And you just got in the Spit and flew a few circuits, it was quite the fastest thing . . . It was as though you'd been kicked from behind into the air!
> Flying a Spitfire was the be-all and end-all of the single-seater

fighters. It had a very compact cockpit. It was difficult to taxi on the ground. In fact, one of the test pilots said, 'She's a lady in the air, but she's a bitch on the ground,' because she had such a tall, long nose. You had to weave to see where you were going. But the minute you got up in the air, oh, it was wonderful. You always took off with your cockpit open and when you throttled back to get to normal cruising speed you shut it. But you only had to touch the column and she did what you wanted. It was as near to being a bird and flying oneself as you could possibly get.

She was now a fully qualified ATA pilot ferrying expensive aeroplanes all over the country, but Joy was from an ordinary rural background, unlike many of the sophisticated and wealthy women who'd joined the ATA early in the war.

We were a very varied bunch in the ATA, even at Hamble, which was an all-women's pool. There were people who'd flown pre-war, very moneyed people but not necessarily very sociable. Flying was their life. In fact it was said that we divided into 'It girls' who did a lot of socialising, went up to London in the evening and got back in time to fly the next day; and there were the 'head girls', who thought about nothing but flying. Well, I was neither. I was a sort of third-former, because I was so junior to them. I did have a social life. Certainly not very much during flying times, because if the weather was nice, one was flying to all hours and you went back to your billet and that was enough, you were tired.

Ferrying aircraft for the ATA wasn't anything like as dangerous as flying in combat situations, but the weather could be hazardous and Joy had some close shaves. Was she ever scared in the air?

I never was. I would have gone on flying for ever. I never wanted the war to end. I know it was very wicked of me, but I wished it had gone on. I'm very thankful that I did what I did and got the chance to do it but it was still only very minor to what a lot of our senior women did.

Workers in essential occupations in manufacturing, farming, mining, the public services or government were exempt from call-up into the armed forces. Ron Jones, a wire-drawer with GKN in Cardiff and married 18 months to his childhood sweetheart Gwladys, was one of them. His was a specialist job involving both heavy manual labour and engineering skills and GKN was in full production making parts for tanks and aircraft, so there was no question of Ron being called up.

> I was working nights and I was in bed [when the post came]. Gwladys came in and she says, 'There's a letter here,' she says, 'it looks from the War Office.' I opened it up and it was my call-up papers. I couldn't believe it because I was in a reserved occupation. I went down to the works to see the personnel manager. He couldn't understand it, because we had forms to fill in. Anyway, to cut a long story short, my form hadn't been sent in, the silly typist had put it in the incoming mail instead of the outgoing, so there was no account of me at the labour exchange. I got called up, and that was it.

Over his six months square-bashing in the Brecon Beacons, his GKN managers made sterling efforts to rectify the error, but to no avail. Ron was in the army now and within nine months he was on his way to the Middle East with the South Wales Borderers.

With so many working men being called up, factories had an insatiable demand for workers. Even heavy industry started to draft in women. Kit Sollitt, now a young woman of 22, found herself in a Sheffield steel foundry making parts for tanks and battleships.

> It was an old-fashioned foundry. They hadn't even a canteen when I first went. You had to have a billycan and mash your tea from a boiling thing in the yard. And you'd have your food where you sat. I was going to be trained as a sand miller. There were a chap on it; he'd been called up and he'd got a week to teach it me.

She 'couldn't remember picking up a barrow in her life' but she had to wheel a barrow to stocks of sand, collect different kinds in certain proportions and mix them together with a treacle-like chemical in a huge machine and then wheel the mix along the earth floor to the skilled moulders making castings.

> Wherever there's molten metal it's got to be earth, otherwise it would hit the floor, bounce up and burn everybody, but if it's earth it settles. So you've got to go through this depth of earth with old-fashioned barrows. If you'd to go past this Bessemer [converter], you'd have to go underneath, and if it were full on I used to have to put a wet sack over the whole of my head. Then I'd take the mixing to the moulder and tip it up in a heap . . . Everywhere you look, sand, dirt, smoke and the fumes from the castings. No windows, no hygiene. You wore trousers with clogs . . . After the first day, I says to this chap, 'I'll never stick this.' He said, 'Oh, you'll get used to it. You'll have muscles like me.' I says, 'I hope not.'

The intense heat of the Bessemer converter and the risk of molten metal splashes made it a dangerous and unpleasant place to work.

> It would be like the top of a volcano and all the sludge showering all over the place. Wherever it dropped it burned and it didn't burn flat. It used to go into your skin like a ringworm. And you'd get loads of them little ones. You'd hear your hair hissing and you'd have a cap on and it'd go through the cap, burn your hat and into your hair. You had all that to contend with, and then the fumes didn't do anybody's chest any good. And there were spills, when the Bessemer would just tip up and . . . molten steel everywhere.
>
> So it's not like working in a factory. No, it was a work in hell. And that were my job. From seven in the morning till whatever time casting was finished – five, six. Lucky if you got away at five. One break. No tea breaks. Saturdays, Sunday mornings. All your life was work. I did that for three years. It were non-stop.

She was so tired after work she would wash and have her tea, then sleep on the settee in her mum's front room until bedtime. The men could make money in the foundry, but the women's wages were always much lower. There was harassment as well as discrimination, though Kit took it in her stride.

It's a different world in a steelworks. You hear words you never heard before. It was all bad language and you'd to take no notice of what they said to you. Some never accepted women, these moulders that were getting on in years. You imagine a bloke in his fifties having a woman coming to labour for 'em. They either hated them or they took to 'em. And if they hated 'em they made the woman's life a misery, I tell you. Moulders, they're a breed on their own, but I got on fine with most of them.

Soon Kit was in the pub with them after work. Eventually she married one of them in 1944. They were hard years and, though she has no regrets, this was a time to be endured rather than enjoyed. 'It became your way of life. You lost your youth. You lost them years. They were just humdrum.'

Enid Wenban's gentler work as a civil servant at HMSO was clean and safe, but unstimulating. Around her, young women were joining the services and she wondered whether she should too, but her father had died suddenly in 1941 and she felt duty-bound to stay at home to support her mother. But by 1943 the demand for service personnel was so great that the Civil Service was prepared to release a quota of employees. This was Enid's chance.

By this time I was relieved to get away, away from London, to a different life. And I was glad by then to be able to do my bit for the country.

She joined the ATS and, after aptitude tests, was sent to the Isle of Man for training.

We were told absolutely nothing, just that we were joining the Royal Corps of Signals. We had to learn Morse up to a high standard, theory of radio, radio waves, all this stuff, which I found interesting. Some of the girls found it boring but I loved it. We were there through a winter and we were accommodated in hotels on the front. We had no hot water and my friend and I used to go down into the town and pay sixpence for a hot bath in the public baths.

We had to sign the Official Secrets Act and we were even told not to talk to each other about it, to make sure we didn't start talking about our work when we were out somewhere. We never discussed the work we were doing, at all. We just accepted it, right from the beginning. You sign the Official Secrets Act and you don't talk about it. That was it, you accepted it.

Enid was about to find out what 'her bit' was to be.

Some specialist kinds of war work had invaluable propaganda value. Dorothy Bohm, who'd arrived in 1939 as a 15-year-old German-Jewish refugee, had just finished a photography course in Manchester and found work in a portrait studio. Now still only 18, Dorothy felt a debt of gratitude to the country that had taken her in.

I remember going to find out if I could join the army and I was told, 'What are you doing? You're a friendly alien!' Then I was told that portraiture was very important because we were photographing a lot of the soldiers for their families and I worked incredibly hard. On a Saturday about 60 people, can you imagine? But a wonderful thing happened to me and I wanted to do something for the war effort. At some gathering we talked about the war and the Nazis a lot and a chap came up to me and said, 'I'm the head of the Ministry of Information for northern England. I'd like you to join a group of speakers. You'll be the youngest.' I was aghast, but he said, 'The English are very slow to hate. If we make you talk about what you know about fascism, when they see you, a kid, and what you saw, what happened, they'll begin to understand what we are fighting, and that it's worthwhile.' And I said, 'Do you think I can do it?' He said, 'I know you can.'

My first talk was at the public library in Manchester. I told them what I'd experienced, what happened to lots of friends of my father's. How when anybody disappeared we were told that they'd committed suicide. I began to try and find out more what was going on in Europe and because of my father's connection, the Lithuanian ambassador was very friendly and he kept me informed about things going on there. So not only did I talk about what had happened and why the Nazis had to be defeated, I was able to tell them what was going on there too.

I did an awful lot of travelling in the blackout, all over Lancashire. And it was interesting. I got to know the country, we were going to workers or to Rotary Clubs, and I remember going to the miners. And I found it fascinating, so for me it was an education. I was never afraid in the blackout and I must say the people I talked to, whether they were the gentlemen of the clubs or the miners or the factory workers, I was able to find contact with them. When I was introduced as a speaker, they said, 'Dorothy tells you what she knows. We don't censor anything.' Now you tell me any other country that during the war would do that! The reaction was wonderful. They used to come up to me and thank me and I was speaking from the heart. I had no notes and the MOI actually at the time offered me a full-time job but I said, 'I'm a photographer!'

She was doing something uniquely worthwhile, but there was an emotional toll to speaking in public about her family, of whose fate she knew nothing.

When I was brought home, there wasn't any sleep. It did upset me quite a lot, but I began to love the country and the people. The MOI made me change my name. They said, 'We can't have your real name in case your parents might still be alive.' Don't forget that I was still very young and being alone was pretty terrifying. There were times when I thought, no, I can't make it, I can't carry on, and then I thought my father would be ashamed of me and I became stronger. But it was tough, very, very tough. And I don't think that in any other country I would have been able to continue the way I did. I made lots of wonderful friends. I always made sure that they knew I was Jewish, they knew my background. My love for this country is due to what I remember during the war and the way people behaved.

Others got a chillier welcome, even if they came from the empire. Earl Cameron, an adventurous young Bermudan of 22, had arrived in England by chance. The British merchant ship he'd joined as a seaman was in port for repair at Buenos Aires when it was recalled by the Admiralty. It docked at Woolwich on 26 October 1939 and from then on, apart from periods at sea, London was Earl's home. 'I loved London. Why? It's a big city and I'm from a small island. I fell in love with London.' Initially life was good, he had his wages to spend and he was enjoying the capital's nightlife. Chasing after a girl from Tiger Bay, he jumped ship and soon found himself workless and penniless.

That was a different experience. It was almost impossible for a black person to get a job in London at the early part of the war. I'm talking late 1939, early 1940. There was an attitude from the people in the twenties that all the black people, in spite of the fact that many of them had fought in the First World War, should be returned to their homes in the Caribbean or Africa, or wherever they came from. That was a terrible thought but that was the way it was. So the bunch of [black] guys I met in and around Soho, some of them had been in England a long time and what I noticed was that most of them walked with these heavy walking sticks, you know, and I thought this seemed a bit Victorian somehow. I said, 'Why do you guys always walk with these sticks?' He said, 'Look, man, this is a weapon, because you never know when you're going to be attacked in this country.'

After menial jobs and another stint as a merchant seaman, he
returned to London. He'd escaped being torpedoed and now he
was back in time for the Blitz. Like many Londoners at the time,
he became almost nonchalant about what they had to face there.

War is a funny thing. Like during the Blitz, the air-raid alarm
would go, sometimes you're in the pub and you just keep on
drinking. Some people will run for the shelter but I would say the
average person in London just went on, you know, they just kept
up the conversation. You become philosophical about things. If
you get all nerves, you wouldn't survive.

Even the Blitz hadn't stopped people finding distraction from
the daily grind and London nightlife thrived. Margaret Rhodes
and the cream of London society haunted the smart 400 Club in
Leicester Square; others found humbler pleasures. Earl was living
close by in the heart of theatreland.

A friend of mine gave me a ticket to see a show called *Chu Chin
Chow*. I saw the show and went backstage and saw Harry Crossman,
who'd given me the tickets. I said, 'Harry, can't you get me in the
show?' I was more or less joking, you know. He said, 'No, Earl,
it's not like that, you don't get into show business like that.' I said,
'Come on, now. What you guys are doing, I could do.' They were
just in the chorus. He said, 'You're not a member of Equity, there's
no way I can get you in the show.' I was mainly joking, but I
thought hoofing would be a lot better than washing dishes.

About three weeks later I was in the club in Wardour Street
and Harry turned up: 'Earl, your big chance has come – Russell
didn't turn up for rehearsal and the director says get someone
else.' I said, 'You're joking.' He said, 'No, I'm serious. Come on.'
He took me to the stage door of the Palace Theatre. The director
looked me up and down and said, 'I guess he'll do.' And believe
it or not, within a matter of half an hour I was on stage, just like
that. I broke into show business!

Another young man was just about to get his break in show business. After his Quaker school in York and volunteering with the Friends' Ambulance Unit, Brian Rix went into his wealthy father's shipping firm at 16, 'to see if I liked it'. Within three weeks he knew he didn't. At 18 he signed up for the RAF Volunteer Reserve and was accepted as a pilot/navigator/bomb-aimer but told to go away for ten months. His mother was from a theatrical background and his sister Sheila was already in a touring company with the great Shakespearean actor-manager Donald Wolfit. When they were playing in Hull, Brian took his chance.

> I knocked on his dressing-room door and I asked the great man if I could possibly join his company because I had ten months' deferred service. He took me straight on to the stage and asked me if I had an audition piece. The only audition piece I knew was a piece of poetry I'd recited the previous Sunday in a troop concert which my mother had put on. It was called 'Bessie's Boil'.

Brian can still recite the comic Lancashire dialect piece, which he launched into for Donald Wolfit. It seemed to do the trick.

> After that I was in *King Lear* and *Hamlet* and *Twelfth Night, A Midsummer Night's Dream*, on that ridiculous audition piece, but that's because young actors were in great demand of course, because they were all called up. So I was with Wolfit and then a letter came from the Air Ministry to say I wasn't wanted for another year.

So he carried on acting. One troop tour was particularly memorable:

> I think it was Tidworth. There were a lot of very raw American troops there, having just got over here. And the curtain went up on *Twelfth Night* and within five minutes, apart from the front row of officers, the entire audience had gone out, moved out. They didn't want to see *Twelfth Night*, and we were there for five nights!

Wolfit complained bitterly to the commanding officer, and he said, 'OK, I'll fix tomorrow night.' And the following night the place is packed. Dead silence. Nobody moves, nobody laughs, nobody coughs, nobody does anything. Curtain comes down at the end of the first act and we look, we're thinking, what's going on? And we peer through, and the military police are walking up and down the aisles with guns! So it really was a totally captive audience – and it was like that for three more nights!

———◆———

Keeping the home front entertained and informed was an essential tool in maintaining morale. Here the BBC Home Service played a dual role: upbeat music, variety and comedy programmes cheered listeners up at home and in the workplace; and trusted, unsensational (but undoubtedly censored) news from home and abroad kept them informed of the progress of the war.

Already an established live performer and recording artist with the premier dance bands of the late 1930s, Miss Vera Lynn soon became a star of radio too. A BBC Forces Programme radio request show, *Sincerely Yours*, cemented her reputation and her wartime repertoire became indelibly written into the history of the home front.

I suppose the songs were plain, simple, easy to remember, easy to sing along to, not like the songs are today – about sex and everything – they were just good songs, well written and nice words. Radio was very important because during the war people didn't like to go out too much, everybody used to be at home by eight o'clock because of the sirens starting. I chose all the songs myself. I never allowed anybody to tell me what to sing. I only sang what I felt I could sing and that I felt right singing, you know, that they meant something to me and they'd mean something to the boys. Lyrics were very important. There were never any war songs, they were all optimistic, full of hope.

She chose well. Songs like 'We'll Meet Again' and 'The White Cliffs of Dover' expressed those basic human sentiments – love, longing, loyalty – that ordinary people found hard to express, even to loved ones far from home. That they also contained a strong patriotic subtext was no hindrance to the war effort. If the Ministry of Information had invented Miss Vera Lynn, they couldn't have had a better vehicle.

Her songs reminded servicemen what they were fighting for: country, home and loved ones. And they kept hope and romance alive for loved ones listening at home.

Love affairs – as opposed to opportunist wartime couplings – were often sweet, romantic and chaste until marriage. Men inclined to believe in the idea of 'love at first sight' and 'the one for me'; women, constrained by fear of pregnancy or parental displeasure, discouraged any 'messing about' and kept themselves for their wedding night. Ron Jones had met his wife Gwladys at chapel, where she played the organ. He'd been keen to 'try before you buy' but was rebuffed. 'I tried very often. "No. No." That was all I had: "No."'

Fergus Anckorn had never gone out with a girl before he met his future wife while he was in hospital with a high fever.

> In the bed next to me was a fellow and we were talking. He said, 'You engaged or anything?' And I said, 'Oh God, no. I don't have anything to do with girls. Nuisance they are, really.' So he said, 'Are you never going to get married then?' And at that moment a new nurse turned up. She came through the door and I said to him, 'No, I can't imagine I'll ever get married, but if I do it will be to that nurse.' I'd just seen her for two minutes. And that's how it turned out. So I was right. Love at first sight, it really was.

While he was in concert parties touring the country, he saw Lucille as often as he could, sometimes walking 18 miles to see her 'just to have a cup of tea' if she was on duty. They got engaged just before he was due to be posted overseas. This was often the pinch point for many couples: it was tempting to get married as they had no idea when they'd next see each other. And they didn't know what the future might hold.

She wanted to get married and I said, 'No, I don't want to do that because if we get married, next week you could be a widow,' because we were heading overseas. We were supposed to be going to the desert. So I said, 'Well, I don't know what will happen, where I'm going, but wait. I'll come back.'

We were together more or less until I went abroad, but love affairs in those days were entirely platonic. In my circles, sex was never mentioned. And not even thought of really. So we used to have the most wonderful times, just being together, going to the cinema, going for walks. Just to be near each other was good enough.

Gladys Parry didn't know much about sex but she knew it made babies.

There was no way that was going to happen to me. So many a time I'd be going out with a bloke, I'd say, 'Before I go out with you, I'm making one thing straight. No messing about, 'cause I'm not having it.' So I used to go out with the blokes, they'd kiss me goodnight but that was the lot. So my being like that, you see, I did go down the aisle in a white dress and I meant it.

Bill Graves courted his sweetheart Eileen during the early years of the war when she was in the Land Army and finally they got engaged. The ring cost him £25, 'a damn small fortune in 1942', but he recognised love when he saw it.

A feeling of compassion, a feeling of warmth, the feeling of security. It's a combination of individual feelings that come together as one and you feel it inside. You feel it in your chest. You feel it in your brain. And that's what I had. She wasn't a saint, I'm not saying that, but she was as near a saint as you'd ever get. She was . . . she was absolutely fantastic. She had a strength that you can't describe. She would do anything for anybody. She never took credit for anything or blew her own trumpet. That's the difference between us.

An engagement was often sufficient commitment for the girl to allow sex. Bill and Eileen were both virgins when they made love for the first time after their engagement.

Well, it was a disappointment, I mean, we hadn't the foggiest idea. We were a pair of twits fumbling around and finally did it and thinking, Well, what the bloody hell was that all about? Partly you felt you shouldn't have done it. Partly you felt a bit triumphant that you had done it and that you'd now joined this band of people who were sexually active. What you didn't admit is, you were bloody useless at it!

Was there a wartime imperative to consummate the relationship sooner rather than later?

You've got to remember that many of the people of my generation and at that period were going away and never knowing whether they'd ever come back again and the girls knew this. The girls wanted, in my opinion for what it's worth, they wanted to prove that they were still going to be there: 'You can go away, but don't get yourself killed and you know I'm here and this is what we'll do when you come back.' . . . It's a declaration that we're together for the rest of our life.

Self-restraint, aided by ignorance, inexperience and lack of opportunity, meant that the majority of loving couples waited till their wedding night, or at least a formal engagement, to sleep together. Whilst it is true that the war precipitated an increase in sexual activity and illicit liaisons (illegitimate births doubled between 1940 and 1945), for most of the single young people of this generation, pre-war moral standards and the romantic ideal of true love prevailed.

Connie Hoe, still only 19, was thrilled when her sweetheart Leslie came back on leave after a long voyage with the Merchant Navy in spring 1941, but bemused when he expected their marriage arrangements to be in full swing. He hadn't even proposed!

He thought that I'd received his letters and I thought he'd received mine – but nothing. We didn't receive any letters so they must have gone down in convoys or something. Because in 1941 the Atlantic war was very serious and a lot of the ships were lost, and of course I was overjoyed to see him, that he was alive after not hearing anything.

Leslie's leave was short and there was no time for a church wedding, so it was a hasty trip to the registry office in Oxford and a frugal reception for the few guests.

After the ceremony we walked along St Giles' where there was a rather nice cafe, Cadena, where they had an orchestra and a lounge, so we went there to have our wedding breakfast. The waiter came up with a menu, which was sardines on toast or beans on toast. So we sorted out how many sardines and how many beans, and then he came back and said, 'Oh sorry, sardines are off. You'll all have to have beans.' So that's what we did.

In the evening they went back to Leslie's digs in London. A raid was on so they spent much of their wedding night in a public air-raid shelter in Baker Street; it was 3 a.m. before they got to sleep together for the first time.

The situation for Charles Chilton and his girlfriend Penny, evacuated by the BBC to Evesham, was complicated. Charles was married and his estranged wife Bess was unwilling to give him a divorce. But this wasn't going to stop Charles and Penny being together. Called up to the RAF in 1941 as a wireless operator, Charles's background in radio put him well ahead of the other trainees and he was soon a wireless instructor posted to Blackpool, but he stayed in close touch.

I wrote to her every day. The only time I didn't write was when I was with her on leave. We got leave every three months 'if convenient' but often it wasn't if the RAF was busy. I used to sleep in the bandstand in Evesham, wrapped up in a groundsheet. I'd have breakfast in the BBC canteen and go and see her in morning.

Letters were a vital – and apart from the odd telephone call, the only – form of contact for lovers kept apart by war and were as important for morale on the home front as for troops fighting far away. So important were they to many relationships that couples married for 60 years and more still have their precious wartime correspondence. Penny and Charles kept all theirs and, after a long and happy marriage, Penny spoke about the role of letters in their early relationship.

We felt we had to write to each other every day, even when you went to India. You wrote very expressive letters and the way you told me about the things you were doing, you made me feel that I was with you. Sometimes you wrote to me twice a day. We went on writing like this because there was nothing else we could do. In this letter to you I'd drawn a picture of two people embracing and I've written here: 'I long to be in your arms, my Chas, and to feel you close to me. I shall give you a great big special hug like this on Christmas Day. I love you and I hope that you will feel it, I think you will. God bless you.'

Letters didn't only help keep romance alive. For established married couples like Hetty and Reg Bower they were a vital link with home and family.

I wrote to him every night before going to sleep. Some still exist but many were lost. One night they bedded down in what they thought were trenches and they turned out to be irrigation channels and a lot of my letters were swept away in water and goodness knows what . . . They helped keep me going, oh yes, because he wrote lovely letters. I wrote to him about the things the girls were doing. One time Margy was dancing about on the bed settee and the furniture. I told her, 'If you knew what it cost to buy an armchair now, you'd stop doing that, so that Dad can have an armchair to sit on when he comes home.' And he wrote back: 'Will you please tell Margy to stop dancing on the furniture. Tell her to wait till I get home and then we'll both dance on it together.' That I never forgot. He was such a lovely man.

Letters from her fiancé Tony were what Diana Athill lived for in the early years of the war whilst he was stationed in Egypt. She had already committed herself physically to their relationship and believed they'd be together for the rest of their lives. She wrote regularly, but over the months his long, loving letters had gradually dwindled and then stopped altogether.

I went on writing into the silence. I didn't know what had happened. It was not knowing that was so painful.

Finally, a letter arrived.

Mother brought the letter up to me in bed. Would I kindly consider our engagement over as he'd met someone else? It was a terrible shock. I had an image of a long bridge being held up by two supports and one of the supports had been taken away, and there was the bridge, still sticking out . . . and it was bad. It wasn't just that he didn't love me, it was because one's career had gone. It was like a job had been taken away.

That was very, very bleak. I felt so completely and utterly alone and I was going to be alone for the rest of my days. After that, I thought, if I can stand this, I can stand anything. It's a good thing to learn, actually, to know you can stand being alone. I never cried in front of my friends or family. Nothing was said, they all tried to behave as if all was well. One tried to go on being normal, not being normal at all.

Diana had seen her future as an RAF wife snatched away. She now had to reinvent herself and find a new, more satisfying future.

> After that, I discovered one could have nice little flirtations that really cheered me up. I went through a stage of being quite promiscuous but it was better than nothing. I did fall in love passionately with a married man. I knew it was fatal, he was married and it was wartime. I was his wartime folly and I knew nothing would come of it, but I just couldn't give it up. Wartime affairs were managed by the man – he arranged dates and booked hotels and so on. I suppose I needed the sex really. I never went out after anybody, men came to me.
>
> I started to realise I could be perfectly happy not being married. It dawned on me at that stage that what would suit me would be not to be married, but to meet a Greek shipping magnate who wasn't in England very much – that would be my perfect life! I could get the sex, have a nice friendly person, but I could live my own life. I got used gradually to living my own life, not somebody else's.

For gay men there was no question of living their own lives. Homosexuality between men was illegal at home and a court martial offence in the services. 'Queers' and 'pansies' were the subject of ribald jokes and whispered rumours. Young gay men like George Montague had difficulty coming to terms with their sexuality, such was the ignorance and social stigma of homosexuality at the time. In adolescence George knew he was more excited by the pictures of men than the women in *Health & Efficiency*, a naturist magazine, but apart from a vague feeling of shame, he had no idea what it meant. He hadn't even heard the word 'homosexual'. In September 1941, when he was 18, he enlisted in the RAF Volunteer Reserve.

> The very first time anything registered with me was when I was a corporal and the corporals didn't mix with the other ranks. We used to sit in the veranda at the end of the hut. They were all

talking and I heard the end of the conversation: 'I've got one in my hut,' and then somebody said, 'I've got two in mine, and if I catch them together, I'll cut their bollocks off!' I said, 'What you talking about?' And they said, 'Brown hatters.' I said, 'What's that?' They told me and I was disgusted, absolutely disgusted.

It would be some years later, after many girlfriends and wartime encounters with prostitutes, that George started to acknowledge his sexuality and explore the subterranean world of queer London.

Life went on, sometimes in the most difficult of circumstances. Connie Hoe, pregnant with a honeymoon baby, gave birth prematurely and alone in her Oxford billet during a blizzard in November 1941.

I had these terrible backache pains. I woke the lady that I lived with and she went out in the blizzard – no phone in the house – to phone for the midwife. And when I stood up, Christine was born. I didn't know anything about childbirth. The cord broke when she fell on the floor. I just wrapped her up and I knew I had to wipe her eyes, so I did that and then climbed into bed [with her] and waited. I was sort of in a mist . . . I realised then that we'd had a child in wartime and Leslie might not come back. That's why we never had any more children, because of the precarious position we were in: no home, no money and no prospects really.

◆

From its extensive investigations, Home Intelligence concluded that people's ability to withstand the continuing privations of war depended on the availability of basic necessities: hot food, decent shelter and a good night's sleep. All those things the public and voluntary services could help provide with British Restaurants (a nationwide scheme of communal kitchens), rest centres and rapid temporary repairs to damaged homes. But more important, it depended on imponderables that not even the Ministry of

Information's most sophisticated propaganda could secure. Critically, morale on the home front depended on demonstrable equality of sacrifice, trust in the leadership and belief in victory. It also depended on the promise of a better life in peacetime.

After risking their lives for their country, no one was prepared to return to the pernicious social inequality of pre-war Britain and the five 'giant evils' identified by William Beveridge in his radical 1942 Report. Beveridge held out the prospect of a post-war settlement in which a new system of social security would vanquish Want, Squalor, Ignorance, Disease and Idleness. The inequities of the first half of the twentieth century would be gone for ever. This was to be the people's reward for staying on the long road to victory.

Personal qualities undoubtedly played their part in maintaining public morale. The war years in Britain imposed every conceivable kind of test on those on the home front. Not only were millions subjected to physical assault from the air, everyone shared a degree of discomfort, dislocation and deprivation. The social and emotional strains of separation and bereavement could be harder to bear, but putting on a brave face was preferred to self-indulgent displays of emotion; hoping for the best and doing one's best the surest ways to win through. On the bleakest days there were always shards of light: hope, laughter, comradeship and love. Memories of these are what survive perhaps most vividly alongside those of the darker times.

9

Prisoners of War

Get through today. Don't think of anything else. Get through today. And that's what I did for the best part of four years.
Fergus Anckorn, POW of the Japanese 1942–45

In June 1940, in a field outside Saint-Valery-en-Caux, the massed remnants of the 51st Highland Division were on their knees with hunger and exhaustion after the debacle of Dunkirk and their forced surrender. Shocked, dispirited and humiliated, they were some of the first British combatants to be taken prisoner in this long war and among the almost two million Allied troops captured during the German invasion of the Low Countries and the Fall of France alone. Many more were to follow. They would experience a new dimension to the depravations of war: some would see cruelty and suffering nothing in their lives thus far had prepared them for, and nothing in their lives thereafter could completely erase.

David Mowatt was one of several thousand Highlanders in the field as they were ordered to form up and start marching, under instructions to accept nothing from the local people who held out food and water in the summer heat as they passed. Although he didn't know it, this was just the start of their long trek from the French coast to Stalag XX-A at Thorn (Toruń) in Poland.

We'd had nothing to eat or drink and we were desperate. We were raiding piles of vegetables on the roadside. We reached a pile of turnips all covered in soil. That heap had a life of its own, it just moved. It disappeared as we went past. And we ate blighted potatoes but they nearly killed us. I was very ill with diarrhoea. We were going through a village. The man in front of me was a Scots Guardsman and he put his left hand out to accept a sandwich from this lady and a guard happened to be just behind him and smashed the back of his rifle on his wrist. The guardsman turned round and gave him one of the finest right hooks I've ever seen delivered and lifted that guard right over the wall and left him lying in a garden. That guard caught up with him and right in front of me he shot him through the stomach. You'd expect it of the SS, but this was just an ordinary *Wehrmacht* soldier. He just killed this man. It was a dreadful thing to do. The body was just left by the roadside and we all had to step over him . . . We were all dragged right down. We didn't know how far we were going to march. The days just blurred into each other. We were filthy, lousy. I can't describe the despair. It was terrible.

To be taken prisoner meant shame and humiliation, but that was just the start. Everything from mind-rotting boredom to the extremes of human suffering followed for the estimated 300,000 British and empire combatants taken prisoner by the Axis powers between 1940 and 1944. The degree depended only on where and by whom they were captured, at what point in the war, and whether their captors were signatories of the Geneva Convention and, if so, whether they were prepared to honour its provisions. In the ghastly hierarchy of suffering, millions of others – notably Russians, Slavs and Jews – fared much worse and far fewer survived their imprisonment. But the fact remains that no British POW who lived to return home came through the experience unscathed. It was the ultimate test of human sanity, endurance and ingenuity.

Like David Mowatt, Jim Purcell had also been at Dunkirk, but he'd been lucky enough to escape back across the Channel. After a period at home on invasion duty and practising some philanthropic safe-breaking in the Bristol Blitz, Jim was posted to the Middle East to join the escalating war in the eastern Mediterranean and the deserts of Egypt, Libya and Iraq. As a Royal Engineer attached to the 6th Battalion, Green Howards, his job was to travel with their convoys, mine-clearing and blowing up infrastructure and equipment to keep them out of German hands. Out in the Western Desert, with the Germans now under the command of General Rommel and supposedly less than 50 miles away, their patrol ran straight into an ambush.

We had enough petrol to reach 500 mile, in tanks. We also had enough blinking explosive to blow half the towns up. We were coming along the top and it led through a wadi [valley or dry river bed]. Nobody had told us this but the Germans had filled the wadi with soldiers; either side was a lot of machine guns, artillery and everything and they were pounding us with everything they had. We were at the back. Our young officer, I think he lost his rag a bit. You could see the trucks burning, you're seeing blokes lying on the bottom, so he shouted, 'Engineers forward!' And it crossed my mind: Someone tell the Germans to stop firing! We moved forward and we were on our own. Everybody was wide open. The truck got hit about six times. My friend Peter Kennedy, the lad I'd been with all the time, was on the other side and I heard him cry out. I stood up, for to get across him because there was stuff in the road; just then the driver got hit and the truck veered off and nosedived straight into the wadi where the German soldiers were. Well, I fell off, landed on my feet. I could see the Germans in the trench, so they started to throw hand grenades. We were in the middle of it, the five of us. I got Peter off the truck and he was crying in pain – the bullet hit his hip and went up near his heart – and I've got him in my arms and I'm underneath the truck, and I thought, It's full of explosives – let's get out of this! Coming down the bank, head first, was our corporal, Wynn Frost, keeping shouting, 'Jim! Help!' He'd caught a full blast, right across his body, his legs were hanging off. So there I am, and he's shouting my name, I canna touch him. I've got another bloke on me. And I'm only blinking 20 year old. What am I doing?

Worse, they were now about to be captured.

> When the battle was over, it would be about four o'clock in the morning, this little fellow came – he was dressed in a polo-necked navy blue pullover, grey flannels, glasses, proper Nazi type, on his armband was the swastika – and he pulled me up. Well, I had cramp in my legs because I'd been having Peter in my arms for nearly three hours. And I learned a German word there, it means 'sick' – it's *krank*. We got put in a line; they searched us and they took our wristwatches off us, because if you escape, you can use your hour hand in the sun as a compass. I was looking for my friends and nothing seemed to blinking worry me. It hadn't sunk in yet. It never sunk in for nearly 24 hours, I was so busy helping other people.

Their watches had been taken but when a soldier tried to take a cigarette lighter from a prisoner, he was reprimanded by his officer and ordered to give it back. That was to change: on their way by truck to Tobruk they were told: 'If you've got anything valuable, hide it because we're handing you over to the Italians.'

Mussolini's Fascist forces had not had a good war so far. Their leadership was poor, they had a reputation for surrendering at the first opportunity and morale was low. Rommel's men, it was said, were taking pity on them because they hadn't managed to take any prisoners of their own and handing over some Brits would raise their morale. So Jim and his comrades were leaving the disciplined custody of the Germans for much worse treatment at the hands of the Italians. It started with the trip by boat from Tobruk to their POW camp in the north of Italy.

> They would give you water [once in] every 24 hours. You could get it six o'clock in the morning, you got it six o'clock the next day, at night, so you had the problem of thirst. So you'd drink the salt water in with tins of corned beef, and I took ill for the first time I think since I was three. I took dysentery. Mind, I wasn't the only one.

It was the start of almost three years of sickness, deprivation and forced labour that would end not in Italy, but in the German-controlled coal mines of Czechoslovakia. Initially downhearted, Jim made a decision: he might have been captured, but he wasn't going to be beaten.

> When I got to Italy, I found out I was a prisoner of war. I looked at the Italians – I wasn't very friendly with them. But then I thought, I'm on my own now, but nobody's going to get me down. Nobody. I've had a tough life. I've been condemned to death when I was three. I've had poverty. Whatever happens, I'm going to win through and I'm going to get home. 'Cause I'm Jim Purcell, nobody's going to stick Jim in the gutter.

Also posted to fight the Desert War was Ron Jones, who'd been called up by mistake from his reserved occupation in the steelworks of South Wales. By September 1941 he was attached to the 1st Welch Regiment and on a convoy from Liverpool bound for Cairo.

> We had our Christmas dinner in Benghazi and about a week or so after, we heard that the Germans had come out there so one day Sergeant Major Corkbill said to me, 'Take a section up the road and see what's going on.' So I took a section of about ten men up the road and we'd walked up there for about four or five hundred yards and there was a big tank coming down the road with a man standing up on the front, and when he saw us he pointed his machine gun at us and in perfect English he said, 'Drop your guns, boys.' He said, 'For you the war is over.' And that's how I got it.

Like Jim Purcell, he was soon handed over to the Italians and only the intervention of a *Wehrmacht* officer prevented them being robbed of their watches and rings. Thereafter, every time there was a search, Ron hid his signet ring 'up my arse . . . the other lads were doing the same'.

By the time he got to Tripoli he realised the rest of his

regiment had been captured too and they all were shipped to a transit camp in Altamura in the heel of Italy. Conditions here were dreadful. There was no heating or hot water and the latrines were exposed to the elements: 'just a bar over a trench. Local people passing by would laugh at us doing our business.' There was no work to occupy them and without occasional Red Cross food parcels they would have gone hungry. Even so, making use of the parcels without implements or cooking utensils tested their ingenuity. They made plates by flattening food tins, knives out of tent pegs, mugs out of dried-milk cans and a 'blower' – an improvised cooking stove out of wood, wire, groundsheet, a strip of boot leather and two sardine tins.

In March 1942 Gwladys received a telegram from the War Office informing her that Ron was missing. Towards the end of that year, Rommel's run of success in the Desert War ended with Montgomery's 8th Army victory at El Alamein. The Italians then moved their POWs north to Macerata near Monte Cassino, where Ron stayed until the summer of the following year, by now weak from lack of food, exercise and purpose. Humiliated, given only scraps to eat and denied medical attention, Ron describes them as 'physical wrecks'. When an interpreter came round in July 1943 asking for men with engineering experience to work in the car factories of Milan, it seemed an opportunity to get away, use their skills and be better treated. Ron was among the 200 or so who volunteered. As they were put on an ordinary passenger train that summer to a new destination and the prospect of a better future, it seemed as if they'd made the right decision.

———◆———

So far, Fergus Anckorn had had an untypically congenial war. His talent as a magician marked him out for special service in his regimental concert party entertaining enthusiastic audiences around the country and, apart from some light invasion duties, he'd seen no real military action. This was just as well as Fergus wasn't a natural combatant: he thought soldiers and soldiering were horrid and recalls his sergeant major in the Field Artillery telling him often, 'We'll never make a soldier out of you, Anckorn.' Very early in the war he was in London's Regent Street when a travel agent's window caught his eye.

They had two big posters. One was 'Come and See the Black Forest'. And I thought, That's awful, because that's probably where I'm going. And I'll probably end up dead in this wonderful Black Forest. Next to it was another big poster: lovely dusky maiden with a banana-leaf hat – 'Come to Sunny Siam'. And I thought, If only someone would wave a magic wand and I would end up in Siam till the war's over.

There was now another reason he didn't want to go to war: he couldn't bear to leave his nurse sweetheart, Lucille. They'd reluctantly agreed not to marry until the war was over. When he was posted to the Far East in the autumn of 1941, their parting was a model of English self-restraint.

We got on the train together. The compartment was full and I sat here and she was sitting there, the other side. Not with me. And we just sat on that train, we didn't say a word. There we were busting to get together and we were going away and this is the last time I'm going to see her. And I remember thinking it could be the last time I'm going to see anybody. She got off at New Cross. I closed the door and stuck my head out of the window and said goodbye, and we kissed. She turned round and walked away and I sat back in the carriage and I could have burst in half with emotion. A man in the carriage said, 'Are you just parting?' so it must have shown. I said, 'Yes,' and he said, 'Never mind.' And that was the parting. I didn't see her again for four years.

Fergus was bound for the garrison island of Singapore, strategically vital for British access to the Far East theatre in Malaya and Burma. The sea convoy took three and a half months, manoeuvring its roundabout way to avoid U-boats. Though they avoided attack, there were other hazards.

> I remember even in the North Atlantic when it was terribly dangerous and there was a storm and I thought, What happens if we get sunk now? I said to a member of the crew, 'How far is the nearest land from here?' And he said, 'Two and a half, three miles.' I looked round and I said, 'What direction?' He said, 'That one.' Two and a half miles, three miles to the bottom of the ocean. And that was it.

Early in 1942 they finally edged up the Strait of Malacca within sight of Singapore.

> It's very narrow, the whole convoy had to go in line astern. As far as you could see there were ships. And that's the first time we got attacked. As we went through these straits I remember I was just standing on the boat and suddenly the guns started firing like the dickens, *bang-bang-bang-bang*, and I didn't know what was going on. I looked round and I couldn't see anything. The guns were pointing upwards and I looked up and there were about 30 little black specks: Japanese bombers. We sailed into Singapore harbour and we came down the gangplank under fire and at the bottom was a young Chinese girl. She spoke English. This air raid was going on and I said to her – this was ten o'clock in the morning – 'Have you had any other raids yet this morning?' And she said, 'Yes. Ten.' So that was the state we were in. We were being bombed all the time. The Japanese bombers had no opposition of any kind, they were just flying round in groups of 27, looking for targets and unloading their bombs. So that was the start of our action.

Their colonel's pep talk was ominous:

> 'Now,' he said, 'the game of cricket is all over. There's no hanky-panky. You get in there and cut their throats and bayonet their

blooming heads.' So we were sitting there in this horrible state, ready to kill anything that moved and we were put in this bungalow and we opened a wardrobe full of clothes and out rushed about eight cockroaches and we all ran like hell to get out of the door away from these cockroaches. They were quite big ones. And I can remember thinking, Well, that's the end of the horrid tough soldiers. We'd just been told how you kill anything that moved and we were fighting each other to get away from these cockroaches.

Some time later, unaware that some of his colleagues had already had orders to try and escape, Fergus was driving his armoured lorry and towing field guns when he came under attack and found himself in the centre of a cluster of bombs, 'with shrapnel flying around my cab'. He was hit in a number of places but the worst injury was to his right hand.

My hand was hanging off and blood was pouring out like a bathroom tap. The artery had gone. I lay on the seat and kicked open the door and jumped. In mid-air I was shot in the knee and ended up in a ditch. A friend of mine from the regiment turned me over, pronounced me dead, took off my dog tags and escaped. I found out later he got to Sri Lanka.

They lay me on the wing of a lorry and two of them hung on to me and shot off at 40 miles an hour. The pain was terrible and we were under fire all the time. At one point a bullet creased my nose, went into the engine of the lorry and stopped it dead in the street. So they had to get me off across the road; I put my arms round their necks and they got me into Fullerton Buildings and a post office with a long counter. The place was full of battle casualties but I was the first to be looked at because I was bleeding so much. They put me on the counter and the surgeon said to me, 'I'm sorry, son, I can't save your hand. It's got to come off.' So I said, 'Well, get on with it.' The orderly looked at me: 'Aren't you the conjurer we saw in Liverpool?' 'Yes,' I said. 'You can't cut off his hand, sir, he's a conjurer!' What I didn't know was the Japanese had just come into the place and all I heard the surgeon say was, 'I'll see what I can do.' Next time I woke up, I was in the Alexandra Hospital.

The Alexandra, Singapore's British military hospital, was about to witness a notorious massacre that set the tone for the Japanese conduct of the war in the Far East.

I was in a bed and my hand was hanging from the ceiling with a great dressing on it like a boxing glove. There was a man next to me on the floor on a stretcher and there was another one under the bed because we were being shelled in the hospital by our own guns because they knew the Japs were there. At one point out comes all the walking wounded followed by a soldier with a bayonet. They were all tied together and they were all walking out of the ward silently. No one saying a word. And I said to the man next to me, 'Isn't that a Japanese soldier?' I'd never seen one, because in the artillery your enemy is three miles away, so I'd never actually seen a Jap. He said, 'Yes, he's a Jap soldier.' I said, 'What's going on? What's he doing?' 'Oh,' he said, 'he's taken them out on to the front lawn and he's killing them.'

And that's what they did – they took them to the front lawn, tied them all up in one lump and bayoneted the lot of them. Then they came into the ward and started doing the same. They were killing everybody. Doctors, nurses, the lot. And they were coming up the row of beds, everyone got bayoneted. I knew it was my turn because they were only about three beds away and I must say that at a time like that there is not the slightest fear at all. In my case I knew I couldn't move. No question of running or anything, so I know in three seconds I'm going to be dead. I'm not going to be on this earth any more. So there's no point in being frightened, it's all over.

There but for the toss of a coin would have been Dr Bill Frankland. After his medical training in the 1930s, he'd come out to Singapore with the Royal Army Medical Corps in the autumn of 1941. He'd arrived on 1 December, a week before the Japanese attack on the American base at Pearl Harbor in Hawaii.

I was attached with another doctor who I'd come over in the troop ship with. After a few days another officer came and said, 'Now, you're going to do some hospital work. There are two hospitals. One's the Tanglin hospital which is mainly skin complaints and the other's the main military hospital, Alexandra Military Hospital, where you'll be an anaesthetist. I said, 'I don't like giving anaesthetics and anyhow I want to go to Tanglin,' and the other doctor said yes, he preferred Tanglin. So the officer put his hand in his pocket, got out a coin and asked me to call and I called heads. It was heads so I went to Tanglin. The other doctor went to the Alexandra to give anaesthetics. When the Japanese came over he was murdered – the patient was murdered first on the table, he was murdered, and so on. They were all just murdered in the hospital. I escaped that time by just the spin of a coin.

Fergus was about to suffer the same fate. His final thoughts were calm and rational.

I remember saying to myself, You'll never be 25. I don't know why that was important. I thought when you're 25 you must be a big man and I said, Well, I'll never be that. And then I passed out again. The surgeon hadn't had time to do anything, he just put a tourniquet on me, not a very good one, so my hand was pouring with blood all over my chest, on to the bed and then down . . . a pool on the floor. And when they came to do me they saw all this blood. They thought they'd done it and they walked off. And when I woke up I was the only one alive in the ward.

It was St Valentine's Day 1942 and by the end of the day over 300 patients and medical staff were dead. Fergus was one of the few left alive, albeit barely.

I must have passed out again, which I was doing all the time, and I woke up lying on the floor in a Chinese girls' high school. No idea how I got there or who took me there. Did the Japs do it? Did our people? In that room lying on the floor were 15 other badly wounded people. I asked the fellow next to me what was going on. 'Oh,' he said, 'we're in the bag.' And I said, 'What do you mean? What bag?' I'd never heard this expression before. He said, 'We're prisoners.' And that was the first time I realised that now I was a prisoner of war.

The next day, following ten days of fighting, British and empire forces were running out of food and ammunition. A counter-attack was out of the question. In what Churchill later described as the 'largest capitulation in British history', the garrison's commander, Lieutenant General Arthur Percival, surrendered to the Japanese. Fergus can't find it in his heart to blame him.

Our general took a white flag and handed us over to the Japs . . . It was the only thing he could do. We were down to our last 20 shells.

Together with Fergus, Bill Frankland was now one of the 80,000 Allied troops 'in the bag' in Singapore.

I was taken prisoner of war on the 15th of February 1942 by the Japanese. I think the public know how prisoners of war were treated so abominably in so many ways and I can tell you one little episode. If we were caught stealing food or some misdemeanour, then we as officers were all lined up in front of our men and bashed by the Japanese. One of these bashings was the best I've ever had 'cause I never felt a thing, I was knocked unconscious. But I was told afterwards that I got up from the floor with clenched fists and it looked as though I was going to hit the Japanese officer who'd bashed me, and the little Japanese private standing beside him was just going to bayonet me. For some reason, I don't know why, the officer stopped him. I never felt a thing but I knew I'd been bashed because I had to spit out a tooth. My officer commanding said, 'Oh, we thought we'd lost you, Doctor.'

Despite tacit promises, the Japanese did not honour the provisions of the Geneva Convention. In any case, their military culture required death before the dishonour of surrender: prisoners of war were considered subhuman, to be treated accordingly. Fergus soon came to understand their mentality.

> We were in disgrace. They despised the very thought of us. That here we were, big strong soldiers going under a white flag. In the Japanese Army that couldn't happen. It ends when the last Japanese soldier is dead. They welcome death. They think nothing of it at all, it's a wonderful thing to get killed – you're going to meet your ancestors.

Nevertheless, the Japanese were taken by surprise, both by the British surrender and by the sheer number of prisoners they suddenly found themselves responsible for, together with the million Chinese already on the island. Food was an immediate problem – and a continuing obsession of POWs everywhere, as Bill explains.

> I always say that when you're a prisoner of war the main thing you think about all the time is food, food, food. Ninety-five per cent of all your thoughts are food: How can I get food? I always remember one Japanese came and told us we might get some food but it was getting very short – I think it was 700 calories a day or something. And this Japanese was fat, so it didn't matter what he said, we just thought, Silly man – why should he talk about the difficulty in getting food? Because he was getting plenty himself.

For Fergus, as for all of them, hunger drove a new attitude to what was acceptable to eat.

> We had no food for six weeks, nothing at all. During that time I ate grass, leaves, scorpions, cockroaches, slugs, mice, rats, cats, dogs. I ate a sparrow and snakes. Anything that moved I ate. The great thing about starvation, when you are starved, the first three

of four days are horrible pain and after that, nothing at all. There
are no pangs or hunger, you just get weak. Weaker and weaker.
But it's the first three or four days when you could eat anything
which is the hardest part. People often say to me, 'What does a
maggot taste like?' Who cares? When you're starving and there's
a maggot, eat it quick before someone else sees it. So that's how
we started our prisoner-of-war days.

But sharing what food there was became a matter of honour and
dignity.

You never ate anything on your own. If you found half a loaf of
bread you'd tear it up into pieces so you all had one. If you got
any food from anywhere you shared it with your mates. I mean,
I used to catch snakes and eat them. I got expert with snakes. I
knew all about them in the end. I'd catch a snake and bring it back
and we'd all eat it.

Unlike those in Europe, POWs of the Japanese didn't have the
Red Cross food parcels that were a vital supplement to meagre
camp rations. The few that managed to survive convoys to get
through to the Far East never reached those for whom they were
intended. To eke out their starvation ration of rice POWs foraged,
bartered and stole. Home-made cigarettes, watches, jewellery –
anything of the slightest value or utility – were traded for scraps
of food. Later in his captivity, Fergus discovered a valuable new
bargaining chip.

When I got down-country, which was a much more peaceful place,
I was practising magic left-handed, because I thought I'd never
have the use of this hand again. And the Japanese camp commandant
was a bit of a magic buff. He saw me practising my magic and I
was sent for into his hut. Tiny little hut; he had a table in there.
He asked me to do some magic. All in sign language. And I hadn't
got anything at all. I'd just got that loin cloth on, so I said to him,
you know, 'I haven't got anything.' So he just said, 'What do you

want?' and I noticed on his table there was a little tin of fish, sardines I think they were, and I asked him for a coin. So he gave me a coin and I vanished it, as you would, and then I reached across and took the tin of fish, opened it and took a coin from it. Now I got the fish because they wouldn't touch anything that we'd touched. We were verminous and filthy and scavenging, so I got this tin of lovely fish full of protein and vitamins. That was wonderful. So the next time I got sent for I looked to see if there was any food around. The only thing I could see was a bunch of bananas, and I do a trick with a banana. I'm the only magician who can do a trick with any food you like to name! So instead of taking one of these bananas I took the whole bunch and held them against my chest, pulled one off and I did my trick with it. And afterwards he gave me the bananas, so there's some more food, more vitamins. The next time I went there was no food around but he'd got a packet of cigarettes so I took a cigarette out and vanished it and all the rest of it and he just pushed the packet [to me]. Now that's currency, so I was able to get something with those. So whenever I had to do magic, I made certain that if there was any food around I'd do something with that.

He worked it up into a fine art.

The commandant told me that he wanted me to do magic that night because there were some generals coming – he wanted to show off, give them a cabaret. So I said to him, 'I can do a very good trick with an egg, but I haven't got an egg.' Now, an egg was three months' pay working 18 hours a day and I was going to get one – think of the vitamins in an egg. So he got a little chitty and wrote on it and told me to take it to the cookhouse. So I took it to the cookhouse, and the Japanese cook sergeant said, 'What do you want?' – all in sign language – so I thought, Well, it can't have on there 'one egg', can it? He's asking me what I want, so I stood there and I thought, What the devil can be on there? I thought, Well, perhaps it says, 'Give him what he asks for.' So I said, 'Fifty eggs.' So he gave me 50 eggs. Now that's two years' pay, so I went straight back to the hut with all those eggs, tipped them in a bowl and we made an omelette.

The morning after the successful magic show, the commandant sent for him.

In English he said, 'You do magic one egg. Where forty-nine eggs?' I thought, Well, I'm dead now. I've got five seconds to live, because you could get your head cut off for stealing a potato, you've got to do something. And out of my mouth came these words: 'Your show was so important I was rehearsing all day long.' And he let me go. Whether he knew damn well what had happened or whether the story was good enough to save his face I don't know, but he let me off.

Sickness was a constant problem: humidity and insanitary conditions were exacerbated by malnutrition, forced labour and mistreatment. Men were exposed to cholera and diphtheria as well as tropical diseases like malaria, dengue fever and beriberi. More mundane conditions such as infestations of vermin, dysentery, boils and tropical ulcers were so common they passed without comment. Prisoners had to look after their own, with no medicines or equipment: what medical supplies the Red Cross managed to get through were appropriated by the Japanese. It was Bill Frankland's job to do what he could for the sick and injured at his camp on the island of Pulau Blakang Mati.

We called it Hell Island. We all had dengue, which was a nasty disease, and most of us had malaria, beriberi, but we were all starving and people went out on to these work parties and were very badly treated. Any camp I was in, thank goodness, didn't have cholera where the death rate was very high, but there was still a very high death rate and the lot that went on [building] the [Burma–Siam] railway, one-third of all those died of malnutrition and bad treatment.

My job was to look after them medically. With all the malaria and dysentery and other things going on, they were of course very feeble and I had to put them off sick. If my sick parade got too large – I remember one day I had 30 people – the Japanese would send a non-medical private to take my sick parade. If a man could stand and didn't faint, he was fit to go to work the next day. These are the sorts of things you get used to, but it was strange, I knew personally every single man in the camp, why he was feeling so ill, why he was relapsing with malaria . . . I knew them all personally and to me it was a great privilege to treat these people and for them to have confidence in me.

When he was first taken prisoner, Bill was able to take a meagre supply of drugs and portable equipment with him, including his microscope, which was subsequently stolen. But very soon he had no access to new drugs and had to use what was to hand.

The most magic treatment of all that you had – or rather you didn't have – was antimalarial treatment. One tablet of mepacrine the antimalarial was worth a month's pay, officer's pay, so it was more valuable than food. But I'd been taught in the early days when I was at St Mary's, Paddington, that saline dressings – just salt and water – on an ulcer would be a good curative thing. The one drug we had was seawater so I used a lot of seawater on the patients who got tropical ulcers and it was my proud boast that, right at the end of the war, there was only one person, Corporal Kerman, he got an ulcer that when he got back to this country he had to have a skin transplant, but all the other ulcers healed.

Inevitably, they suffered dramatic weight loss.

I had the weighing scales and people used to weigh themselves. In the end this obviously wasn't a good idea because we were all down to skeletons, literally skeletons.

Random beatings and cruel punishments for misdemeanours or for nothing at all became a way of life for Bill, as for every prisoner of the Japanese.

I remember once we were made to sleep on the road all night as a punishment. You sometimes knew what the punishment was for, but sometimes you didn't. I think they just made up a story to make our life difficult. One day, and I don't know why this was, a Japanese private, I'd never seen him before, came up and said, 'I'm going to kill you!' And he started to bash me and of course you couldn't reply. I put my arm up and he was bashing a chair on my head. He may have broken my arm, I don't know, but I managed to run down and I saw this Japanese officer as a last resort and he stopped it. I have no idea why . . . The Japanese had just lost their first battle in the Pacific to the Americans and I wondered, was that it? Had he heard some bad news? I just know I'd never seen him before. He said he was going to kill me but he didn't succeed.

Fergus describes his arrival at Changi, Singapore's main POW camp, and the regime he soon got used to there.

They got hold of me and threw me into the back of a lorry, and I mean threw like a sack of potatoes and with these two bones poking out. Very painful. Drove up to Changi which was about 20 miles, bumping about in the back of this lorry with this broken arm and when they got to where the prisoners were they threw me out on to the pavement, just like a sack of rice. It's a wonder I didn't fracture my head in.

There were prisoners everywhere, thousands of them, milling about like zombies. At first it was obvious the Japanese couldn't handle us, there were so many of us. Right through prisoner-of-war days, we had to do everything for ourselves. Cooking, everything. Any infraction of the rules you could get killed. They could kill us any day without any questions. If you gave them a nasty look they could kill you if they felt like it. That was the worst feeling, that they could do anything they liked with us at any time and we had no chance of doing anything. We weren't allowed to laugh, we weren't allowed paper, pencils, razors, scissors, nothing. If you saw a Japanese guard, even if he was a hundred yards away, get

down quickly. Try and get your head on your knees, bow as low
as you can, and don't dare think about coming up till he's out of
the area . . . You had no rights to anything at all.

In the face of this degradation, men had to call on every reserve
of strength and resilience. They soon learned not to waste precious
energy on resisting, questioning or worrying about the future;
they had to conserve everything they had for the effort of survival.
Those not mentally strong enough quickly succumbed to illness
or despair. Bill Frankland had the advantage of his vital role in
helping save the lives of his fellow prisoners. His survival plan
was simple: 'keeping busy' with his medical work and 'living in
hope' that one day they would be free. Fergus Anckorn, thoughtful
and pragmatic, made his own plan.

> I remember thinking when we were taken prisoner, What's going
> to happen to us? I expect we'll get bashed around a bit, and the
> first time I got bashed around and my face slapped I remember
> thinking, Well, I was right about that! So instead of being horribly
> upset, you accept it. Later on, it became the norm and so it didn't
> matter. I thought, How am I going to survive? And I thought,
> Well, whatever happens, don't think of yesterday, it's all history,
> yesterday has gone. Nothing can change it. Don't think of
> tomorrow. You might not wake up in the morning, 'cause a lot
> died in their sleep. When you wake up in the morning, good. Get
> through today. Don't think of anything else. Get through today
> . . . I didn't even think of home because I thought it would take
> my mind off surviving. I might never get home, so let's not worry
> about what's going to happen. Just get through today.

His family nickname was 'Smiler' and he decided to live up to it.

> I decided to be as natural as I could and to have a pleasant smiling
> face. A lot of people used to wander round like zombies with no
> purpose. I decided, I'm not going to do that. What I'll do now,
> I'll walk over there to that tree and when I get there I'll then walk

over to that tree and when I get there I'll walk back to this spot, so everything was positive. I wasn't wandering, I was going to that tree. I decided that within five minutes of waking up I would be washed and shaved. Now, we weren't allowed razors or anything like that. A friend of mine who'd been a barber made me a razor out of my army knife. It took him three days on a stone, and it was as good a cut-throat razor as you could buy in any shop in London. No soap of course. No hot water. Just cold water. In fact you don't need all these lovely, fancy things they have now. I still shave every morning as soon as I get up with water. Nothing else.

Early in 1943 Fergus was put on trains with hundreds of others for the five-day journey to what is now Thailand to work on the Burma–Siam Railway.

Standing for five days and five nights, 30 in every truck. Everybody had dysentery. Two people died. You could do nothing about it. One of the first jobs I had was on what is now called the Bridge over the River Kwai. There's no such place: *kwai* means 'river'. It got worse. I was sent up to another camp called Wan Po, where we built a viaduct round the top of a mountain 100 feet up in the air. There's me with vertigo, and we were working 18 hours a day, sometimes longer, in 120 degrees, even at night. All that on 60 grams of rice. So the death rate was just growing all the time. You weren't allowed to be sick. We had to blast the mountain away with gunpowder and it was the only job I was on where we actually had elephants to help us because it was teak we were building this viaduct of. In every joint we put a little box of termites, hoping they'd eat the viaduct when we'd gone. I only found out recently they don't like teak, it's too hard!

The stupid thing was, we had to creosote it, so you had to climb up and they gave you a five-gallon tin of creosote. Very, very heavy and if you got a drop of it on your hand you got a blister straight away in that heat. The Japanese told me to climb up and creosote it. Now I hadn't got the use of this hand, so how am I going to carry five gallons of creosote? I said no, all in sign language, I told him I was sick, and that cut no ice with him. He expected me to climb up that lot, 100 feet up, and don't forget I had the most tremendous vertigo. The only way I could carry the creosote was on my elbow, so I carried it there, like that. He went and got a bamboo to beat me up with so I started climbing. When I got there, I couldn't move, the whole earth was spinning round and he was down there shouting at me. If God had told me to get on with it, I'd have to say no. So he came up after me like a monkey within 30 seconds and threw the creosote all over me.

All I can remember is waking up in the river with fellows washing me because I was huge blisters everywhere – I was just like the Michelin Man. They'd carried me and got me down into the river. And that was one of the good things that happened to me, because I was taken off the railway, down-country, and I was never on the railway again. I remember going to my friends to say cheerio. I said, 'I'll see you around.' And my best friend said to me, 'You won't.' I said, 'Why not?' And he said, 'We'll all be dead.' In three weeks they were. If I hadn't had that creosote, I would have been dead with them.

Just as their attitude to food changed, so did their attitude to death.

As far as we were concerned, death was nothing at all, you would step over dead bodies and that was nothing, it was a fact of life, and to illustrate that, they wanted a volunteer in one of the camps to prepare the dead for burial. This was in the monsoon time and I volunteered for the job because I knew you'd get a little hut out of the rain. The corpses would be brought into my little hut and I'd put a rice sack over the lower half of them and another one over the top half and then sew them together and then they would be buried. I had that job for eight months and there wasn't one minute of that eight months that I didn't have ten to twelve corpses in that little place with me and I used to sleep on top of them at night, out of the mud.

It was a good thing when someone died, you got a water bottle or you got a blanket or you got a haversack. Death? Nothing: I get a water bottle. So death was a way of life and it had no effect on you at all. Your friend died: 'I'll have his watch,' whatever.

———◆———

David Mowatt was posted missing after Dunkirk and details of his prisoner registration, usually so meticulously kept by the Germans, had been lost. So it wasn't until late 1941 when his first Red Cross letter arrived that his family in Scotland knew he was alive and a prisoner of war. In Stalag XX-A at Thorn his health had suffered with repeated attacks of gastroenteritis. Roped to his bed with no medical attention, he owed his life to his comrades looking after him. As soon as he recovered, he was assigned work in a rail-yard, then on a farm. Farm work was familiar to him but harder than at home, and his diet and living conditions were poor. Already a small man, David's weight plummeted. He had a major accident when horses he had in harness bolted and dragged him along the ground by his neck. Life as a prisoner in Poland was cold, harsh, hungry and filled with hard labour. After being captured so early in the war, it seemed as if his incarceration would never end.

POWs weren't just put to work in Poland. After a couple of years in an Italian POW camp Jim Purcell found himself in the Prinz Eugen coal mine in Czechoslovakia. True to the promise he'd made to himself not to let anything get him down, he made the most of it, finding short cuts and skives where he could – and making new friends.

At the end of the shift there was a fellow there called Josef and I got friendly with him. It's marvellous how you can get talking to a Czech bloke and you don't understand a word you're hearing. He had two children and sometimes we used to get Red Cross parcels and I used to give him the chocolate for his bairns. And we became very friendly.

Meanwhile, after nearly two years in Italian POW camps, Ron Jones was on his way to what he hoped would be better conditions working in Milan's car factories. So he and the other 200 volunteers were surprised to find themselves tipped out of their train at the Brenner Pass on the Austrian border and handed back to the Germans. It was August 1943, only weeks before Italy's capitulation to the Allies. Instead of releasing their 70,000 POWs, they were gifting them to their old Axis ally.

At home, they all thought I was coming home, but of course I went to Germany. They stuck us in cattle trucks, 40 of us to a truck, no latrine and all of us had the runs. I used the tail of my shirt to wipe my bottom with, we used one corner for a toilet, the humiliation was appalling. We pulled up at this place, we didn't know where it was, eventually of course we found out it was Poland. There they cleaned us up – don't forget I'm still in khaki shorts and shirt – and took all our clothes and burned them because we were covered in lice and fleas.

Everyone below the rank of sergeant did the work. There was about 130,000 to 140,000 prisoners of war in Poland, they worked on farms and coal mines, railways, all sorts, so one day they picked out a few hundred of us and said, 'You're going to work in a dye factory, IG Farben dye factory.' So we got on a train. When we got off the train we were marching down the road and we saw these men in pyjamas – this is October '43 and it was cold – and they were digging trenches. We said to one of the guards like, 'Who are they?' 'Juden,' he said. And we said, 'Pardon?' 'Jews,' he said, as though we should have known. We didn't take much notice and we went to our digs. Then someone said, 'This is Auschwitz.'

Auschwitz was a town-sized complex in three parts: it housed POW camps, slave-labour camps for the IG Farben Buna chemical works, and an extensive facility for exterminating human beings. Ron Jones and his fellow POWs found themselves in Auschwitz III, Monowitz, in POW camp E715, the part of the complex dedicated to the IG Farben plant. A few miles away was Auschwitz II,

Birkenau, the concentration and extermination camp where by the end of the war over a million people, mostly Jews, were starved, worked or gassed to death.

> We didn't realise what Auschwitz was or what was happening to the Jews, it must have taken us about three to four weeks before we actually accepted that it was a death camp and they were gassing them. We wouldn't believe it. One day the wind was in our direction and the smell was terrible, and someone said, 'What the heck is that smell?' And one of the Poles said, 'Oh, that's the crematorium.' We used to talk to the Poles in the works, of course, and then we realised what was happening there. When they told us that, I said, 'Don't be so daft, they couldn't. They wouldn't gas them and burn people like.' We thought it was daft, but eventually of course we learned it was true.

They couldn't see what was happening at Birkenau but they could smell it, and at Monowitz was the railway siding where the 'selections' were made from the cattle truckloads of humanity arriving for their ghastly fate. Two-thirds were routinely processed straight to the gas chambers. The able-bodied were used as slave labour at the Buna works. Ron and the British POWs sometimes worked alongside them but not for long.

> They did all the menial work, digging trenches, laying cables and all sorts of things like that. And what we realised was, after about a month or six weeks, when they were too weak to work, we used to see them put on a lorry and they used to pass the road and we used to say, 'Poor buggers, they're going up to the death camp, to the gas chambers.' If you could have seen the way they treated those Jews in the works, their lives were ten a penny, terrible. They had *kapos* with them and these *kapos* were political prisoners, they used to knock them about and treat them terrible, push them around. I saw one actually beat a Jew to death. If they saw one coming they used to cringe, absolutely scared to death . . .
>
> We weren't allowed to speak to them. If we spoke they'd hit

them about, but we did talk to them when they weren't looking. If we had food parcels in, which we did occasionally, I wouldn't eat the German rations so I had a piece of sausage one morning so I took it down to work and gave it to one of these Jews, he said his name was Josef. After a couple of weeks he disappeared, so I said to one of his colleagues, 'Where's Josef this morning?' And this is exactly what he said: 'Gas chamber, kaput.' So they knew about it, they knew exactly what went on. They were frightened to death to get injured. If they got injured and they couldn't work, they were taken to the gas chamber. Oh, we felt terrible. We used to boo and shout and when the *kapos* came round we called them everything. They took no notice of us.

Though their conditions were relatively humane, Ron and the British POWs were still working 12 hours a day, 6 days a week. Their rations – ersatz coffee, black bread, sausage and a 'foul and inedible' soup which they gave to the slave workers who had even less – gave them boils and rotted their teeth. Only their Red Cross food parcels prevented more serious malnutrition.

Sundays and sewing were Ron's salvation. He'd picked up the basics from his seamstress mother and took to embroidery in the long, empty hours in the Italian camps, improvising with scraps of calico and threads pulled from rags. On their only day off, after a church service – important to Ron with his Welsh chapel background – they played football.

Someone made a rag ball so we started kicking a ball about because there was a few professional footballers in the camp; myself I'd played in goal for my local team. So someone gave the guards a couple of packets of fags and they came out with us to a field. When the Red Cross found out we were playing football – they used to come there every couple of months – the next time they brought four lots of shirts, English, Welsh, Scots and Irish, some boots, socks and shorts and a few decent leather belts. It became a regular thing and we used to look forward to it. We had the Welsh team – we weren't all Welsh but most of them were – and

I was the goalkeeper. There was crowds around there, factory workers, even the guards used to come out, cheering. Oh, it was terrific, it used to make us feel that we were back home.

Ron didn't have a proper shirt, but he embroidered the Welsh feathers on his jersey. A photo taken by a Polish maintenance worker in 1944 shows a smartly kitted-out Welsh team with Ron and his embroidered jersey in the back row. In every camp, even those suffering the very worst conditions, men made their own diversions to alleviate boredom and despair and keep better times in mind. Ron had his football, Fergus his magic. There were sports, musical entertainments and educational classes, all improvised with available talents and materials. If they were lucky, Red Cross supplies of books, equipment and instruments followed. Even in Changi, which had no such luxuries, Fergus recalls concert parties in the early months. It was all part of the necessary armoury for survival.

Of all the diversions, letters from home – arranged through the Red Cross – were the best of tonics for Ron and the POWs held in Europe. They were allowed to write and receive a short letter every month.

Sometimes we used to go two, three months without a letter and then we'd get two or three at a time, the mail was pretty grim. There wasn't much news. If you put any news in there it just got blacked out. Gwladys didn't know I was at Auschwitz or anything, she just knew I was a prisoner of war, that's all.

Though letters from loved ones were longed for, men lived in dread of news that their wives or girlfriends had got fed up waiting for them and had found someone else. They all knew the Yanks were 'over there' and feared the worst.

Gwladys sent me a letter once and said that she used to go out dancing and I used to get a bit jealous naturally, of her with another fellow's arms around her. I just said, 'Be careful,' because the Yanks were over there and girls used to go off with the Yanks, but Gwladys was wonderful, she didn't do that.

POWs of the Japanese may have had similar worries but no means of receiving or sending news. There were no Red Cross letters for Fergus Anckorn.

I had no contact with home at all and I purposefully never thought of home because that would lessen my efforts of trying to stay alive. But I had this photograph of Lucille. But I had to have it hidden because we weren't allowed anything. If the Japs had found it they would have taken it away. So that was hidden in a bamboo. I thought, We'll put it in there and now here I am, close to Lucille again, we're together again. And all the rest of my days that was just hanging there and I could look at it. It was very comforting.

But his parents *had* received news of Fergus.

The man who'd escaped from Singapore got home and contacted my parents and gave them the sad news that I was dead. And to prove it he said, 'I was the one who found him. I turned him over and he was dead.' So my parents were then told that I'd been killed in action, and that's all they knew for two years.

Uncharacteristically, one day the Japanese allowed Fergus a Red Cross card to send home.

They wouldn't allow us to write on it. It was a preprinted card: 'I am well'; 'I am unwell'; 'I'm working for pay', things like that. And you just crossed out what was not applicable, but we were allowed to sign it. I took the card to my colonel, who was a saint, and I said to him, 'Can you see anything wrong with my card?' And he looked at it and said, 'No, why?' And I said, 'There's a code in it.' So he examined it thoroughly and he said, 'I can't see anything.' So I said, 'Good. I'll send it.' And that's what I did.

My parents called me Smiler, and I remember when I left to

go into the fighting, my mother said, 'Whatever happens to you, you keep smiling, you'll be all right.' And suddenly this card turns up home from the jungle and there's my signature on it. My mother got the card and she said, 'Well, he really is dead, because that's not my son's signature!' So she took herself off to bed, my name not to be spoken. Ten minutes later she was screaming the house down, 'He's alive, he's alive!' She'd been sitting looking at this card and suddenly she spotted that I'd changed the shape of certain bits of it to get curves so in Pitman shorthand I could write 'Still smiling' as part of the signature. And in all the crossing out, I'd put [in shorthand], 'Building a railway from Bangkok to Rangoon. Don't worry.' On the front of the letter where I'd got 'Britain', I'd put inverted commas which said, 'Wounds better.'

Within the space of a preprinted card designed to convey the minimum of useful information, Fergus had used his ingenuity and his shorthand skill to reassure his parents of his existence, his good health and good spirits (even if both were in truth severely depleted), and impart details of his work and its location. It was a triumph of the human spirit.

Like many thousands of other POWs, David Mowatt, Jim Purcell and Ron Jones in Europe and Fergus Anckorn and Bill Frankland in the Far East had developed their own ways of coping with the enforced normality of an unhealthy climate, hunger, physical punishment and the removal of everything comforting and familiar. As the war carried on around them, their ordeal must at times have seemed never-ending, their future uncertain.

Even as an Allied victory turned from glimmer of hope to racing certainty, their freedom from captivity would be hard fought and not without new horrors, their homecoming far from the unalloyed joy they'd long dreamed of.

IO

The Road to Victory

1943–1945

> What surprises me is that we were all totally convinced we were
> going to win this war. What was problematical was how long it
> was going to take.
>
> Russell Margerison, gunner, Bomber Command

It is hard to find anyone who lived through the war who didn't
believe that Britain would come through in the end. Even Gus
Bialick's doubts in the early days, when the country fought alone
under threat of invasion from a far stronger power, were less
about the likelihood of victory than the long haul it would take
to achieve.

> I found I couldn't visualise victory at that time. I realised it was
> going to be a long time before we could get the better of Germany
> because they had vast armaments where we were only halfway
> through rearmament by the time the war broke out. It left me
> feeling this is going to be a hard, long struggle.

The defeats and disasters of 1942 – the convoy losses, Rommel's
successes in North Africa, the fall of Singapore – should have
challenged faith in the conduct of the war and paralysed morale.
Yet morale held up. People who were there at the time credit their
conviction to Churchill's skilful rhetoric. His striking images of a
proud unconquered people with the will to defend their land to
the death, and of the 'broad sunlit uplands' of victory, had already

done their work, helping Britons visualise what, in the depths of 1940, might have been unimaginable. Gus acknowledges their impact.

> Churchill did a great deal for the morale of the people. He lifted their spirits up and made them feel they could win this war. His use of the English language, the way he gave illustrations of what might be, helped me to think, We'll win this war, but it will take a while. Churchill and Anthony Eden had the foresight to understand that Hitler could be beaten if only we had the will to do it, and he created that in his speeches.

Inclusive and invigorating, they were invaluable in helping Britons keep faith with their leaders through the worst of times until the tide of the war started to turn in 1943.

In the difficult years before the road to victory could be glimpsed, the only way of taking the fight to the enemy was to send long-range British bombers into Germany. Underpowered in men and aircraft and fraught with technical problems, early RAF raids were scattershot. Air crew took a long time to train and aircraft production had concentrated on fighters to meet the demands of the Blitz. The Area Bombing Directive in February 1942, and the appointment of Air Marshal Sir Arthur Harris to carry it out, changed that.

Bomber Command, still controversial after more than 70 years, became the key instrument in a sustained effort to damage German war production, divert strategically valuable resources and break its people's morale. The degree to which it succeeded or failed is still a matter of dispute. The bravery and resilience of the 125,000 men who flew its 364,514 sorties to carry out some of the most difficult and dangerous missions of the war is not.

Teenager Russell Margerison was first attracted by the glamour.

> We'd watch the Spitfires and the Hurricanes in the Battle of Britain and I thought, Yes, I'd like to be part of that. Thousands of us

did. It was a bit of a glamour job in fairness. The girls used to go for air crew. So that's why I joined. I volunteered when I was 17 and a half and I was called up two or three days after my eighteenth. They were short of air gunners but I didn't know that, did I?

Londoner Bob Frost, former Boy Scout and fire service volunteer during the Blitz, had resolved to stop fighting fires and do something to help stop the war that was causing them. His father was already in the RAF, so as soon as he was 18 on New Year's Day 1941 he'd signed up.

When I went to the recruitment centre it was suggested to me that I apply for air crew. I thought you had to be superhuman or something to do that but I said, 'Well, I'll give it a go,' and I was accepted for all trades – pilot to air gunner. They reckoned it would take 18 months to begin pilot training and the same for navigator but if I came in as an air gunner, I'd be on a course straight away, so I said yes, that would do me fine.

There were a number of close shaves in training, including a couple of forced landings, one where the port engine on their Wellington failed.

We took up crash positions, shot over a village, being catapulted over it by the tops of some trees, and landed in a barn on the other side. I'd been knocked unconscious at the back of the aircraft, the gunsight had come back and hit me, and as I pulled myself together, Scotty the navigator was coming down the side of the burning aircraft to get me out. That crash taught us that we could absolutely rely on each other.

Training could be as dangerous as an operational sortie: some courses lost as many as a quarter of their trainees before they graduated. For Russell Margerison it was the inevitable flip side to the glamour.

Bit of a dicey job when you're all novices and you're starting flying. You're all learners, you're going to have lots of accidents. But it's always somebody else that's going to get it. You're going to make it. I was very confident I was going to make it, I don't know why.

That unshakeable confidence was to help Russell and many an airman face the daily risk of death or serious injury. The attrition rate for Bomber Command, at 44 per cent over the course of the war, was higher than for any other part of the armed services.

We had to do 30 raids: that was a tour. You did 30 then you went on instructing. When we went on squadron it had been going about eight months. Not one crew had finished a tour, nobody had done 30. After we'd done about seven ops we were being briefed for a raid by the wing commander and he said, 'Before we start this evening, gentlemen, I have some good news for you. Flight Lieutenant Middlemiss and crew have completed a tour of operations from this squadron.' And everybody cheered because they'd managed to get through 30 and we all said, 'Well, if he can do it, so can we.'

That's not to say that the men were fearless or in any way casual about the job they had to do. Bob Frost certainly wasn't.

It was frightening. I never met anybody in Bomber Command air crew who enjoyed doing it, not one. And the crew room, before you went off on ops, was usually a pretty quiet sort of a place, chaps were making their own thoughts, there was no light-hearted banter or anything going around. You were just wanting to get your ops done. You never saw anybody there long enough to get to know them, you stuck with your own crew. Most crews went by the time they'd had 14 ops. We lasted for 22.

Rituals and superstitions were common: Russell Margerison had to dress in a certain order.

After you'd done a few operations you became superstitious. The rear gunner always used to wash his hands before he got in the Lancaster and he'd bang his hands on the ground. We all did something, silly things. I'm not superstitious in the least, but I had to put my left sock on first and I remember once or twice when I got completely dressed – and as gunners we had an awful lot of clothing on – I thought, Did I put my left sock on first? I couldn't remember. They'd be waiting for me in the crew bus and I'd start all over again.

The young Polish-Jewish refugee who'd come alone to Britain as a 16-year-old in 1939, Andy Wiseman, lied about his age and volunteered as a bomb-aimer. A good-luck golliwog knitted by a girlfriend went with him on every operation.

We all had something. My friend had a used condom to help him remember happier times. Everybody had some ritual, some would hug, everybody smoked. You did whatever made you happy. Camaraderie on the station was really good. We didn't show our fear to others – we went out as a team, a strong unit. We knew everything about each other because our lives depended on it.

That sense of comradeship and interdependence was important to Russell Margerison.

The camaraderie was fantastic. The more so because we were very much a mixed bunch: Australians, Canadians, New Zealanders, Jamaicans, southern Irish, Northern Irish, the lot. It was a very, very good atmosphere and a very close-knit thing and it developed more and more into a close-knit unit. We always said the most successful crews were the mixed crews. Mix it together and it works. And it did work. It was great, it really was a good place to be. I loved being with them.

As the area bombing of Germany gained momentum through 1942 and ground on through the following two years, the air crews of Bomber Command would come to rely on that comradeship and a faith in their own survival to see them through.

———◆———

As Ron Jones and Jim Purcell discovered when they were taken prisoner by the Germans in the Western Desert in 1942, the North Africa campaign was not going well for the Allies. The Desert War was important to Britain: it couldn't afford for Egypt and the vital British-controlled Suez Canal supply route to fall into enemy hands. After early success in pushing the Italians out of North Africa, the Allies faced much stronger resistance from General Rommel's Afrika Korps and by the spring of 1942 they were in retreat, demoralised. It looked as if Suez might be lost. Two battles at El Alamein, a small railway halt outside Alexandria, proved critical. The first, in July, ended in a stalemate. The second, fought over two weeks in October–November, with the 8th Army now under new leadership, was decisive. Dunkirk survivor Freddie Hunn of the 12th Lancers was there for both of them. Before that they'd suffered months of demoralising defeat and loss.

> We did the retreat all the way from Benghazi and Gazala battles. Each time you were losing friends, and you had to leave them there, because you were on the way, getting out of it. So you were losing your armoured cars, and friends, and losing battles and there was nothing you could do about it.

In the desert, miles from anywhere, getting supplies through was a logistical nightmare and living conditions were difficult.

> The supply line was so long that by the time the food or water got to you with the flimsy tins bumping over the 200-mile desert you'd lose half of it . . . So for breakfast you'd have a slice of corned beef and you'd fight. Lunchtime you'd have another tin of corned beef, shared with the other crew, with biscuits. That'd be your lunch. At night you'd then have another tin of corned

beef, cut in three, fried, break up the biscuits with a hammer, put them in a dixie, put a little drop of water with them, stir it up, and that was a stodge. That was your supper. And we lived like that for about three month.

Water was a persistent problem.

The water supply quite often didn't appear. I got to the stage where I would drain some water from my radiator, which would have been in the armoured car, oh, 12 month. You'd drain it off, it'd come out red-rusty, and you'd give the driver and myself and the gunner probably an egg-cup-ful and you'd drink that. That's how we were living. One day I found an armoured car, belonged to a sergeant, Silky Sparks. His car had been destroyed by the Germans. I saw it and straight away I went and drained the radiator. Came out like lava out of a volcano! And we made a drink with that. You never washed or shaved for three or four month. I saw Silky Sparks about a month later and I said, 'I found your armoured car out in the desert. I drained the radiator.' 'Did you?' he said. 'What was it like?' I said, 'Oh, pretty awful, but it was wet.' He said, 'I'm not surprised, we drained it off three times, washed and shaved in it, and poured it back.'

Even before El Alamein, they'd been engaged in fierce skirmishes.

On one occasion we were being chased by 27 tanks and they started shooting and the shots were coming by like, you know when you're on a station and an express train comes through? Well, the shells were coming through and that's what it sounds like. And suddenly, *boof!* Right underneath us. I grabbed my mascot, put it in my pocket and said, 'Right, bail out, start running!' We started running and five shells dropped over on my right. Explosion, yellow smoke, flame and everything. And through that came a lorry loaded with high-octane petrol and ammunition, driven by Trooper Wilkes. He drove through that and he'd seen what happened from way over, changed his direction and came all that way, when he saw us running, to pick us up. Taffy the gunner jumped on the right running board, Jock jumped on the left. I couldn't get on the back. He saw me running still, so they slowed down and let me jump up and we got away. That was one of the bravest things I saw happen in the war. Wilkes was driving a time bomb with all that stuff on board.

The run of defeats and retreats ended with the Second Battle of El Alamein under Lieutenant General Bernard Montgomery, a meticulous planner.

Montgomery rehearsed everything before we went into battle. Through the minefields, we'd done it at night, done it in the daytime, so we knew what was happening. And it opened up with a tremendous barrage from Alamein down to the Qattara Depression, which was a natural defence of petrified forests and soft sand, impassable by any reasonable vehicle, you'd do it in a jeep but nothing else. So that was our left flank. The rest of it was fortified with minefields and guns. And I remember the whole length, of about 20, 25 miles, and all the guns of the 8th Army were lined up, side by side. At twenty to ten they all opened up, a tremendous barrage for 20 minutes, and all you could hear non-stop was these shells coming over, *boom, boom, boom, boom* on to the German defences . . . We couldn't do anything till that line was broken. And that went on for a number of days.

It was an anxious time waiting for a break in the line but no one wanted their nerves to show.

We were sitting on the edge of a minefield waiting, just waiting to go through. And we used to sit reading a book. I'd sit with my back leaning against the wheel of my armoured car. And in front of me, 100 yards away, was the squadron leader and he'd be there reading a book, but he had a deckchair. And a shell dropped over there, then another one, and another. And they started dropping, and I thought to myself, I'd like to get in my armoured car. And I was looking at the squadron leader and I thought, I wish he'd get in his armoured car, 'cause I didn't want him to see me get in mine whilst he was still sitting out there, otherwise he'd think I'm windy. So there I was, waiting. Then suddenly a shell dropped in between us. But it didn't go off. There it is, sticking in the ground. I looked up to speak, but he was in his car, gone. So I got in mine quick. That evening we drew alongside and he said to me, 'What's the matter with you, have you gone mad? Why were you sitting out there with those shells falling?' I said, 'Because if I'd got in my car you'd have thought I was windy.' He said, 'Well, I was thinking the same thing!' There we were, both thinking the same, wouldn't give way until the other did!

The victory at the Second Battle of El Alamein was to be a turning point in the Desert War and the first British success in a terrible year of defeats. Rommel was on the run and would be out of North Africa altogether by the spring of 1943. They could take pride in the 8th Army's achievement.

> We'd won a victory. If we'd lost they would have taken Egypt, so we felt good about it, that we'd defeated [Rommel] and he was on the retreat. And our 8th Army was, as it should have been, on the winning side. As Churchill said, it was the turning point of the war. We never looked back from then on.

———◆———

In September 1942 Bob Frost was on his twenty-second bombing operation, to the heavily defended industrial city of Essen.

> We crossed the coast, light flak, nothing to worry about, and then running in towards the target – we're a few minutes away from the dropping area – a box barrage and we were right in the middle of it. Well, you can't do anything in the middle of a box barrage except get through it, but that put the port engine out of action,

the [gun] turret went dead. We were so near the target that Bill [the pilot] said, 'Let's press on, drop the bombs and then get the heck home as quickly as possible.' If we could make the coast at least we might be able to pick up Air Sea Rescue.

Over Belgium the starboard engine packed up and we were about 13,000 feet. All Bill could say was, 'Well, so long, chaps, this is it. Bail out,' and out we went . . . I saw the aircraft go away and then eventually I saw a crash on the ground and I thought, No blighter's going to fly you any more. And then the ground came up and hit me in the shape of a large Belgian field.

I'm laying on the ground with not much wind left inside me and there's this big white parachute drifting about, and I hadn't been best pleased on the way down. It was a Thursday night and we were due to go on leave on the Friday and I saw my leave disappearing, so by the time the ground came up and hit me, I was absolutely hopping mad.

Bob soon had more important things to worry about. He was in enemy-occupied territory. He found his way to a village where he saw painted on a wall the Resistance symbol, the Cross of Lorraine – a hopeful sign. He found refuge in the home of the local mayor and, after interrogations to establish that he wasn't a German spy, he was placed in the hands of an escape network run by the Belgian Resistance, the *Comète* ('Comet') line. Given new clothes, a new identity and false papers, he was sent to a safe house in Brussels where, miraculously, he was reunited with two of his crew. The plan was to get them out via *Comète*'s well-tried relay through occupied France and neutral (but pro-Fascist) Spain to British Gibraltar. On the way, he had several close shaves with German guards, accompanied always by his calm, quick-thinking Resistance minders. If he'd been discovered he would have been shot.

How did he cope at these tense times?

I wasn't frightened. The very manner of the people who were looking after me was so normal and so natural, so I followed their lead. Anything they asked me I didn't question them, I told them everything. I thought, I'm putting my life in your hands, and you're doing the same for me. So our trust was absolutely implicit all the way through. It was what I wanted to do, it had been in the back of my mind when I got shot down, I was going to Gibraltar. And so it was.

He was passed on to another safe house in Paris for the long train journey down to the Spanish border.

There were six of us airmen going down from Paris to the south-west corner of France and we were taken by a girl of 17, Janine. She was our guide. Like all wartime trains, it was absolutely crowded. The corridor was at one side, with little compartments leading off, each holding about eight people and the six of us were in there with Janine and we'd been chugging along for a bit and our Canadian co-pilot got up, opened the door and offered a lady standing in the corridor a seat: 'Say, ma'am, would you like my seat?' In English with his good old American accent. She said thank you and sat down, and he stood out there. I glanced around the rest of them and Janine, she hadn't turned a hair. We all thought, All hell's going to break loose in a minute! Not a thing happened and we continued on our way.

At Saint-Jean-de-Luz, they began the trek across the Pyrenees into Spain with a local and one of *Comète*'s young Belgian organisers, Dédée de Jonge.

At this real old working farmhouse we were given a pair of rope-soled shoes, *espadrilles*, and a stick. Then we tied our shoes by their laces round our necks and set out to follow Florentino, a real Basque smuggler, and Dédée. I'd met her in Brussels and I met her again down there at that farmhouse and I spoke with her, sat on the back doorstep of the farm, and I asked her, how did she manage to do this very dangerous work? Because if they were caught it was the whole family – I'd seen notices up in Belgium and France, what would happen if they were caught helping the 'Terror-fliers' as we were called. And she said, 'It's there to be done.' Simple as that. She wanted her country free. I felt reassured in their company. They were people I could rely on. I made better friends in those days I was with them, than many, many people I've known for years. They were the real friends.

The journey across the Pyrenees was arduous, but Bob was prepared.

Well, that was tough going but having been out on night exercises with the Cubs and Scouts, that sort of background was all there, it wasn't unknown to me. I did manage to fall into a damned great hole and Florentino lifted me out like a drowned rat and plonked me on the side. From time to time he stopped, fished out a bottle of cognac from behind a bush and we all had a swig, the bottle went back in the bush and we carried on. Coming down the other side of the Pyrenees, looking at Spain and the lights were on, there was no blackout and oh, that was liberating! For me that was the moment of freedom: liberation is here, I'm on my way home!

It was an exquisite moment for Bob: he'd survived being shot down over enemy territory and five weeks later he was on a USAAF Dakota out of Gibraltar clutching a bottle of sherry he'd been given as they passed through Jerez. Still only 19, he was alive, free and on his way home. His Bomber Command comrades Russell Margerison and Andy Wiseman wouldn't be so lucky.

———◆———

Back on the home front, life for the majority was cheerless. Though the Blitz was over, there were still sporadic raids. Food was bland and monotonous. Petrol for cars and coal to heat homes was in short supply: imported supplies were mostly lying at the bottom of the world's oceans. Though mining was belatedly designated a reserved occupation, the work was hard, dangerous and badly paid. Mines were privately owned and poorly managed, and industrial relations were bad. Young men who would otherwise have followed their fathers into the pits chose the services or cleaner, better-paid work in munitions factories. The industry had lost 36,000 miners by the middle of 1943 and production was down at a time of unprecedented demand. In the 1942–43 winter 'coal crisis' the situation was critical. Something had to be done to get more coal out and faster. Conscription was the answer and Minister of Labour Ernest Bevin was put in charge.

Names were randomly selected from those due for call-up. Four out of ten appealed but few were successful. Conscripts from across the social classes were sent far from home into unfamiliar communities often with their own culture and language. Because they had no uniform the Bevin boys, as they became known, were treated with suspicion and derision as 'conchies' or 'shirkers', their contribution to the war effort unrecognised and unrewarded. They were among the last to be demobbed and, unlike servicemen, got no demob suit or gratuity. It was an essential job, but a hard and thankless one.

Not all Bevin boys were conscripts and not all had bad experiences. Public schoolboy Brian Rix, most recently treading the boards with Donald Wolfit's theatre company, made the most unlikely volunteer. It happened more by accident than design. Brian was about to join the RAF, but there was a problem.

> They did medicals, of course. When I was a kid of eight I'd had measles very badly and that gave me terrible sinusitis – I always had problems with sinus throughout my life. Anyway, they said I wasn't fit to fly because of the altitude, so I was grounded and offered alternatives: glider pilot, paratrooper, cleaning out the cookhouse and going down the mines. So I went down the mines.

He was sent to Askern Main colliery in Doncaster, the deepest pit in Yorkshire. Unlike older Bevin boys, Brian didn't work at the coalface, but on the 'roadway' leading to it.

We shovelled rocks into tubs. We were labourers really, it was no more sophisticated than that. We lived in a sort of hostel in Doncaster and went by bus to the pit every morning. I quite enjoyed it, actually, because you put on sort of 'character' clothes: you put on steel[-capped] boots and you wore a snap tin with your food in and your Davy lamp hanging from your belt.

He found it an eye-opener.

It was the first time I met a genuine socialist. They were lovely, these guys. We were all mainly public school or grammar school, and they were very nice to us. I suppose it was the first time I realised how the other half lived and it made a great impression on me. To meet these guys and seeing where they lived and how they lived and what a bloody life it was really. I admired them, I thought they were incredibly brave. You're working shifts, covered in coal dust, breathing in coal dust. How the hell do you do that for a living, all your life?

By September 1943 the Ministry of Labour estimated that 22.75 million Britons were engaged in the services, in civil defence or in essential war work. War service at home could take very different forms. While Brian Rix was digging coal to keep Britain's war machine moving, hundreds of young women in the ATS, WAAF and Women's Royal Naval Service (WRNS) were engaged in a huge wartime endeavour that they could tell no one about and, at the time, knew very little about themselves.

After six months' training on the Isle of Man with the Royal Corps of Signals, ATS girl Enid Wenban was posted to Beaumanor Hall, a small country house in Leicestershire, its many outbuildings camouflaged to deceive air reconnaissance.

The area was set up to look like a farm, complete with cows grazing, but I don't think that would have fooled the Germans if they'd seen the huge dipole aerials we needed to receive signals from across Europe!

She'd already had to sign the Official Secrets Act and she knew she wasn't to talk to anyone about the work, but at that stage 'we had absolutely no idea what the work was going to be'. In fact, Beaumanor was one of four military listening stations – the so-called 'Y Stations' – and her job was to intercept enemy communications from Germany and across Eastern Europe.

I was allocated to C Watch. Watches were diabolical because you had four different watches over three days and then a day off, so you had no proper sleep pattern and ended up spending your day off asleep. I hated that. But we just got on with it. We worked in pairs, taking Morse messages through headphones, in code of course, in blocks of five letters. It was boring up to a point, but we knew it was important. We'd occasionally have a pep talk where they gave us some information which was probably quite harmless, about messages we'd intercepted, but we were aware that this information was absolutely vital.

All their encrypted messages were sent by teleprinter or dispatch rider to Station X: 'We knew it was somewhere in Buckinghamshire, but we didn't know it was Bletchley Park.'

In 1942 middle-class Jean Valentine from Perth was nearly 19 and thinking about signing up before she was conscripted.

Having spent a lot of time knitting socks and working in soldiers' canteens and trying to be helpful, I thought, If I don't volunteer soon, I'm going to be put in a munitions factory or I'll find myself digging potatoes. So I went into the Women's Royal Naval Service recruiting office in Dundee.

After basic training, when jobs were being allocated, she was sent to London but not told anything about what she'd be doing. For the first few days she saw the sights and enjoyed a visit to the House of Commons.

> Up in the Strangers' Gallery, fascinating, and then we saw somebody stand up and it was Winston Churchill, and it was very difficult to understand what he was saying. He was a bit incoherent, mumbling. Eventually one of the backbenchers said, 'Oh, sit down, Winnie,' so he sat down!

Soon she was introduced to a large machine at an installation west of London, a new outstation of Station X.

> My heart sank, because I knew I couldn't reach the top of it. It was over six feet tall, eight feet wide, and they said, 'This is what you're going to learn to operate.'

This was a 'Bombe', the decryption machine originally designed by Alan Turing to help break the daily-changing German Enigma codes. At 4 foot 10, Jean had to stand on a raised plank to reach the top. The work was exacting. Enigma coding machines generated random letters; the chances of finding the right one was infinitesimal. The Bombe was a clumsy electromechanical device but a revolutionary advance in the intelligence war. If set up correctly it could eliminate the many millions of incorrect possibilities and so reveal that day's Engima settings.

> You didn't have to be very clever, but you had to be very, very accurate, so we were very careful about setting. We got what was called a menu to set up our machine, which would go through all the possibilities and that machine had 36 drums on the front of it, all with letters of the alphabet round about, all set up to agree with this menu, and the back of the machine was plugged up again to the menu so that all these possibilities could be covered. You were waiting for the machine to stop. When it stopped, it

was saying in effect, 'We've got a possible answer.' We put it through a checking machine and if it was a possible answer then it was sent through to a telephone number. None of us had any idea where that was going. Years later I discovered it was literally going across the lane to another hut, Hut 6, where people would then apply this to the encrypted message. If it was correct they were able to read off the message. Then the telephone rang and somebody at the other end said, 'Job up!'

By the time Jean was working on her Bombe in Hut 11 at Bletchley, there were a hundred or more machines there and at five outstations, employing more than 700 Wrens.

All our machines had names, but you were never told the name of the machine that had been successful, nor the people who'd been handling the machine. You never got a pat on the back for anything. It was nice when they said 'Job up', but we didn't know if we'd had a hand in it. I'd never heard the word Enigma at that time. As far as we were concerned it was a German encrypting machine and we were trying to find our way into it, but none of us had heard of Enigma.

How was it possible to keep it all so secret, for so long?

Because of discipline. If you'd been told by people in authority that you do not do this, you didn't do it. You respected them. Everybody respected the fact that we had to keep quiet. We knew it was important, we were doing something rather special and we were quite proud of that. We didn't swap names or anything, so there wasn't any communication really and that's how you keep your secrets: by keeping your knowledge to yourself. I'll tell you another thing: nobody actually asked me!

The Bombes, cumbersome and labour-intensive as they were, aided Allied intelligence in the most difficult early and middle stages of the war. As German encryption machines themselves became more complex, the introduction of the Colossus machine at the end of 1943 increased efficiency and heralded the electronic computer age. Bombes kept working throughout the war and some were retained for the cold war that followed. None of this could have happened without the hundreds of young women like Jean and Enid who took the messages, worked the decryption machines and kept the secret for decades afterwards. As Jean says:

> When the Bombe was first produced it was manned, if you'll excuse the expression, by men. They thought women couldn't do this. Well, gradually women were introduced and before long there were nothing but women doing it, many hundreds of women using a Bombe 24 hours round the clock. And I think we did quite well. If we hadn't, the men would have pushed us out, wouldn't they?

———◆———

With good intelligence and a run of Allied successes, by the summer of 1943 the tide appeared to be turning. In July Allied forces attacked the weakest Axis partner. Within weeks of the invasion of Sicily Mussolini had gone but Italy wasn't to be overrun without a fight. Gus Bialick was part of the invasion force with the Pioneer Corps, who landed some of the worst jobs.

> My job in my unit was to look for mines. We dug into the sand with our bayonets and when we hit something metal we knew it was a mine. Two kinds: the Teller mine, it was the size of a soup plate and it was for blowing up tanks, artillery, heavy stuff. If they went over these the vehicle was blown up. The other was an anti-personnel mine in the shape of a cocoa tin with three prongs sticking out at the top. It would be buried in the sand with the three prongs exposed. When an army boot pressed on it nothing happened. The moment they took their boot off it, it shot up in the air and burst, and that's how we lost two of our boys – friends of mine from Ireland – the first 20 minutes we arrived on the island of Sicily.

Worse was to come. They were bombed and shot at by Stukas on the slopes of Mount Etna but, most shocking, Gus saw men from his own side commit rape and other abuses against the local population.

> You won't find these things in the history books, but they're true. I saw them. I was an innocent when I went into the army, but war changes everything. You see a different side of humanity, the good sides and the bad. I found myself in some terrible places seeing horrible things.

Though the south had been overrun and Italy capitulated in September 1943, Hitler poured German troops in to protect Rome and the industrial north. It took four Allied attempts before the Gustav Line protecting the capital was finally broken at Monte Cassino in May 1944. Orphanage boy Matthew MacKinnon-Pattison, now a non-commissioned officer (NCO) with the Argylls, was part of the final push. The men were keyed up, but in good spirits.

> The night before the Fourth Battle of Cassino we're all called together and we're in this orchard. And this truck pulls up in front of us and on the truck are Canadians – the tank corps. They have a bit of a band and they have us all singing along, all the old cowboy songs, and then as the evening wears on one of the Canadians comes to the microphone and says, 'Now, I want you all to sing "Ye Banks and Braes o' Bonnie Doon".' It's a Scottish song. So we all sing, and when we're finished he says, 'Now I want to you all to just sit there and hum the tune.' So we hum the tune and he gets on the microphone and he starts to talk to us with this lovely background music of us all humming away there. And he starts to tell us: 'Tomorrow we're going into action. You boys are really going to go through it because we can't bring our tanks over until we get past a certain point. I want you guys to know that if you meet the enemy, don't stop and fight them. Keep down. Send for us and we'll come up and sort them out with our tanks.

Scots and Canadians are brothers, we're kith and kin and we're going into this battle together. And we'll be with you all the way.' And I'm not kidding you, there was hardly a dry eye in the bloomin' house because it was so emotional. The music took you back home. It was wonderful. Moments like that you never forget and they're moments that live with you all your life.

Prayer, learned in childhood at the Quarriers Homes, became an instinctive response for Matthew in the heat of battle.

When you go into action, you don't let the other lads know that you're doing your prayers, you keep that quiet. That's between you and God. Even if you rejected Him ages before, you remember your childhood training and go back to praying to God. You go into battle as a young boy full of bravado but you're going through a baptism of fire and you're going to be converted into somebody with adult caution. That's when you pray, you realise you need help. People say prayer doesn't do any good. Of course it doesn't every time. But it did most of the time for me.

———◆———

By the spring of 1944 the endgame in Europe was starting to be played out. The Eastern Front had cost many German lives. Italy was overrun. The long-planned invasion of France was imminent. Bomber Command was about to be diverted from area bombing to tactical support for the Normandy landings, but their operations were no less perilous. At the end of March 1944, in one of the last big area bombing raids, nearly 800 bomber crews set off for Nuremberg. Among them were Andy Wiseman and Russell Margerison. Russell remembers:

That night we'd hardly hit the course before we had the fighters dropping flares over us and when they start dropping flares you get a lot of the crews dropping their incendiaries and lighting up the route, which was precisely what we didn't want. So we ended up in a situation where we were lit up from above and lit up from below and the fighters moved in. That particular raid was the only time, I must admit, I was getting a bit emotional, there was that many aircraft going down. It was frightening seeing so many blowing up, going down. Most of them were shot down early in the raid. A lot of them never got to Nuremberg that night.

Bomber Command lost more men that night than in any other raid during the war. Like Russell, Andy survived to make it over the target. The sight of the medieval city of Nuremberg burning beneath him was something he couldn't get out of his mind for weeks afterwards. Then in April, on only his seventh operation, Andy's aircraft was hit by a German night fighter over Tergnier in France. The aeroplane quickly caught fire and bailing out was chaotic.

I remember getting to the exit and counting to six and then jumping. Four of us jumped, the pilot and other two crew didn't make it. I managed to land on the only tree in a big field and bundled my chute down a well. The next day and night were spent hiding in a forest. I had a map printed on silk and some French francs so I found north and started walking. I tried a farmhouse but they told me to bugger off. They knew they'd face the death penalty if they helped me. On the third day, I tried another one. Wrong choice. I opened the door and saw lots of German soldiers sitting round – it was a German base. I made my excuses and left but they soon caught up with me and handed me over to the Gestapo.

Andy was sent to Stalag Luft III in Silesia, only weeks after the celebrated 'Great Escape' after which 50 of the 73 recaptured escapees (3 got away) were shot by the SS. Despite this, conditions in POW camps for airmen were generally considered the most relaxed. Even after the Great Escape, Andy found his guards amenable, perhaps because they too could see the end of the war in sight.

They didn't shout at us or beat us. They even apologised for the behaviour of the SS. The feeling was that we all had to live together so we all tried to establish a degree of live and let live. They had us, but we also had them.

A month after Andy Wiseman was shot down, Russell Margerison was on his nineteenth operation: Duisberg in the Ruhr valley was the target.

We used to call it Happy Valley. It was anything but happy. There was always loads of flak and loads of fighters. You knew if you were going to the Ruhr you were going to get hammered.

They turned too early, missed the target, dropped their bombs and found themselves in front of the bomber stream, 'where you don't want to be'. Within half an hour they were caught in a box barrage.

A box barrage is an anti-aircraft-guns concentration on you, and we didn't half get clobbered. We got through it all right and we were about 20 minutes from the coast and as clear as day I head these cannons, *dug-dug-dug-dug* . . . The firing probably lasted a mere second but it was more than enough. We'd been hit from the front. We had our two port engines on fire, flames were sweeping down the side of my turret. We were in trouble. 'Abandon aircraft!' And you can bet your neck I left that turret as quick as I possibly could. You have to remember you're part of that turret, you can't just drop out like that, you're connected to it with your oxygen mask, your intercom, your electrically heated suit. You need to unplug everything . . . By the time I'd done that I could see the big tail fin, there was pieces of metal just rolling off, red hot, just flying away.

He went inside the burning body of the aircraft to get his parachute.

Young women played a major role in the defence of Britain during the war. Joy Lofthouse (back row, second left) ferried planes to RAF airfields all over the country for the Air Transport Auxiliary.

Like this young worker, Gladys Parry built parts for fighters and bombers at the Avro factory in Manchester.

Jean Valentine, shown here demonstrating a rebuilt Bombe machine to the Queen in 2011, was one of thousands of young servicewomen at Bletchley Park working to 'break' enemy signals.

Life at sea on the merchant convoys carrying vital supplies to and from Britain was perilous, with the constant threat of attack from the waves, the weather and German torpedoes. John Harrison, a Royal Navy ordnance artificer (*above left*) and Austin Byrne, a gunner in the Merchant Navy (*above right*), were lucky to survive enemy attacks on their ships.

Storms like this one, which struck David Craig's Russian convoy in February 1943, were common on 'the Russia run'.

In 1942, during the Desert War (*above left*), Jim Purcell (*above right*) was taken prisoner by the Germans. The Second Battle of El Alamein the same year, in which Freddie Hunn fought under General Montgomery (*below, receiving the German surrender from General von Thoma*), was the first British land victory of the war.

War in the Far East. *Left*: Major General Percival surrenders Singapore to the Japanese in 1942. Fergus Anckorn was one of the 80,000 Allied troops taken prisoner. His scrapbook (*below*) shows his armoured car in action in Singapore and himself in Suez after three years in a Japanese POW camp: at this point he had managed to get his weight up to six stone.

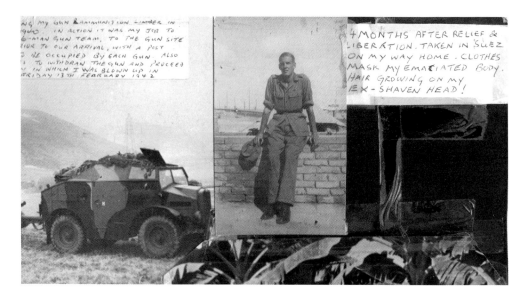

NG MY GUN & AMMUNITION LIMBER IN GUNS. IN ACTION IT WAS MY JOB TO 6-MAN GUN TEAM, TO THE GUN SITE PRIOR TO OUR ARRIVAL, WITH A POST O BE OCCUPIED BY EACH GUN ALSO S TO WITHDRAW THE GUN AND PROCEED IN WHICH I WAS BLOWN UP IN FRIDAY 13TH FEBRUARY 1942

4 MONTHS AFTER RELIEF & LIBERATION. TAKEN IN SUEZ ON MY WAY HOME. CLOTHES MASK MY EMACIATED BODY. HAIR GROWING ON MY EX-SHAVEN HEAD!

Left: in Burma in 1944, men of the 'Forgotten' 14th Army are entertained by Miss Vera Lynn, who carries an improvised bouquet of jungle flowers wrapped in surgical gauze.

On his nineteenth operation for Bomber Command, air gunner
Russell Margerison (back row, third from right) was shot down, taken
prisoner and then put on a forced march before eventually being
repatriated in 1945.

Above left: D-Day, 6 June 1944. Frank Rosier of the Glosters (*above right*)
was in the second wave of troops landing on Gold Beach and lost an
eye in the ensuing battle for Normandy.

Rationing meant that wartime weddings were often frugal affairs, nevertheless couples still made the most of their happy day. *Clockwise from top left*: Bob Frost and Daphne; Gladys Parry and Cliff; Bill Graves and Eileen; Fergus Anckorn and Lucille.

Margaret Rhodes' 1950 wedding to Denys (*above*) was rather more lavish, attended by her uncle and aunt King George VI and Queen Elizabeth, with Princess Margaret as a bridesmaid.

Above left: housing was a post-war problem after so many homes were damaged or destroyed by wartime bombing. Jim Purcell felt fortunate to get his Jarrow council house in 1948. He is still there after nearly seventy years. *Above right*: the new holiday camps offered a break from the austerity of 1950s Britain.

David Croft, left, and Jimmy Perry, right, were responsible for some of the most successful television comedies of the 1970s and 1980s – including *Dad's Army* and *Hi-de-Hi!* – which drew on Perry's wartime and post-war experiences and played on Britain's class sensitivities.

The return to normality. *Clockwise from top left*: actor Earl Cameron, his wife Audrey and their children; after a long career in publishing, Diana Athill made her own name as a writer; Dr Bill Frankland worked with Alexander Fleming, conducted pioneering research into allergies and started the Pollen Count; Brian Rix and his wife Elspet campaigned for a better deal for learning-disabled people after their first child, Shelley, was born with Down's syndrome.

Everything on the inside was on fire. I couldn't see up front, everything was burning and flames were licking round my parachute . . . I couldn't get it on. I tried a second time. I couldn't get it on. The heat was intense, ammunition is exploding all over the place. And I said to myself, Russ, this is it. And then something in my head, I can never explain why or what: Russ, what the bloody hell are you doing? To be honest, I think it was my dad. I got the chute, I banged it on and it stayed on. I dropped to my hands and knees, crawled to the back door. I didn't jump out. I didn't roll out. I was sucked out. And I'm flying about 2,000 miles an hour – or it felt like it – an icy-cold wind in my face. I pull the metal handle, there's a flapping noise and I'm stopped dead. I knew I'd got away with it.

He'd got away with his life, but not his liberty. Russell landed in Belgium and was in hiding for more than six weeks, hoping to get on an escape line as Bob Frost had done. But he was betrayed to the Gestapo and rounded up with 40 other air crew, some of whom had made it as far as the Spanish border. On their train journey as prisoners through the ruins of Germany's devastated cities, the airmen could see at close quarters the strange fruits of Bomber Command's long campaign: scenes of utter destruction devoid of people. It made Russell wonder how much longer the Germans could carry on.

◆

By the early summer of 1944 the Red Army was advancing from the east and the British and Americans were preparing to land in the north and south of France. But another war was still being hard fought in the Far East where the 14th Army had the sticky job of pushing the Japanese out through the jungles of Burma. They had good reason for calling themselves 'the Forgotten Army': they were very far from home and got little of the attention given to fighting forces in Europe. Letters, Red Cross parcels and Entertainments National Service Association (ENSA) entertainments were thin on the ground. In May 1944 Vera Lynn, by now the best-known performer in Britain, decided to do something about it.

> My radio programmes were going overseas to the boys and I was getting a lot of letters from them and I thought it would be nice if I went out and sang to them personally, so I approached ENSA. I said, 'I don't want to go where they already get a lot of entertainment, I'd rather go where it's a bit scarce.' So they said, 'Well, would you go to Burma?' So I did.
>
> Morale? Oh, it was wonderful. They were so pleased to see me and of course taking messages, 'What's it like at home?' and 'How's the bombing going?' and 'What's the food like?' and all sorts of things like that. So I was able to say, 'Well, fine, we're doing great and getting on with it, none of us are starving!' I was able to reassure them and it was nice for them to see someone from home. Some of them had been out there since before the war started so of course they hadn't seen a white girl for years, because all the nursing was done by men on the front line.

Conditions were steamy and primitive. She slept on a camp bed in a tent or in a hammock in a bamboo basha during the monsoon rains.

> I wore khaki men's trousers held up with a belt – they were more practical than anything else – or shorts. It wasn't worth putting make-up on, you just perspired it all off, so I went around with a lipstick, that's about all I could manage. I washed my hair in a bucket. I had a perm before I went away because I thought it would keep my hair nice, but of course it wasn't the right thing to do because I couldn't set it. It was just wash and go! But I never had any health trouble, never any gyp, so I must have been quite healthy to start with.

The piano suffered more than she did.

The heat changed the key, but fortunately it changed it lower, not higher, so I was able to cope with that. It had to be carted around in a car and of course the roads were so bumpy. When we arrived at one of the places the sides fell off and the boys had to jump up on stage and hold the piano together so I could carry on with the show.

'The boys' always received her rapturously and feted her with whatever came to hand: she has a treasured photograph among them holding a 'bouquet' of jungle flowers wrapped in surgical gauze. Her biggest audience was 6,000, the smallest two patients in a casualty clearing station.

They were too ill to be taken to the hospital so I went to visit them and I sat talking to them and they said, 'Will you sing "We'll Meet Again" to us?' It's the most requested song I ever had, during and after. Wherever I went I had to sing it. I never tired of it. Because that was what was most in their minds, that they'd meet their families again. It wasn't written for the war, it was written before, but it was very appropriate to the boys going off, and that's why I took it for my signature tune.

What impressed her most?

How relaxed the boys were. They didn't seem to be stressed at all. You couldn't hear anything, but the fighting was quite close. Kohima, where the fighting was, was at the top of the hill and we were at the base at the bottom. They were just getting on with the job and making the best of it.

———◆———

Vera returned from her exhausting three-month tour of India and Burma in early June. For much of the previous year plans had been in hand for the most important development of the late war years, the opening of the so-called 'second front' designed to hasten the end of war in Europe. The invasion and liberation of France from the beaches of Normandy was one of the war's most closely guarded secrets. ATA pilot Joy Lofthouse had a bird's-eye view of last-minute preparations.

> For several months before there'd be no travel allowed to the south coast because they didn't want the general population to see the build-up to D-Day and have careless talk about it. But from the air of course we could see it, all the military vehicles building up along the lanes of Hampshire, the landing craft lining up – you could have walked across them to the Isle of Wight! Obviously the Germans could see this from high reconnaissance but we were clever – they still didn't believe we'd go anywhere but the Pas-de-Calais, the shortest route. We flew on the morning of the 6th of June. The Solent was empty. One felt in one's heart, one knew what was going on on those beaches. All the strategic bombing hadn't made Germany give in. We knew we wouldn't win until we got a foothold back in Europe. We knew however bloody it was, that we had to go there.

Frank Rosier was there on 6 June, with 2nd Battalion 'the Glosters', on the second wave at Gold Beach, an 18-year-old who'd joined up in 1943 and spent the months since training for the invasion. He was fighting fit, but all the PT instructors in the world couldn't stop him being seasick. As they approached Normandy all he wanted to do was get off the landing craft on to dry land. But what he found there appalled him.

> The carnage on that beach was something that an 18-year-old should never see. It brought me to a halt for a couple of seconds. It was horrifying, what I saw. Well, I hate saying it . . . a red sea. Heads, legs, bits of this and bits of that, not exactly clean cut, if you know what I mean. And it was just horrible.

Frank survived weeks of sporadic action during the Battle of Normandy, including hand-to-hand fighting with SS troops ('I won't disgrace an animal by calling them animals'), but one later close encounter will stay with him for ever:

> Out of the hedge stepped this young German boy. To this day, why didn't we say 'Good morning' and leave it at that? We were sent to kill, weren't we? To cut a long story short, I cut him in half. Killed him. I sat on the ground and I cried, and I was sick. I killed a human being face to face. It's awful. From that day on, I understood my father's generation, because the First World War was eyeball-to-eyeball, bayonet stuff. I understood the First World War for the first time.

But Frank's luck ran out in late August when, scavenging eggs from a farm, he was hit by a mortar bomb. Dazed and unaware how badly injured he was, he managed to walk back to his unit.

> I remember getting [there] and the lads must have seen my face and come running out of the trench, 'cause that's the last thing I remembered. Went out like a light. [Shrapnel] hit my skull, went up through my face and come out through my eye.

The first Frank realised he must have lost an eye and done serious damage to his face was in hospital back in Britain when he started on his weekly NAAFI ration of 50 cigarettes and saw the smoke come out of the bandage on his eye. The ward sister called him a stupid boy and took his cigarettes away. It was the start of years of reconstructive plastic surgery. Frank was only just 19.

Fred Glover had joined up at 16 after Dunkirk. Fed up with picking potatoes and clearing bomb sites with Young Soldiers battalions, he passed fit to join the elite Parachute Regiment.

> Once you joined a regiment like that, where everybody is there because they want to be there, then your chances in my book are greater for survival than anywhere else because of the camaraderie: men you could rely on, trust. I would have moved heaven and earth to get back to my unit.

In the early summer of 1944 he knew he'd let himself in for a hard time when the CO told his company they'd only be taking unmarried volunteers on this special operation to crash-land inside an enemy gun emplacement. And they'd be using gliders not parachutes. It was an audacious, if not foolhardy, plan. Fred volunteered anyway.

Weeks of intense training following. When the time came for action on 6 June several gliders had mishaps along the way but Fred's at least reached the target and cast off.

> As the glider pilot flew over the battery we're engaged by a 20-millimetre flak gun and I received wounds in both legs . . . . We come down, skim over the minefield and crash into an orchard about 250 yards away from the battery . . . Although we were presented with something entirely different from what we anticipated, training came into play. Everybody dispersed for cover, returned fire. I crawled to the lip of a bomb crater and returned fire . . . My boots were full of blood.

The Paras fought ferociously and the Germans withdrew from the battery, leaving two wounded men behind. Fred was put in charge of them whilst the rest of his unit moved on.

> You get this astonishing transition from the combat situation to when everything dies down. When you're left with prisoners, unarmed, wounded, what's the right thing to do? There is only one right thing to do.

Fred, wounded himself, administered his own supply of morphine to the more severely wounded man and shared his chocolate ration. At that moment, a German patrol approached. From being in charge of two prisoners, he was now about to be taken prisoner himself. He'd disabled his Sten gun, but still had his fighting knife and a Gammon bomb on him and 'things were ugly, shall we say'.

Then the wounded German spoke up and pointed. I couldn't understand a word of it but the whole situation changed straight away. They got stretchers, shook hands and I was transferred to an advanced dressing station. Didn't leave me my knife though.

He was later taken to the Hôpital de la Pitié in Paris, where shrapnel was removed from his legs. By August Paris was close to falling to the Allies. Nevertheless, Fred's one thought was to get away, back to his unit. The Resistance were active everywhere: with their help he escaped from the hospital and was holed up in a safe house, still badly wounded, until the city was liberated on 25 August and he could return to Britain. After a few weeks in an American hospital he was transferred to Shaftesbury Hospital, where, courtesy of the bed baths given by the Voluntary Aid Detachment (VAD) nurses there, he could 'lay claim to be the most excited and joyful private in the British Army!'

When he finally got back to his battalion after convalescence, he reported to his colonel, who said, 'Where the devil have you been since June the 6th?'

All this time, his foster mother thought he was dead as he'd been posted missing in action and she'd heard nothing further from the War Office. The silver ring that Fred had bought her on Brighton seafront had started to crack and she took this as an omen that she would never see him again. When he finally did turn up on the doorstep, the reunion was overwhelming for both of them, with years of emotional reticence put aside.

We weren't a particularly emotional family but . . . we held each other and I said, 'I love you, Mum.' . . . She said, 'Well, I love you too, son.' I often regretted, after I'd joined the army, that I hadn't uttered those words earlier.

———◆———

People at home enjoyed the morale boost of D-Day and the symbolic liberation of Paris. There was now the comfort of knowing that the long war was drawing to its inevitable conclusion. But Hitler hadn't abandoned his attempts to break British resolve: V-1 flying bombs plagued London and the south-east, killing more than 6,000 people.

Once again, women were in the firing line. Dorothy Hughes was under canvas on Camber Sands on the Sussex coast with her anti-aircraft battery. They'd already had a direct hit from a V-1 and lost six of their comrades. They were no match for the German missiles, and there was another danger too:

> The V-1s were coming over at 400 miles an hour and 1,000 feet and if our guns pointed at a certain angle we had to stop firing. We had an American battery behind us and they completely ignored these instructions. They talk about 'friendly fire' now, well, these men were firing almost horizontally and they took our NAAFI tent away. That was really essential because you could have cups of tea and cocoa at night from there, but with the NAAFI tent gone we had nothing, it really hit us hard. Plus the fact we could have been killed.

Eileen Younghusband, now a commissioned WAAF officer in charge of her own team of plotters at Fighter Command HQ, Stanmore, was busier than ever tracking the V-1s' murderous approach. But then without warning in September 1944, into London came an even more deadly weapon, the world's first long-range ballistic missile. The secret operation to combat the V-2 was code-named 'Big Ben'.

> We were warned that . . . we wouldn't be able to track it because it was supersonic, but we would know where it was going to land and possibly radar could pick up the top of the curve and we might be able to extrapolate the curve to the launch site. If we ever got the warning by a radar station that they'd picked up one little spot of that trajectory, they would say 'Big Ben' and the first filter officer to get that message had to stand on a chair and shout out 'Big Ben!' three times. And guess who got that first message? It was me.

> We couldn't do anything about them. All we could do was
> bomb the launch sites.

Successful identification and disabling of launch sites by the RAF and disinformation about landing positions meant that the thousand or so V-2 missiles aimed at London over the remaining months of the war did considerably less damage than they might otherwise have done.

Prisoners of war in Europe, many of whom followed the BBC's war news on clandestine radios, were looking forward to liberation. At Stalag Luft VII in Silesia, where Russell Margerison had been since the previous summer, life was 'boring beyond description' but by Christmas they could hear the Russian guns going and even the camp guards were talking about deserting: they'd treated Russian POWs appallingly and expected retribution. On 19 January 1945 Stalag Luft VII was evacuated.

> We had to leave camp and march to central Germany because
> Hitler had ordered no Allied troops must fall into Russian hands.
> So we all set off. After a few days we'd completely run out of
> food. It was bitterly cold. The march was horrendous, there was
> 1,500 of us and we did 240 kilometres walking in deep snow, driving
> rain, driving winds and we refused to go any further.

To complete the journey to a new camp in Brandenburg they were packed into cattle trucks for three days without food, water or sanitation.

> Quite a few of the lads developed dysentery . . . We arrived in
> Luckenwalde in a pitiful state. To get to the latrines there you had
> to go up two steps. I had to go up on my hands and knees at 19
> years of age. I couldn't walk up those two steps, that's how bad
> it was.

On 21 April the Germans abandoned this camp too and the Russians arrived shortly afterwards. The situation was chaotic:

fighting was still going on around them; there was no food; local women were coming into the camp and offering sex with the POWs in return for protection from rapacious Russian troops. The Russians seemed both callous and disorganised. An American attempt to liberate the camp was rebuffed. There was no immediate prospect of release, let alone repatriation. The word was they were to be repatriated via Russia. There was only one option.

> Six of us broke out of camp. We wanted to get to Magdeburg and across to the Americans. The trouble was we were tied up with literally hundreds of thousands of refugees, you couldn't escape them.

On the way they took refuge in a house where two frightened women were sheltering. Whilst they were there three Russian soldiers arrived, discovered the women, raped them both and left one dead. The brutal chaos continued. Magdeburg was a ruin, its bridge over the Elbe destroyed. A temporary pontoon, the Roosevelt–Stalin Bridge, served instead – the Russians on one side, the Americans on the other.

> We got to the Roosevelt–Stalin Bridge and the Russians wouldn't let us across to the American side. 'Nyet. Nyet. Nyet.' They didn't want to know. We were at Magdeburg five days. Two of us tried to swim the Elbe but the currents proved too powerful and there was bodies floating because the Russians were shooting them left, right and centre. Anybody that moved. And the women were being raped left, right and centre as well. It was the worst time of the war, even though the war had ended. On the fifth day an American Dodge truck was down below where we were staying by the bridge and a voice came up, 'You guys wanna go home?' We jumped on that truck and in two minutes we were over the Roosevelt–Stalin Bridge.

On the same day that Russell started his forced march in January 1945, the Germans evacuated those Jews at Auschwitz–Birkenau and Monowitz who could still walk. Ron Jones and the other POWs were left behind until the 22nd, when he started his own gruelling march, passing the bodies of dead Jews on the way. The winter was the worst in Eastern Europe for a generation and they had no food.

> I was on the road for about 17 weeks. We marched something about 800 miles and they stuck us in barns at night-time. And we ate what the animals ate. We ate potatoes. I kicked a pig out of the way and ate the potatoes he was eating, covered in muck and all I suppose. When you're starving, believe me, you'll eat anything.

They trekked over the Carpathian Mountains, through Czechoslovakia, Bohemia and Bavaria. Of the 230 or so POWs who left Auschwitz, scores perished, mostly from dysentery and exposure. They were all lice-infested, starving and frostbitten; sacking replaced their rotten boots. But they kept going, trying to care for the sick and dying as they went. Bizarrely, at one point they were given a leaflet urging them to join the fight against the Bolshevik Communists. After months on the road, they reached Regensburg in Bavaria and on 28 April they finally met up with a US 9th Army tank commander.

> He asked: 'Are you boys all right?' and we said, 'We are now!' We were cheering and shouting but they couldn't give us any food. All they had was bloody chewing gum and cigars! It's difficult to express the joy and exhilaration of freedom when you've been deprived of it for so long. No more guards, no more pushing around.

On the same march westward, but from Stalag Luft III, was Andy Wiseman.

> I think 'march' is the wrong word. It was the long shuffle. As it went on and on, past three months, you began to care less for the others and more for yourself. It really became a personal battle

– the survival of the fittest. It was no longer a war between the Allies and Germany, it was you, the individual, fighting for life. You no longer had the strength to look out for anyone else.

Looking out for himself too was David Mowatt, captured after Dunkirk and now, in early 1945, on the march as well. After nine days in freezing weather with nothing to eat or drink, he escaped after hiding under snow in a ditch and was on the run in Poland for two weeks. Recaptured, he was rescued from an SS firing squad by a *Wehrmacht* officer and finally liberated by men from his own regiment, the Seaforth Highlanders: 'When I saw that badge, that was the best thing I've ever seen in my life!'

POW Jim Purcell, who'd been put to work in the mines, was spared forced marches but he too witnessed the chaotic vacuum between the collapse of one belligerent and the establishment of the rule of law. Once his guards had fled from the Russians, Jim celebrated at the home of Josef, the Czech he'd befriended.

> We just woke up one day and there were no guards there. The Russian troops were in a wood at the end of the village . . . but when they got drunk, it was chaos, they were picking children up and raping them. You'd be coming through the town, they'd see a young lassie, maybe 15, 16, they'd pick her up and throw her on the back of the cart and then we'd see them ripping and she was screaming. What could you do? They had guns, we hadn't anything like that.

But when a Russian officer tried the same thing with Josef's wife as they all walked out one night, he couldn't just stand by.

> He'd be about 25, drunk as a noodle. And he stopped with a blinking screech of brakes, ran and grabbed her and started dragging her towards the truck. And he was just getting her on to the truck and I thought, I can't allow this to happen, so I ran forward and parted them. She ran back up the road to her husband and he pulled his revolver out – and me and him struggling with

the revolver, then Josef ran across and smacked him on the chin, and down he went. I said, 'We've just knocked out a Russian officer, what do we do?' He says, 'Run like hell!'

Jim Purcell, the skinny Jarrow lad who'd decided that being a prisoner of war wasn't going to get him down, survived Axis camps, Czech mines and the brutal aftermath of the German collapse. He was finally repatriated in spring 1945 by the Americans, when thousands of other POWs in Europe started coming home. Hundreds didn't survive the camps: an estimated 2,000 died on the forced marches. And those like Bill Frankland and Fergus Anckorn in the Far East still weren't free.

Japan had yet to be defeated but the long struggle to pull Europe back from Nazi domination was over. France was liberated, Hitler was dead, Germany and her allies overcome. Their belief in victory vindicated, the war generation could at last put the losses and sacrifices of the past behind them, celebrate their success and start looking to a better future.

II

Victory and the New Jerusalem
1945–1965

> To my way of thinking, that was a terrific time to have lived in.
> It was full of energy: 'Let's get out and do it. Rebuild the country.'
>
> Frank Rosier

Special Wireless Operator Enid Wenban knew the war was really over when, one day at her listening station in the spring of 1945, she intercepted a message of surrender from a U-boat in plain unencrypted German.

Churchill made the formal announcement of victory to the House of Commons on the afternoon of 8 May. Bells were rung, the lights went back on and everyone took to the streets. After five years of restraint, a night of wild celebration with whoever and whatever came to hand seemed the natural thing to do. Enid and the girls from C Watch went out on the town – or what passed for it in rural Leicestershire.

> We piled into an open tilly [utility truck] and drove up and down, headlights blazing, singing 'There'll Always Be an England' at the tops of our voices. The street lights had come on in the village after the blackout. The relief that the war was over was enormous. We'd beaten Hitler!

Bob Frost celebrated by opening the bottle of sherry he'd been given in Spain on his escape from occupied Europe. He and his WAAF girlfriend Daphne were in London.

On VE Night we danced the night away . . . Daphne was put on the top of a set of traffic lights in Piccadilly by some sailors. It was quite a celebration!

Nearby at Buckingham Palace, King George and Queen Elizabeth gave special dispensation for their daughters to join the crowds. The girls' cousin Margaret Rhodes, who'd been staying at the palace while she worked as 'a small cog' in M16, was with them.

It was a mass of people all cheering and saying 'Whoopee!' We made up a little party. There were about eight of us and we had one of the King's equerries as our escort. He was a splendid old boy with a bowler and an umbrella, very formal, looking terribly out of place amongst the cheering crowds. We walked right up to Leicester Square where everybody was kissing everybody and putting policemen's helmets on their heads. Princess Elizabeth was wearing her ATS uniform with her hat well pulled down so that nobody could recognise her. It was just a wonderful night out . . . It was the end of drabness and blackness and misery and it was like a sort of awakening, a phoenix rising.

The royal party danced the conga, the Lambeth Walk and the hokey-cokey with the rest of the revellers, the Princesses enjoying their unaccustomed anonymity.

We ended up coming back to join the crowd in front of Buckingham Palace and I think [Princess Elizabeth] must somehow have sent word from the sentry or the policeman at the gate that we were outside – 'Please could Mummy and Daddy come out on the balcony?' So we had a grandstand view when they did come out and we all waved and cheered and hurrayed . . . everybody was euphoric.

ATS gunner Dorothy Hughes was also in the crowd.

Four of us girls agreed we'd go up to the West End to celebrate. We were near Horse Guards Parade so we thought we'd go to Downing Street to see Churchill and we got behind this stationary car, not realising he was going to be in it to go to Buckingham Palace. The police didn't stop us. We had a lift on the back of the car, out of Downing Street down to Pall Mall, then we got off and walked behind it to Buckingham Palace where the King and Queen came out, and it was fantastic because we were all sort of letting go after five years of living with death. It was a wonderful feeling to really be ourselves . . . We sang 'Land of Hope and Glory' and did the conga. The beer ran out but we had some Americans join us and they had Spam sandwiches and I'd never tasted Spam before in my life . . . A day you'll never forget.

When the revelry stopped and reality returned, the business of 'getting back to normal' was uppermost in people's minds. After five years of dislocation and grim news from abroad, the focus turned inward to domestic matters. Families fractured by war had to be put back together, those divided by death, divorce or long estrangement reconfigured. Demobilisation was slow but gradually lovers were reunited and husbands came home – sometimes to changed partners and children they didn't know or hadn't fathered. The physical environment of many urban areas was wrecked, but the human landscape too was in disarray. The rebuilding task was immense.

The most poignant homecomings were those of the POWs, some of whom had spent much of the war in captivity. They had all been changed by the experience. David Mowatt, captured after Dunkirk, was barely recognisable to his family when he finally returned to the Highlands.

Mum was in the garden. Well, she nearly collapsed and I did as well, because it was nearly six years, wasn't it? She was shocked. I wasn't the boy she'd remembered that had left home in 1939. She had to get to know me again.

Margaret Rhodes' much-loved eldest brother John, an officer in the Black Watch captured at Saint-Valery with David Mowatt, now returned, 'a strange, gaunt figure', from his imprisonment in Colditz.

The horror of German concentration and death camps was now revealed to Britons at home in newsreels, and to service personnel on visits to recently liberated camps. A week after VE Day Eileen Younghusband, now stationed in Belgium, was given the 'grim task' of showing people round Fort Breendonk, a concentration camp notorious for torturing Resistance fighters. The experience still gives her nightmares. In Germany, Fred Glover was taken to see Buchenwald.

> It was felt that some of us should have first-hand knowledge of what was happening there, and really it supersedes anything you could possibly imagine. There were people lying about everywhere starving, some of them skeletons already. People in the huts were corpses, just lying there . . . indescribable really. That a cultured race could be brainwashed to such an extent is unbelievable. You can't imagine the human race can do such a thing.

The Russians had liberated Auschwitz in January but released no details. In any case, the press were already absorbed by the inhumanity uncovered by the British liberators of Bergen–Belsen. After witnessing some of Auschwitz's horrors, Ron Jones had endured a desperate 800-mile march across Europe before being rescued by the Americans. Now he couldn't wait to get home to Gwladys in Newport. As the taxi drew up, he could see the balloons and 'Welcome Home' banners.

> Who should come out of the back door but Gwladys. She was going to the outside toilet. I caught hold of her, she caught hold of me. We couldn't believe that we were together again. I didn't let her go for ages. She didn't get to the toilet! But oh, what a relief. Marvellous. My whole family was there, of course, made a big fuss of me. Eventually she took me to bed and put me in the

bath. Oh, and she started to cry. I was like a boy from Belsen, I was just skin and bone. I was only about seven and a half stone from a thirteen-stone man and before the war I was extremely fit, I used to lift Glad up and down in my hand. And then I couldn't get in the bath myself, could I? I said, 'Oh, don't cry, I'm here in one piece. I left men out there who are never going to come home.'

Ron's recovery was slow and painful.

I wouldn't be here today if it hadn't been for Glad, 'cause I was in a hell of a state. I used to get blackouts, and for 18 months I was covered in abscesses and boils. When I say I had them everywhere I mean everywhere. Instead of being a fit man I was a physical wreck. I used to lose my temper, in fact one day I caught hold of her by the hair and shook her. Gwladys didn't like it when I came home. She understood about it and she was marvellous but I wasn't the same man as she married.

Five years of temper, nightmares, anxiety and physical distress followed. Just as he did in Auschwitz, Ron found solace in sewing: Gwladys encouraged him to finish embroidering a tablecloth she'd started. Embroidery calmed his anxiety and helped him learn to be more at ease with himself.

After witnessing Russian atrocities in the final chaotic days of the war in Europe, POW Russell Margerison was flown to RAF Cosford near Wolverhampton to a memorable homecoming.

It was a wonderful feeling because the Lancaster taxied up straight outside of this great big hangar and over the hangar it had 'Welcome Home, Boys, You've Done a Great Job'. There were loads of officers and airmen there slapping us on the back, 'Well done, lads.' We were taken into this hangar where there were trestle tables full of sandwiches, cake, and these ladies going round with great big teapots, 'Tea, coffee, love?' 'Help yourself to a sandwich.' 'Try one of these cakes, I baked them myself.'

And what were we so-called heroes of the sky doing? We were crying. We had our head in our hands on the trestle tables and we were sobbing, to have such a friendly, friendly welcome. No more *'Raus!'* from the Germans, no more *'Nyet, nyet'* from the Russians. It was a wonderful feeling. I've never experienced such an emotional scene as in that hangar. If I had to make a film of my experience I'm trying to convey to you I would fade it out in that hangar at Cosford with those ladies going round, 'Have a top-up, love,' 'Have another cake.' Wonderful feeling.

Prisoners of the Japanese had longer to wait: the Allies were still at war with Japan and there was no immediate end in sight. By the summer of 1945 Fergus Anckorn was in a camp in Vietnam.

I belonged to a circle of six. Five of us were Dutch and there was me. We used to meet in the jungle every fortnight at midnight and exchange news. There were some French-speaking natives in the area so I could speak to them, we'd take money to them and they'd give us war news. One day it was a job getting out and back undiscovered. I got back and I said to the others, 'I'm not doing that again. These natives are messing us about. They're taking our money and giving us war news they think we'd like. One of them told me today that a bomb had been dropped on Hiroshima and had wiped it out and the bomb was called *"bombe atomique"*. Now, I know *"atomique"* is something pretty small and Hiroshima is about the size of London, so clearly they're messing us about.'

Now, if we had but known it, that was the end of the war, but we took no notice of it. And it wasn't until three or four days later that we were summoned on to the square and told that the war was over. I'd always envisaged that we would stand there chucking our hats up in the air, hugging each other and singing and dancing. Course, we hadn't got the hats anyway, but when it happened and they told us, we couldn't take it in because all through those years the Japs sometimes would say to us, 'War finish, war finish,' and it wasn't, so we never believed it. When we were officially told by the Japanese officer that night, 'The war is over, you will soon be going home,' we just stood there with our hearts bursting. There was nothing we could say or do. There was no cheering, no dancing. We just stood there and I remember thinking, I'm free. At last I can say 'No'. Up till then if you say 'No', you're going to get beaten up, so I'm free. I can say 'No'. And that's how it ended.

The two atomic bombs on Hiroshima and Nagasaki ended the war in the Far East. The Japanese surrendered on 15 August. VJ Day celebrations were more muted than those on VE Night but relief that the world war was finally over was palpable. At last the thousands of men, fighting or in camps, could come home and all those standing by to be drafted could be stood down. In hospital in Gloucester, D-Day veteran Frank Rosier was up and about after an operation on his eye. He joined other injured servicemen, allowed out for the celebrations. Treated to free drinks in all the pubs they visited, they were in the mood to party.

There's some American boys and we were having a fine old time, 'cause you know Americans, they always carry a bottle, don't they? So that was going round. Suddenly out of the blue come some snowdrops – that's American military police, they wear a white hat – in a jeep. And they started laying into these American boys for no reason at all. That did it. We saw these snowdrops off, and turned the bloody jeep over!

Though the atomic bombs unleashed on Japan killed almost 200,000 people and were controversial, even at the time, Fergus Anckorn is convinced that they were a 'lifesaver, not a life-taker' because, he argues, many more thousands of lives would have been lost in the event of an attempted American invasion of Japan, and all POWs would have been killed. Nevertheless, their repatriation was a strange, hole-in-the-corner affair. Skeletal and wracked with tropical abscesses and disease, they were thought too shocking to be seen at home straight away so they were sent to warm places to be fattened up. After three months' recuperation in Egypt, Fergus managed to get his weight up to six stone. Even so, the prisoners' eventual homecoming was so surreptitious it seemed as if their country was ashamed of them.

> We arrived at Liverpool in the dark, no one was allowed to see us, we came down the gangplank covered, into lorries that took us to a church hall where we were fed and stayed the night. The next morning we were put on a train to London, all the window blinds were down, doors were locked, carriages reserved, so no one saw us.

He was met by his family and Lucille at the station but it was an uneasy first meeting.

> I just said, 'Hello.' I didn't go near Lucille. It was weird, I was sitting on the train and we just spoke casually about things and I didn't get the chance to touch her even . . . No one quite knew what to say, it was weird and awkward, but it was one of those things, you know, typically English.

After a few days Fergus started to talk about some of the things that had happened to him, but his family struggled to comprehend.

> That was one of the most difficult parts of it all, coming home. We couldn't identify with people here who hadn't known what we'd put up with. I remember my mother telling us of the horrors of this country, how they only got two and a half ounces of bacon a week. Now, if someone had offered me a [tiny] piece of bacon rind, I would have thought Christmas had come. My sister said to me, 'Well, I suppose you got plenty of fresh fruit out there.' We got 60 grams of rice a day.

For some time Fergus withdrew, preferring to spend time in the woods he loved rather than in the company of others. He lost his memory and didn't know who he was. He broke down while having dinner in a Lyons Corner House.

> I couldn't believe that a few months ago I was lying in the mud without a hope of living and here I am: look at those silver knives and I don't have to steal them! I just dropped my head on the table and burst into tears. I could not believe that I'd been there, lower than a pig, and now I'm in this beautiful place. I'd been used to living in the utmost squalor with no means of washing, no clothes, very little food, mud, rain, bashings, and now I'm in the height of civilisation. It didn't work . . . It was a nasty period, there were times when I'd think, I wish I was back in the camp. We were all together there, we all knew what was what. Coming home was so different.

Doctor Bill Frankland coped with his Japanese POW experience in another way. He didn't talk about it then and he didn't talk about it for the next 65 years.

> I would never talk about anything to do with what happened to me as a prisoner of war. I just wanted to forget it and think of a new life that I was going to lead and not mope about the past or hating the Japanese.

————◆————

Weeks after VE Day, with the war in the Far East still going on, the wartime coalition government fell and an election was called for July. The Conservatives expected to capitalise on Churchill's wartime record; Labour promised to deliver Beveridge's social welfare reforms. Confident Conservatives fatally misjudged the public mood: while people cheered Churchill to the echo for bringing them through the war, they were quite prepared to vote against him in an election that was all about the peace. He was the man for his time and that time had now mercifully passed. People wanted to look forward. They'd sacrificed much and been promised much; now they looked for promises to be delivered and the Conservatives weren't trusted. With the military conflict all but over, class differences re-emerged and feelings ran high. Committed socialist Bill Graves took part in an unexpectedly heated discussion on a train after being demobbed from the navy.

> We were coming up from Plymouth and it was packed, as usual. People were sat on one another's laps – servicemen mostly. They'd issued us with a copy of the Beveridge Report. I think everyone had one. I'd read it, I discussed it with Dad when I was home on leave . . . This was all the debate that was going on at the time, and when we were in the compartment the discussion started. Well, there was a cockney tucked up in the corner and he had a WAAF on his lap. And he started getting a bit noisy about it and he said, 'I hope you lot haven't given up your guns!' 'What are you talking about, stupid ass? Of course we've given up our guns.' 'Well, you ought to have bloody kept them because if those bastard Tories get in, there ain't going to be no welfare and the only way you're going to get it is for us to fight for it the same as we fought the Jerries, and then we shall have to shoot some of them perishers including Churchill. Everybody says what a wonderful bloke he was. They forget what he did down at Tonypandy with the miners!' And of course this started a debate then on the merits or demerits of Churchill's character . . . and this was the sort of debate that was going on and it was quite a passionate debate, it wasn't just a casual conversation.

The forces vote was critical and, as Bob Frost could see, this split along class lines.

> In the minds of the average British serviceman, the Conservatives were the party of the officer and the other ranks was the Labour Party and I think they voted along those lines. Churchill, who did a darned good job – I do not deny that at all – lost. My own family had always voted Liberal but I wouldn't have minded voting

Labour, it was my kick against the Conservatives because we saw their party as associated with the officer class.

Russell Margerison wanted Churchill to win but recognised his flaws.

No, I didn't want to see the back of Churchill. I wanted him to still keep leading us as he had been doing. Having said that, I think he was completely out of touch with the working man. I don't think he had a clue what was going on in the backstreets of Britain.

Fred Glover, another admirer, felt the same.

I thought about it a great deal. I thought about Churchill's record during the war, but I felt that that wasn't good enough. We wanted something more after the war, we wanted something happening. I was quite convinced when I cast my vote that I was doing the right thing.

Bill Graves canvassed for Labour in the election and keenly awaited the outcome in his Bristol constituency. The final results had to wait several weeks for the service votes to be counted, but on 26 July they were all in.

At the Labour headquarters there was a big sign outside: 'Penny on the Drum' – every seat we took off the Tories we put a penny on the drum. And that place was absolutely chock-a-block packed and people were outside listening to the results come in. [From canvassing] we realised we were collecting a lot of civilian votes . . . And then the great day when all the service votes came in and were allocated to the various constituencies and the pennies were going on the drum, penny after penny, in fact we ran out of pennies because it was a landslide and we were absolutely ecstatic!

Diana Athill was working as a clerk at the BBC.

One felt quite sad about Churchill being thrown out in a way because he'd been so important, but you could see he was going ga-ga, so this had to happen. No, we were thrilled, I think everybody in the BBC was. I remember we all stayed in the newsroom all night, listening, getting more and more excited. I think everybody was absolutely over the moon about that – a new government.

With the BBC's infant television service not yet resumed, the first glimpse of the new government for most people was on a cinema newsreel. Bill and Eileen Graves were at the Bristol Regent.

They showed Pathé News of Atlee – this insignificant little man Clem Atlee – coming out of 10 Downing Street with the Cabinet by him: Nye Bevan, Ernie Bevin, Morrison, Stafford Cripps . . . There was a cheer from the audience and they started clapping. They were clapping and they were cheering. We'd done it! Not only had we won the war, we'd won the peace, we'd got the people in power who were going to give us the Beveridge Report. We didn't call it 'the welfare state', we called it the Beveridge Report. We were going to get the things we'd been asking for. And there was this state of euphoria for weeks afterwards.

Not everyone was ecstatic.

I remember my dad and some of the old-timers didn't seem to have the same enthusiasm. I said, 'Dad, what's wrong? We won a victory!' 'Yeah, I know,' he said, 'but we got to pick up the pieces of that victory. This country is flat broke. It's on its knees. The Tories don't give a bugger now. Anything that isn't right now is going to be our fault 'cause we're the government now. You'll have the [right-wing press]. The blame will start. You watch it now. Some of you haven't thought this through.' It was true. The old-timers like my old man who'd been around the block and knew the way of things, they knew that it was going to be tough.

In the words of the Treasury that August, Britain faced a 'financial Dunkirk', with a balance of payments deficit of £750 million. The country was indeed flat broke, in huge debt to America and with three million damaged homes and ruined infrastructure to repair. The effort of war had exhausted industries as well as workers, who were no longer prepared to tolerate pre-war wages and poor conditions. Though jobs were plentiful, the homeless needed housing and people were desperate to resume family life on a firmer, more prosperous footing, protected by the social welfare benefits promised by Beveridge. Expectations were as high as the resources available to meet them were threadbare: it looked as if the New Jerusalem would be some time coming yet.

The bitter winter of 1947 was perhaps the darkest hour of the immediate post-war period. Coal shortages meant power cuts and unheated homes in the coldest winter on record. Everything and everyone was affected: industry and agriculture lost production; bread and potatoes were rationed for the first time; radio programmes and magazines were restricted. Enid Wenban, demobbed from the ATS, was back at her old job with HMSO, now in an office opposite Selfridges.

> I remember buses bumping over rutted snow in Oxford Street – no snowploughs then. At home we couldn't get fuel for the boiler and the radiators froze.

But then in a burst of renewed optimism the following year – a year in which Britain hosted the 'Austerity' Olympics – the Labour government delivered Beveridge with a series of radical Acts of Parliament. Enid, working in HMSO's Parliamentary Publications section, helped process every associated report, Bill and Act: 'We saw the founding of the welfare state!' The long legacy of the Poor Law – the hated Means Test, the fear of unemployment and ill health and of dying in the workhouse – was at last swept away. Working people had their own good reasons for welcoming the new welfare state. Fergus Anckorn had to return to hospital for several weeks every year for treatment for the conditions he'd picked up in the tropics.

All free, all on the National Health, looked after very well indeed and without that I'd probably still be having tropical diseases to this day.

For Gus Bialick it was all about security.

They were building new hospitals and people were feeling secure in themselves which they'd never felt before the war. I felt secure in my own mind that if anything happened to my elderly parents, they could go to the doctor and get help.

The impact of the new service was such that it quickly assumed a place of special significance for Diana Athill and her generation.

We had the National Health. That was the most wonderful thing. Anyone who can remember when it began really feels that it is almost a sacred thing, it made such an immense difference to life for so many people.

The NHS was the most visible but not the only pillar of the new welfare state. Joan Wilson was a young clerk who'd returned after the war to her old job with the small children's homes section of Croydon's Public Assistance department, part of the creaking pre-1948 machinery of Poor Law.

When I got back there were enormous problems of abandoned children, fathers not facing up to their responsibilities or perhaps soldiers back from abroad finding unexpected children at home. Nineteen forty-eight was just such an extraordinary year for everything: the National Health Service, welfare services, a proper children's department. At last, they'd got something to help children. The big old children's homes closed and we opened small group homes, started an adoption service and recruited child care officers. For the first time there was a complete consideration of a child's needs.

For Bill Graves it was a matter of principle.

[Poor Law] was a very rough regime. People who were poor were ostracised. It was their own fault: they shouldn't be poor. That was the attitude. The welfare state to us meant equality of opportunity and equality of service. The NHS was going to be free at the point of use. We were going to get security for handicapped people. Elderly people were going to be secure with their pensions. This is what we believed. We thought that it was fair. If you want a free, fair society you've got to look after your neighbour. And . . . if you want the privileges of democracy then you got to pay for them.

Bill Frankland, working at St Mary's Hospital alongside the father of antibiotics, Alexander Fleming, was no fan of the Labour government and voted for Churchill. His research work on allergic reactions to penicillin was little affected by the changes but he was, and remains, a staunch supporter of the NHS.

Education was another pillar of the post-war covenant and reform came earlier with the 1944 Education Act. Remembered for enshrining the tripartite eleven-plus system that later caused so many inequalities, at the time its advances were to make secondary education free for all and to raise the school leaving age to 15 – though its target of 16 wasn't achieved until nearly three decades later. Resources were tight, classes were large and teachers were being hastily recruited, but there was a new vitality in Britain's schools and from the 1950s young architects produced hundreds of innovative buildings to house them.

Ex-servicemen too were taking new educational opportunities and encouraged to retrain for new trades and professions. RAF gunner Bob Frost ended his war as an instructor.

It was put to me by an education officer that I seemed to be naturally inclined to teaching and there was a scheme called the

Emergency Teacher Training Scheme. Would I consider applying? So I thought to myself, Well, I'll give it a go. It was a profession and a job for life, something to go for.

In hospital, Frank Rosier was encouraged to study between operations to restructure his face, and Bill Graves, now a British Rail driver, won a Trade Union Scholarship to Ruskin College, Oxford.

Prospects weren't so good for women leaving the services, as Dorothy Hughes discovered when she was demobbed from the ATS in September 1945 with a fortnight's notice, a rail warrant and 90 clothing coupons.

> The men of course all had their jobs kept for them so they were OK, but the women weren't needed at all so we were feeling disgruntled. The men were given a suit, raincoat, shoes and shirts and quite a good gratuity. We were given £50 and that was for nearly six years . . . and when we did get home we were still very restricted in the jobs we could go into and there were very few vacancies. We did feel frustrated and we hated the idea that we'd given five years of our youth up to the army. It was a big cut out of your life because 'old' in those days was 25 and most of us were 25 when we finished.

It was especially hard for those with specialist skills likely to be done by a man in peacetime, like former ATA pilot Joy Lofthouse.

> I wanted the war to go on, partly because I knew when we finished with ATA, that would be the end of our flying for most of us. There was no place for us in commercial flying when it restarted after the war. The men were pouring out of Bomber Command. They didn't want women. I thought at the time, rightly or wrongly . . . after six long years of war with no flying ahead, I was quite happy to settle down, get married and have children.

———◆———

'Settling down' was the priority for the majority of young people who'd come through the war. The romantic ideal had survived intact. Even for Jim Purcell, who'd never had a girlfriend, the dream of 'the one' was still alive.

> I thought I was going to be condemned to a life of being a bachelor. Then one night I had a dream. I dreamed I would meet the most beautiful girl in the world and that she'd only be young, and we'd be married. And I woke up that morning and thought, I wonder if my dream comes true?

Within weeks of getting home to Jarrow he saw her, cleaning windows in a neighbouring house: 'She was only 18 and at that window she looked like a picture in a frame.' By the end of 1945 Jim and Betty were married.

Long engagements weren't the rule. Couples had had enough of separation and waiting and wanted to get on with married life. Brian Rix was finally demobbed in 1947 and with £1,000 borrowed from his family, started a small repertory company.

> On the 1st of January 1949 I was auditioning people at a club in Dean Street and I sat there, a bit hungover, over a guttering gas fire, and the next person came in and I immediately wanted to marry her, and that was Elspet. She walked in and she looked absolutely fantastic in a green costume . . . That night I was so anxious to see her again I went round to her mother's flat near the BBC where she was staying. It was extraordinary. I proposed to her and I'd only known her two days. I just knew I wanted to marry her.

She was non-committal but – scandalously for the times – they moved in together.

> Elspet and I shared a bedroom and that was unheard of in those days of course. I think we were in the bath together, I was at the plug end and she said, 'You've stopped asking me to marry you.' And I said, 'Well, you never say yes!' She said, 'I've decided I will.'

So within three months we were married and we stayed married for 64 years.

Demobbed from the Pioneers in 1946, Gus Bialick was now 32 and ready to settle down.

My wife came to England on the *Kindertransport* from Germany in 1938 just before the war began, and this good country allowed 10,000 Jewish orphans in, and my wife was amongst them. I was introduced by her brother who was a friend of mine. She was working as a children's nurse in Bedford. I went down there one Sunday morning with him and she came out of the building dressed in a nurse's uniform and I fell for her like a ton of bricks. She was 14 years younger than me. On my side it was love at first sight.

They married at the start of 1948 and spent the next 58 years together.

The loss of an eye and facial disfigurement proved no barrier to romance for Frank Rosier. The year he finally left hospital he met his wife Margaret and they married in 1949.

She never referred to it. She just accepted it. She never knew me any different. And we fell in love and that was it. But it was great. You'd see other weddings, of lads with no legs, or two walking sticks, marrying that nurse they met in hospital who never knew them any other way. A person is a person whether they lost two legs or one eye, or whatever they are.

With rationing still on, weddings were the same modest affairs they'd been in wartime. Bob Frost met his wife Daphne whilst they were both still in the air force. Neither set of parents approved of the match so they eloped. Bob remembers cycling round the countryside to buy eggs to make the wedding cake. Wedding cakes were important but they also took a lot of rationed ingredients; eggs, sugar, butter and cooking fats didn't start to come off ration until 1953.

For Bill Graves's wedding to Eileen in 1945, they had to resort to sacrifice, ingenuity and the black market:

> People gave from their own rations. My grandmother and my mother-in-law got together and they made a two-tier wedding cake, which was exceptional at that time. Most wedding cakes were a little cake inside of a cardboard carton thing, all padded out. But this was an actual wedding cake with marzipan. Don't ask me where it came from – if I did know, I wouldn't want to. My dad got all his mates at the allotment to give lettuce and tomatoes so we had salad, and through a farmer contact of my grandfather's we got a ham . . . So we had as near an old-fashioned wedding as it was possible to get at that time. I suppose one in a thousand had that sort of atmosphere to get married in.

If Bill and Eileen had a one-in-a-thousand wedding then in November 1947 at Westminster Abbey the Princess Elizabeth and her new husband Prince Philip, Duke of Edinburgh, had one in a million. Rationing wasn't an issue: there were 2,000 guests and a four-tier cake that stood 9 feet high. But only naysayers and republicans begrudged the extravagance; for everyone else it was a bright spot in a grim year and a harbinger of better times. Margaret Rhodes was one of her cousin's eight bridesmaids, in dresses of ivory satin and net silk tulle. She can remember little of the ceremony but

> I can remember waving a white-gloved hand through the window of a car at the crowds. It was rather exciting being on the balcony . . . It was wonderful looking out where you could see miles of people, just thousands and thousands of people stretching up the Mall.

Gladys Parry's start to married life the same year was rather different.

> I got married in 1947 and my husband was on £2 10s a week. We had to do everything with that, food and rent. You never dreamed

of getting anything off the state but when they gave us 7s 6d [Child
Allowance] for the second child, I was in heaven. I could eat.

They were all living in her father's house in Hulme, with its bugs
and gas lighting.

And then I'd been married a while and we decided we were going
to be really posh, we were going to have electric in – £12 that cost,
it was like nearly three weeks' wages. But I tell you, what a
difference it made. You could see every cobweb, you could see
every spider!

A month after his return from a Japanese POW camp, Fergus
Anckorn married Lucille. Still withdrawn, he wanted a quiet
wedding without fuss, so they married by special licence in January
1946 and returned to live with his parents. Their marriage was a
balm for the long years of separation and ill-treatment and the
shock of returning to a different normality.

From then on, life was beautiful. We were together again and we
went everywhere together. She looked after me, she knew I was
capable of mood swings and she knew when not to talk to me
and when to let me be on my own. She was the one that got me
going properly again afterwards. She knew exactly what to do.
Life was good.

Because they'd been so malnourished, POWs had been told to
expect problems.

When we first came home a general got up and gave us a little
speech and he said, 'Now, there's one thing I must tell you. You're
all sterile so you won't have children, but just be thankful that
you're alive.' Well, that's what caused the baby boom! Everyone
went home and away they went and there were children being
born all over the place! He'd got it wrong. We came home and I
got married. We went to bed that night in a normal way as though

that's what we'd been doing for ever and we were just together from then on. It was perfect.

Fergus and Lucille went on to have two children. He delighted in family life, teaching his four-year-old daughter Deborah how to hold a snake without fear and sharing his love of nature in the woods he knew so well. There was magic too: in the hollows of trees he'd leave a coin for her to find.

> I used to say to my little daughter, 'The fairies live in that hole, and if you're good they'll leave you something.' I used to put my hand in and say, 'No, they haven't left anything for me,' then she would put her hand in and find sixpence. So every tree with a hole in, she'd rush up, 'There's a fairy tree!' So I'd do it again and she'd come out with a coin. Wonderful!

Though family life could be a joy, adjusting to uneventful routine was a problem for some ex-servicemen like Russell Margerison.

> Settling down after the war I found extremely difficult. I couldn't get used to day-to-day routine. My wife used to say, 'You've got ants in your pants.' I couldn't settle down. It was so abnormal to the life I'd been leading . . . this seemed ever so flat. I was restless.

He found the solution in doing up a succession of old houses 'sometimes full of cockroaches and goodness knows what'. It was hard work on top of a full-time job but he and his wife Betty did up five in all whilst the family lived in them and this 'improved our living standard considerably'.

For those married during and just after the war, housing was perhaps the biggest challenge. With so many homes damaged by bombing and no new building for the best part of a decade, the housing shortage was acute. The majority of young couples started their married life with parents or in rented rooms. The government's solution was mass-produced prefabricated bungalows. They were only designed to last ten years but their popularity and longevity took everyone by surprise. It shouldn't have done: the new 'prefabs' were well designed and full of conveniences unfamiliar to most working-class families. Connie Hoe and her young daughter Christine had been evacuated to Oxfordshire, but now her husband Leslie was back from the navy they needed a home together.

> Somebody told me, 'If you go up to the housing department of the LCC [London County Council], you're eligible for housing.' So I went there and registered. They wanted to see Leslie in uniform, and they gave us a prefab. It was like a small bungalow and they were built on bomb sites, [there were] four prefabs in a row, and the inhabitants all had husbands in the forces so we were all in the same boat. It had quite a big kitchen and a fridge all fitted and a gas stove. We were there for 28 years and the gas stove and the fridge were still working!

Bill and Eileen Graves were thrilled with their new prefab in Bristol.

> We couldn't believe it . . . we were literally gobsmacked. There was a kitchen like something out of *Homes and Gardens*, as far as we were concerned. There was a built-in refrigerator – you couldn't buy a refrigerator then because everything was going abroad [for export]. There was a worktop, there was a stainless-steel sink, there was a swivel tap. Really state of the art it was. An indoor toilet, bathroom . . . We thought we'd died and gone to heaven. My brother and his wife came over and my brother said, 'I was in America and this was the standard of homes there. It's a bloody quality place. You are the luckiest bloody pair that ever put on shoes!'

But prefabs were only a temporary and partial solution to the housing crisis. Thousands of permanent new homes were needed. The 1946 New Towns Act put in hand an ambitious programme for ten new planned communities. These were to be built on greenfield sites to rehouse people from poor and bombed-out areas in the cities. Local councils too started ambitious building programmes: Jim Purcell got a job with Jarrow Corporation building council houses and refiguring the ruined centre of the town. After living in one room with Betty and their first baby, he was rewarded with a council house of his own. It was everything he'd ever dreamed of.

> Life was good in Jarrow. After living with her grandmother for three years we got our little house on Falmouth Drive. And she turned it into a blinking palace. She cleaned, she loved it. She done everything. She was a lover, a mother, a friend. I became a king and she was my Queen.

———◆———

Times were still hard and people made the most of what they had. Little was available in the shops because most consumer goods were made for export. If men were the breadwinners, women often bore the brunt of managing a family on little money in substandard accommodation. In the back-to-back terraces of Hulme, Gladys Parry was well used to hardship but she was less prepared for the physical aspects of marriage.

> Put it this way, my wedding night was not very successful because he'd had too much to drink and I was very apprehensive. So it must have been about three or four nights later that I discovered what being married was like and I didn't like it very much. Took me a long time to get used to that, I'll tell you. And then of course when you have a baby and you don't know how the hell you got it, 'cause in them days I was a bit Victorian. I didn't have a mother to tell me what life was about. You found out off somebody else, a girlfriend. Later on it got all right where you could do it without thinking too much of it, you know, and you could paint the ceiling while it was going on or think about what you're having the next day for dinner, and have I got enough money in my purse to buy it?

Two children later, she was keeping the family together on their joint income of £10 a week, made possible by her thrift.

> I used to get a joint of mutton, which would cost 7s 6d, and I'd cook it very, very slow in the oven that was on the grate and we'd have Sunday dinner, roast, off it. After that, I used to cut all the meat off and put it in a pan, bones and all, and cook it up and tater hash – and more potatoes than meat, I'll tell you, then we used to have that. But I'd leave enough to make two plate pies and we'd have those Wednesday and Thursday.

Nothing was wasted. Every commodity was precious; some creatively recycled.

> I used to use tea twice, because we had no bags in them days. I used to put a drop of gravy browning in the cup so it made it look darker. My husband never found out until I forgot to put the milk in one day when I'm giving him his tea and he could see the fat on the top: 'What's this on the top?' So I was found out.

The tight-knit community around her made life bearable.

> In those days you could leave your door open, 'cause we used to sit on the steps. We could sit outside maybe until one o'clock in the morning talking, laughing, joking . . . The kids used to play out in the street – we were watching the kids as well. We lived house-to-house, almost talking distance. In them days, everybody knew everybody's business. And if we knew somebody was in trouble and needed help, we didn't mess around. We went. So yes, it was a good community. We'd all help in any way we could: if it was washing or cleaning or looking after somebody when they were poorly. Even washing a corpse down. There was a lady that used to wash the corpses down. Today undertakers do all that. In my day it was a neighbour.

As well as everything else, Gladys had to put up with her husband's philandering with other men's wives, but she usually got the better of him and his lady friends with a piece of her mind, occasionally with her fists. Divorce was never an option.

> Well, for a start I couldn't keep the house on with my wages and I never even thought about divorce. I wouldn't divorce him because I really did . . . I absolutely adored him.

Women were still the dependent partners in marriage; few had the resources to leave, even if they wanted to. Divorce was difficult, expensive and shameful. When Joy Lofthouse married her Czech pilot husband after the war, she expected it to be for life.

> In those days, divorce was an unheard-of thing almost. People just didn't get divorced, they stuck it out for years and years. There were very unhappy marriages, I know, certainly with cruelty from husbands in marriages. In those days you didn't get out of them.

Women fortunate enough to be socially confident and financially independent were able to make their own way without having to rely on a husband, but the majority were expected to want to return to domestic duties after the exceptional circumstances of the war. Those who chose not to marry, or who perhaps sought to escape an unhappy love affair, looked for other opportunities.

After returning from her secret Y Station work to her relatively mundane job at HMSO, Enid Wenban was ready for a new adventure and wanted to carry on doing something useful. She joined the Red Cross as a welfare officer in British military bases abroad. Here she witnessed some of the violent results of the post-war shift in the balance of power. She was in Suez in the run-up to the 1956 Crisis. Here jeeps were fitted with vertical bars to break the decapitating wires strung across roads by terrorists agitating to be free of British control. There was violence too in Cyprus where 'they were shooting our soldiers in bars'. While she was in Germany, a trip into East Berlin organised by the Russians before the Wall went up in 1961 was 'an eye-opener', if anything its empty streets bleaker, more wrecked and more poverty-stricken than anything in London. The cold war now cast a frosty pall over Europe, the threat of a new uniquely destructive atomic war never far away.

Independent-minded Diana Athill had by the 1950s established an absorbing career in a small publishing house with émigré André Deutsch. With 'various little affairs' and a new circle of fascinating writers from different backgrounds, countries and cultures, she'd found her perfect métier.

———◆———

Despite or perhaps because of wartime laxity, moral standards and social attitudes hardened in the two decades following the war. Marriage and family weren't just the norm but the only acceptable social unit. Couples 'living in sin', divorced people and unmarried mothers were all social pariahs except in the most bohemian circles. Brian and Elspet Rix, who shared digs together before they were married, were very much the exception to the rule but then actors were perceived to lead louche or unconventional lives. Illegitimacy still carried a stigma for parent and child. Some parents went as far as falsifying the date of their wedding anniversary in order to conceal the fact that their firstborn was conceived (or born) out of wedlock. It was only on his mother's deathbed that George Montague discovered that his parents had married three years after his birth and the man he'd always called Dad probably wasn't his father after all.

If non-conforming heterosexual behaviour was frowned on, homosexuals were so far beyond the pale that most either denied their true feelings or led a secret double life of furtive assignations in private clubs and men's lavatories under cover of confirmed bachelorhood or a 'lavender' marriage. Sexual activity between men wasn't just socially unacceptable, it was a criminal offence.

George Montague had homosexual encounters after the war in men's public lavatories and with rent boys. He was appalled by

Alan Turing's arrest, barbaric 'treatment' and subsequent suicide in 1954, and encouraged by the 1957 Wolfenden Report's recommendations for the limited legalisation of homosexual acts, though this didn't happen for another ten years. George knew he was gay and at times felt suicidal about it. By 1960, after having a stable but covert gay relationship for five years, he was 36 and under intense pressure from his mother to get married. He'd tried to confide in her.

> She sensed I was going to tell her. She may have suspected, you see. She said to me, 'Darling, if one of my sons was like that, I'd rather he didn't tell me.' That was why I didn't tell her and why I got married. She wouldn't have understood, she would have been hurt, terribly hurt . . . Being gay in those days was such a terrible stigma. It was worse than being a murderer. I loved my mother. Most gay people love their mothers. So I got married to please my mother.

In 1961 he married Vera, 'a wonderful woman'.

> But I was living a lie. I'd done a bit of acting and that helped. You have to act, pretend you're heterosexual. You have to do what every other heterosexual does and kiss your wife and give her affection in public. You don't feel like doing all of this, but you do it. She knew I was gay. But she told me she'd rather have a gay husband than no husband. We managed to live a completely acceptable heterosexual life, with three lovely children. I was living a complete lie and nobody had the slightest suspicion. I must admit I enjoyed being married. I enjoyed my children. I love my children. I thoroughly enjoyed married life, but I wasn't in love. It was difficult with my wife, but you just plough through it, and with iron will.

George loved his family but he was leading a double life. Sex in private between men over 21 was finally legalised in 1967 but homosexuals were still reviled and those working in entertainment and public life couldn't risk coming out of the closet. Meeting partners was hazardous: known places of assignation were routinely planted with young agents provocateurs and raided by the police. Despite a number of covert gay relationships, George remained married, his sexuality a shameful secret. He didn't feel able to reveal it until after his mother's death in 1982. Their children now grown, George and Vera agreed to part but they remained good friends until her death in 2002.

———◆———

If homosexuality was a dirty secret, with 'pansies', 'queers' and 'fairies' the subject of whispered gossip and prurient speculation in private, then prejudice on the basis of race was much more openly expressed. It was unexceptionable to be rude or hostile when referring to people with a different colour skin. The *Windrush* generation of immigrants from the Caribbean started arriving in 1948 to fill essential jobs in the new National Health Service, nationalised railways and London Transport. At first a curiosity, 'coloured' people soon faced an unofficial colour bar when it came to housing and jobs.

Earl Cameron arrived from Bermuda in 1939 and spent much of the war in London and in the Merchant Navy. The racial prejudice he experienced then was mainly from white American GIs, though he found getting work difficult. He never encountered direct racism from the British, but that may be because he was moving in liberal circles with actors and performers. Nevertheless, establishing a career as a black actor after the war wasn't easy. He survived on small parts in regional rep before his big break in 1951.

> I got a part in a play called *13 Death Street*. Terrible title, terrible play, but I had to earn a living. While I was with this play I phoned up the casting director at Ealing Studios to see if there might be a part for me in *Where No Vultures Fly*. 'Well,' she said, 'we're not doing that till November, but it's strange you should phone me up because we've seen your picture in *Spotlight* and we're doing

a film you could be right for. Can you get down to Denham Studios about two thirty this afternoon?'

Earl met with the director Basil Dearden and after screen tests got the central role of Johnny Lambert, a Jamaican merchant seaman, in a new Ealing crime thriller, *Pool of London*, 'a drama of the river underworld'. This was a breakthrough for Earl, his first film role, acting alongside established stars James Robertson Justice and Leslie Phillips. It was also a breakthrough for British cinema, the first to portray an interracial love story and racism, with a black actor in the lead.

> *Pool of London* still remains the best part I've ever had in a film. It was important from the fact I was the first black actor to have a relationship with a white girl, although it didn't develop very far, but it was a sort of love story building up, and I think from that point of view I made a bit of history, and also for the first star role for a black actor, so that made a difference.

Earl was already in his own interracial relationship. He'd married Audrey, a fellow actor from a white Jewish background who he'd met in rep.

> She was a beautiful young lady, a very good-natured sort of person. We got on very well together. I got on pretty well with her parents but deep down they weren't very happy about the marriage I'd say. They were both in show business so they were broad-minded but deep down they would have much preferred her marrying a Jewish boy, no doubt about that. But Audrey wasn't bothered about it at all, she did what she wanted to do and that was that.

For others, too, attraction not race was the prime consideration. Someone else who'd embarked on a 'mixed' relationship was Diana Athill. She had met Barry, a Jamaican writer, through her work. They shared a common love of books and ideas and soon became lovers.

I was privileged in that my part of the world, publishing, was full of liberal-minded people so perhaps it's not surprising that no one ever raised an eyebrow as far as we were concerned, but that would have been completely impossible before the war, unthinkable. God knows what other people were saying about it. The thing is, I really have no idea what other people thought. Everyone was much too good-mannered to ever express any opinion.

It was perhaps an experience at Oxford in the late 1930s that helped shape her attitudes to racial prejudice:

I was at a dance and a very black African man was there, and I was afraid that he would ask me to dance and I'd have to. I was talking to another girl about it afterwards and she said, 'Urgh, I think I should be sick if a black man touched me.' I was disgusted by that and it suddenly occurred to me that it really had been very stupid not to want to dance with that poor man.

Earl and Diana's prejudice-free experience wasn't shared by the majority of mixed-race couples, who faced everything from parental disapproval and verbal abuse to physical attacks in the unsettled post-war period. Successive waves of immigration – the East African Asians expelled by Idi Amin and Vietnamese boat people among them – reignited public anxieties, stoked by Enoch Powell and sections of the press, about the country being flooded by foreigners. Casual references to 'coons' and 'Pakis' passed without comment until well into the 1980s, and popular television comedy and light entertainment offered crude racial stereotypes throughout this period. Ignorance fed prejudice. When Earl Cameron was cast for the 1961 film *Flame in the Streets,* about racial tension in London, the director called him in for advice.

He said he'd never worked with 'my people', as he put it, before and he'd just like some feedback on how to handle the script. So I explained a few things to him . . . The one thing that's terribly mistaken with white people's attitude to black people, [is] that they have unclean homes and they're overcrowded. I said the majority of Africans or West Indians are very house-proud and they keep their homes very clean and they don't have overcrowding as they seem to be depicted so many times. So on that line and a few other things I explained to him and he was very happy about that, we got on very well.

The habitual casual racism ingrained in British society for so much of their lives explains a persistent strain of prejudice among many of this generation. Even if expressed in general rather than overtly racist or homophobic terms today, that old suspicion, even fear, is evident in their less guarded comments.

But suspicion of extremism and hatred of oppression eclipses even that long tradition of fear of the foreign. Fighting a fascist regime and witnessing its vile fruits during the 1930s and 1940s had a profound effect. It elicited a strong sense of fair play and the desire to protect the weak from bullies. This concern for the oppressed tempered intolerance, especially when it came to accepting refugees. This may explain why Jews fleeing from Nazi Germany and the children of earlier generations escaping European pogroms feel a special sense of gratitude and loyalty. The work of Dorothy Bohm and others in helping people understand exactly what was happening in Europe sharpened resolve to overcome the Nazi regime but, as she acknowledges, when the chips were down, Britons responded with humanity and generosity.

I have a tremendous love for this country, for what it stands for, what its principles are, the humanity compared with other countries. I'm grateful that I was allowed to be here to have a life which has been certainly demanding but rewarding as well. I have no doubt whatsoever that this for me, and for lots of people, has been a wonderful country and it should stay like that. It lets you be, it accepts you. It has much more freedom, and freedom is important.

Gus Bialick, the child of early-twentieth-century Jewish immigrants from Eastern Europe, saw his father's pride in being recognised as a British citizen:

My father became a naturalised citizen in 1928. And he always said to me he was so proud to get his naturalisation papers, that when he bought his ticket to go back to Poland to see his father, he went through Customs for the first time as an Englishman without having to queue up with all the other foreigners. He said he lifted his naturalisation papers high up in the air and walked straight through without stopping. To him that was a wonderful thing to do.

You know, when your parents are immigrants, and they come from an area of the world where the rulers don't care for their own people, let alone for people of a different religion and a different outlook, you know that this country, England, stood for something better, and you wanted to be part of it. My father lived to be 100 years old and every single day of his life, from the time he arrived in this country, he loved Great Britain. He arrived here as a boy from a barbaric nation, to a nation of civilised people, and that was something he absolutely delighted in.

———◆———

Despite medical advances and the new National Health Service, social attitudes to physical and mental disability remained ignorant and discriminatory. Brian and Elspet Rix were overjoyed at the birth of their first child, Shelley, at Westminster Hospital in 1951 while Brian was appearing in a West End comedy, but

Elspet and I just knew there was something wrong. I went to [the obstetrician's] rooms in Harley Street at six o'clock. The curtain went up at seven in those days. He said, 'Do sit down. Do have a cigarette. Have you ever heard of mongolism?' I had heard of mongolism, but I didn't know anything about it. And he said, 'Well, I'm afraid your daughter is a mongol. Will you please tell your wife?' And that was it. I said, 'What are we going to do?' He said, 'Put her away, forget her, start again.'

I went back to the theatre and burst into tears. [I had] a very large brandy and then I went on, which wasn't very easy. That was the way we were all treated as parents in those days. And that's when we began, Elspet and me, to think what we could do.

In the absence of better advice, Shelley was 'put away' in a private home. Those without resources would have coped with their child at home unaided or had them confined in a mental asylum or hospital for the 'subnormal'. There was an indelible stigma: before the discovery in 1959 that Down's syndrome is caused by an extra chromosome, it was thought the parents must somehow be to blame: 'I was asked if I was drunk at the moment of conception, or if I'd had a venereal disease.'

Their distress turned to a determination to help others in the same situation. As Brian's theatre – and soon television – success grew, so too did their fund-raising and campaigning for the organisation that eventually became the influential charity Mencap.

We used to hold the committee meeting between the matinee and the evening show on the Whitehall stage, me in my dressing gown, full make-up on. I think these bank managers and solicitors and good people wondered what on earth they were coming into! Anyway, we did raise a lot of money.

The money went to improving facilities for the thousands of mentally disabled people in residential homes in the 1950s and 1960s. Attitudes and policies, however, would prove harder to shift.

———◆———

Despite the long struggle for post-war recovery and continuing hardship for many, the country still felt as if it was pulling together as one. For the time being at least, simple pleasures sufficed and enough was as good as a feast. As a diversion from necessary austerity, large-scale communal events brought people together and gave them a welcome glimpse of a better, more colourful future. Ten million Britons enjoyed the 1951 Festival of Britain but the biggest and most spectacular diversion was the Coronation of Queen Elizabeth II in June 1953. A joyous and momentous event in the life of the nation, many fervently willed it to signal the start of a new era of plenty.

Margaret Rhodes, now married and pregnant with her second child, was there in Westminster Abbey.

> I wore my wedding dress which had been let out in the relevant areas and it was awful because you had to be in your seats quite early. And then, what happens when you want to go to the loo? I couldn't think of anything else. Luckily I managed to get through it . . . But it was just an immensely moving, historical moment . . . Somebody you've played with as a child and bossed around or been bossed around by, and you suddenly see this same person with this sort of aura of blessing, being crowned. It put her in an entirely different context. One could hardly believe that one knew somebody who was going through this amazing performance.

For Margaret, as for many others, the Coronation marked the start of better times.

> After the horrors of war, we had a new queen and it was like starting afresh. Everybody felt it was the new Elizabethan age and that it was all going to get better and better, so everybody felt happy.

The BBC television service had resumed in 1946 but sets were expensive and it had yet to capture the public imagination. The Coronation changed that. At her brother's home in south London, Enid Wenban was transfixed.

> For me, the amazing thing about the Coronation was the invention of television. It was the first time I'd seen it. What's more, my

brother had built the set! We all sat round and watched, completely enthralled. It was exciting to see this young couple taking over as the new royal family.

Enid was just one of the 10.4 million people who watched in friends' and neighbours' homes; another 7.8 million watched in their own. The television age had now begun. With full employment and rising wages, this was part of the slow rise of consumerism, boosted in 1955 by the arrival of ITV. The desirable goods now being advertised on the new medium were gradually reappearing in the shops and people at last had money to 'splash out' on unaccustomed luxury – a gas refrigerator or a week's holiday.

Emblematic of this growing prosperity and the longed-for return of the gaiety and leisure absent from people's lives for so long, holiday camps offered escape to another, more colourful world. Butlin's were the biggest and the brashest, offering the first all-inclusive seaside family holidays at prices working people could afford. Now heavily advertised on the new commercial channel, they appealed to many like Connie Hoe, drawn to their promise of a fortnight's fun and non-stop entertainment.

> The very first one we went to was Butlin's, of course, as there was a lot of publicity and advertising. It seemed too good to be true, the adverts. We went to Butlin's in Filey and it was marvellous. There were lovely gardens and the adverts were true. Christine used to be with all the kids, we used to watch the quizzes and Leslie entered a swimming competition. Our favourite was the dances. We used to join in everything because it was such a happy atmosphere. To be with so many people might not be to somebody else's liking, to go into a dining hall where there's hundreds of people, but it was our first visit to a holiday camp and we thoroughly enjoyed ourselves.

Jimmy Perry used his own experience as a young Butlin's entertainer for his hit comedy series *Hi-de-Hi!*

I was at RADA, along with a lot of other ex-servicemen. All young, most of them a bit violent and always having rows – we'd been in a war. We had very long summer holidays so a friend of mine who was there said, 'Look, I'm going to get a job at Butlin's as an entertainer. Do you want to come?' So we hopped on a bus to Butlin's headquarters.

Jimmy with his RADA-trained accent was thought too posh to be a Redcoat but was given a job at the Pwllheli camp as sports organiser.

I was useless. I didn't even know how to referee a football match . . . No sooner was I there than they promoted me to producer. I used to compere the Holiday Princess competition, all the Ugly Face competitions, the Who-Can-Stay-Under-the-Water-the-Longest-Without-Drowning competition . . . I succumbed to the Butlin magic. A wonderful time. All those games. Fun, fun, fun!

For much of the next five decades Butlin's was synonymous with holiday paradise: near enough to home but a world away from the workaday. But perhaps it was never enjoyed so much as by its first fun-starved guests in the late 1940s and 1950s.

◆

By the 1960s, those who had come through the war and now had growing families looked forward to settled lives in increasing prosperity. Their simple, sterling qualities had won a war that now lived on only in war films and boys' comics. Only old soldiers recounted their exploits. Everybody else wanted to get on with their lives in peace.

Prosperity brought an end to old certainties and old allegiances. The world was changing: the empire was now a commonwealth of newly independent nations, America and Russia the new world powers. As Britain's pre-eminent place on the world stage faded and personal goals took the place of national struggle, patriotism went out of fashion, just as the sentimental songs that had made Vera Lynn the Forces' Sweetheart gave way to raucous, energising rock and roll, and that in turn to the Rolling Stones' suggestive lyrics and the Who's anthem to youth, 'My Generation'. The world now seemed to belong to 'teenagers', who were more independent in every respect than any previous generation of young people.

Britain's moral compass was shifting too: prurient interest in the 1963 Profumo affair's corruption in high places went hand in hand with a more universal awakening from the moral stranglehold and class certainties of the 1950s. Now that working people felt more secure in their lives and prospects they no longer deferred to authority, and the unbreachable class barriers of the past looked vulnerable. When one of Margaret Rhodes' brothers observed that he'd 'hardly ever met a plain Mrs', it now sounded like an embarrassing anachronism rather than a social fact of life. The erosion of deference went across the generations: with increasing spending power and social freedom, young adults no longer deferred to parents or automatically adopted their values.

For the generation that had built the peace there were unimaginable new riches to be enjoyed as the 1970s approached and they reached comfortable middle age. And new storms to be weathered too.

12

Living in a Changing World
1965–2000

I was having a lovely time!

Diana Athill

In the final 30 or so years of the twentieth century our generation – now in the latter half of their lives – enthusiastically embraced the brave new world of consumerism and personal freedom, even if this sometimes chafed against values and attitudes ingrained since childhood. The simple post-war pleasures of family life, of managing on little and making the most of what you had, gave way in the late 1960s to more conspicuous displays of prosperity: home improvements, a fortnight in Spain, a new Cortina. Working conditions in traditional industries and in the factories now turning out consumer goods for the domestic market steadily improved thanks to powerful unions, and a rapidly expanding public sector created thousands of new safe, pensionable jobs. With life more secure and more comfortable than ever before, parents felt able to treat themselves and provide for their children the comforts and opportunities they'd never had.

The dream of home ownership was now within reach for those, like Gus Bialick, who'd grown up in insecure rented accommodation. Do-it-yourself, which started as a necessity in the 1950s, exploded in a riot of Formica and Fablon, helping families create the desirable modern homes they aspired to.

It was a happy time because I'd saved up my money that I'd earned and I had the opportunity to put a deposit on a house in north-west London. It was only a small bungalow-type house, but it was great for us. We spent a lot of money and a lot of time working on it. We replaced windows ourselves, I did all the painting and decorating myself. Life was good. Life was interesting.

Austin Byrne, veteran of the Arctic convoys, was by now a foreman in a Yorkshire textile mill. The 1960s were good times for him too.

It were as if things were within your reach. We had good holidays. We started going on cruises. We used to save up like mad and go on P&O cruises. It were a struggle but we did it. I liked to go back to sea – you didn't get the bouncing weather that you got in the Arctic. Oh, it were great. Some people on there thought you shouldn't be there because you weren't as good as them. You always met them, oh yes. But some people were very nice.

After struggling to bring up her two boys in poverty and a less than idyllic marriage, Gladys Parry was at last making her own mark in the world at work and in public life. When her husband died of lung cancer it was an unexpected release. Though she cared for him in his illness and 'felt fastened with him', she welcomed the new opportunities widowhood presented whilst she was still young enough to enjoy them.

I realised I could do all the things I wanted to do. I could go and see who I wanted and I could go places I wanted. I just took off. Holidays abroad. I don't think there's many places I've not been. I found out that I could be very happy, being free of anything. That's why I said I would never get married again. Well, I don't want to go round washing other people's underpants!

Marriages, once sacrosanct and severed only by death, were breaking up for new reasons. From 1969 unhappily married people no longer had to prove – or feign – adultery to get a divorce. Despite enjoying a comfortable lifestyle, Joy Lofthouse and her husband had grown apart and her 20-year marriage was foundering. Her three children were grown or growing up and she was dissatisfied with her life.

> The thought came to me: Look, if I'm ever going to lead another life, I've got to find something to do, so I looked for a place at teacher training college . . . and it was there that I met my second husband, Charles. His marriage was on the rocks too. And that was when I got the idea that perhaps I shouldn't be unhappy for the rest of my married life. Perhaps there was some other way.

Joy made the difficult decision to leave her husband and youngest child, then a teenager – a matter of lasting regret. But moral imperatives and social conventions still trumped personal desires. She hadn't yet embarked on an affair with Charles and they stayed apart until their respective divorces came through and they could be married.

From the late 1960s the gradual liberalisation of attitudes and social policy gave women many 'other ways' of managing their lives and families. The sexual revolution so firmly associated with the young and with the 1960s in fact only started having a major impact in the following decade when contraceptives, including the miraculously accessible and effective new Pill, were made available to all women regardless of marital status.

If the changes in practices and attitudes to sex were driven largely by the young and advances in contraception, the more liberal environment it engendered had a transformative effect on parents too. By then divorce was no longer prohibitively difficult or shameful and attitudes to unmarried couples living together were more relaxed. Demand in the labour market afforded working women a measure of financial independence and the confidence to make decisions for themselves. Though it was less a revolution and more a gradual process over a couple of decades, Joy thinks the start of these developments probably influenced her actions.

> Yes, I suppose in the sixties we were aware that the world was changing a little, but women certainly had more opportunities. It was the time of the Pill, wasn't it, when women began to believe that they could have a family and do something else as well. And I suppose that was still working its way through to us, that there was going to be more freedom in the world, that women weren't going to be as tied to marriage as they'd always been. That may have got through to me subconsciously somehow.

By her early forties, Diana Athill was already an independent woman with a satisfying job in publishing and a live-in Jamaican lover. Was she aware that she was breaking several sexual taboos?

> I didn't care a fuck about that. I knew there were people who wouldn't approve, but in the world I lived in, the world of writers and intelligent people, I never had a hint of disapproval . . . By the time I met Barry I wasn't really thinking whether people were black or white. We published a lot of black writers and I met many African and West Indian people, so I really had stopped by then thinking about black or white, so it hadn't occurred to me that Barry was black. He'd been to Cambridge, but he'd had a fair amount of prejudice since he'd been in England. Apart from the sex, which was very good and very immediate, we talked about writers and writing. We were very much on the same wavelength. And, I must admit, he washed his own shirts and did half the cooking, so that I was having all the plums and none of the pudding! I wasn't going to take on the duties of a wife. I'd hit on a way of life that suited me, a happy time all during my forties and fifties.
>
> In all this time I suppose I was benefitting by what people called the sexual revolution, but I never thought about it in those terms, I never thought, Aren't I lucky to be living now and not earlier? I

was just doing what I wanted to do and I think most people were. It just happened, it wasn't consciously achieved.

Diana was fortunate to move in liberal circles. For everyone else times were changing more slowly. Now pregnancy could be reliably avoided, sex was potentially free of fear. Even so, it would be the final decades of the century before 'shotgun weddings' and the indelible social stigma of unmarried motherhood and illegitimacy were finally eradicated. Nevertheless, from the 1960s onwards the generation who grew up in more socially constrained times were having to come to terms with their children adopting relationships, attitudes and values very different from their own.

Alf Garnett's character in the popular sitcom *Till Death Us Do Part*, which ran in various forms throughout this period, personified the reactionary white working-class parent, the uncomprehending, out-of-touch older generation. Though they may have been perplexed at times at the conduct of modern relationships and disapproving of aspects of the new laxity, Garnett's real-life contemporaries didn't share his extreme views. If anything, they were inclined to envy the young the freedoms they never had and enjoy for themselves the liberating effect of prosperity, opening the way for new ideas, tastes, experiences and relationships.

◆

A striking feature of the period is the way so many of this generation engaged wholeheartedly in different forms of public service, as if the war had given them a taste – perhaps a compulsion – for contributing to the greater good. 'Doing your bit' had become not just a wartime expediency but a way of life.

Whether as a salaried part of the expanding welfare state or in a voluntary capacity – sometimes both – many chose to dedicate their time to the service of others. As one former RAF serviceman who went on to spend his life in social work wrote: 'Maybe we were still soldiers of a sort, only in civilian clothes. Not seeking victory, but seeking to heal.' Enlightened self-interest rather than pure altruism may have been at work here: childhood and war experience had taught them that they were part of a wider community and mutual aid meant survival. Whatever the motivation, the predisposition to serve was probably more ingrained in this generation than in any other before or since.

D-Day veteran Frank Rosier spent much of his post-war life working for others. After leaving the army, he joined his trade union and became a regional organiser, then he spent eight years as a volunteer with the Citizens Advice Bureau and 'a job I was always proud of', sitting on National Insurance Tribunals, making legally binding decisions that would fundamentally affect individual lives. He went on to become secretary of his regional branch of the Normandy Veterans Association.

After his POW experience Fergus Anckorn was content with a 'tuppenny-ha'penny job as a clerk in an office for £8, £9 a week', paying for his mortgage by performing magic shows in the evening. Unfit for military service, he decided to become a special constable in the early 1950s at the time of the Korean War.

> I said to my wife, 'Well, if this war is happening I'd better do something to help out, but I can't go in the army again, so I'll join the special constables.' . . . I knew that we were helping people because we were out doing traffic duty during the day and patrolling at night-time, 'shaking doorknobs' we called it, we were always visible, we'd help tourists and if there was a fight in the dance hall at night we'd be in there settling that, so I knew that we were always needed.

He had a particular approach to the job and his pragmatic attitude to death, learned in the camps, was put to positive use.

> A lot of young fellows, they joined the specials and they think they're tough, you know, and I used to say to them, 'Don't go out and say, "Who can I arrest tonight?" Go out and say, "Who can I help tonight?"' I remember one particular night we got a message that a lady down the road in Westerham, her husband had gone

to a football match in London and had a heart attack. I had to find her and get her up to London to see him. The Green Line bus had just come – that was the last one to London that night. I stopped it and held it there while I went to get this woman. She was in the bath. I called out to her, 'Get yourself dressed, your husband's not well and you have to go to him.' She came out and I said to her, 'Now look, your husband's had a heart attack. You can get on this bus now and you've got an hour. On that trip, think: What am I going to do if they say he's dead when I get there? You must get ready for anything.' The husband made it, and several days later she came and said, 'You couldn't have done better than you did to get me ready for that,' so that was the sort of feeling you got, you can be of help to people. I enjoyed the police. If I'd known how good it was, I would have joined as soon as I came home.

Fergus is typically modest about his achievement over 28 years as a special.

After seven years they said, 'You're a sergeant now,' and after about four more years they said, 'You're an inspector,' and the next thing was I'd jumped chief inspector to deputy commandant and in no time at all I was divisional commander, just like that!

Those who'd loved being in the Scouts and Guides as children wanted to help new generations of children enjoy it too. Former Scout George Montague was looking to make his own contribution with the organisation he'd benefitted from as a boy. 'I thoroughly enjoyed the Scouts and I know what it did for me. It made me a good citizen.' After putting on a Gang Show for children at the local hospital, he started up a Scout troop for boys with physical disabilities and those suffering from conditions like Still's disease, a form of juvenile arthritis, that were considered 'incurable' at the time. With the introduction of steroids through the 1960s these conditions could be treated and as a result the troop gradually dwindled.

I ran the troop for 10, 15 years. I had 30 in each ward, Cubs and Scouts. I used to tell people, 'Oh, they've discovered cortisone, wonderful, we don't get so many kids, and all my kids are getting better and not staying in hospital so long.' It was a funny thing to say but I said, 'With any luck, my Scout troop will have to close.' Which it did.

But George's work had only just begun. On the strength of his hospital work he was made an assistant county Scout commissioner with special responsibility for disability.

So I did that with all my usual zest and vigour and shooting my mouth off, and said, 'We've got to do something about it.' I found these boys with muscular dystrophy. Nothing wrong with the boy's brain, the same as every other boy, but the body was useless. Why can't he be in the Scouts? So we got them into the Scouts. But when it came to camp, that's full of activity, games and tracking and all sorts of things, which is too much for a boy in a wheelchair.

So he started camps specially designed for disabled Scouts.

Oh my God, you need tents, you need nurses, you need medications, you need expert helpers, how can I do that? But we did. The first camp was an experiment and we grew from there. Each year we ran a camp in each county and it was wonderful, wonderful. Each boy had a buddy and that boy was trained to dress, undress, put to bed, give him his medications, get him out on parade. We did parade just the same, kit inspection, tying knots, everything the same as possible. One boy was [a victim of] thalidomide and he was watching another lad peel potatoes. I said, 'Come on, he can do an awful lot with his feet, why can't he do it?' And he did!

If George's primary motivation was enabling every boy to benefit from Scouting as he'd done, it also reminded him that he'd been fortunate with his own family.

I used to think to myself, you know, I've got three wonderful kids, nothing wrong with them, they're perfectly healthy. They don't need me. My wife used to say to me, 'You're spending more time with these boys than with your own kids.' 'Yes, but they're fit and healthy. These kids need me more than my kids do.'

While George was making Scouting more accessible for disabled boys, Brian Rix was campaigning on the national stage on behalf of Mencap for a better deal for learning-disabled children and their parents. It was an uphill task in the early days.

I went to see Enoch Powell who was then the Minister of Health. It was a simple request: that if a child was born with a learning disability in the NHS, the parents would be asked if they would like to talk to parents who were coping with the [same] situation. He turned me down flat. He said it wasn't necessary.

He had better luck with Margaret Thatcher when she was Education Secretary in 1970. The 1944 Education Act, so beneficial in other respects, had branded children with learning disabilities 'ineducable', effectively barring them from all state schools. The best on offer was an 'occupation centre' perhaps miles from home.

We lobbied the Conservatives and Labour and Margaret Thatcher introduced a bill which gave education to learning-disabled children for the first time and it came into force in 1971. So that was a major step forward. Educating the public, of course, was vitally important. The BBC in 1976 piloted a programme which I was presenting called Let's Go! three times a week and these were teaching programmes for disabled people – children and adults. And people with learning disabilities actually took part in them, which was fantastic, a huge step forward. It made a difference at the time. People got used to seeing [learning-disabled] people for the first time on the box and that was huge publicity. It was a fantastic thing for the Beeb to do.

After giving up his very successful theatrical career for full-time campaigning, in 1980 Brian became secretary-general of Mencap and in 1988 its chairman, continuing the struggle to fight discrimination and bring learning-disabled people back into the community.

> What I had been as an actor stood me in the greatest possible stead as boss of Mencap. Because of who I'd been I could invite politicians round to lunch. They all came. I think the really big thing was our Homeless Foundation which started in my time, which led then to housing for people coming out of long-stay hospitals. Our own daughter moved into a Mencap house with three other people and they had a marvellous life. They went out all the time, they went to football matches and the pub, which anyone can do. The achievement was that she was living in the community. She was seen by other people and not pushed away or giggled at or bullied. She was a person, she was our daughter. We've come a long way from 'put her away, forget her and start again'. That's never said any more.

Shelley, written off at birth, lived a fulfilled life until she died in 2005 at the age of 53. It is largely through the efforts of the determined parents of this generation that the unsympathetic treatment of sick and disabled children in hospitals and homes, inherited without thought from a harsher period, was revolutionised by the 1980s.

Jobs in the public services and caring professions were attractive, particularly to single women like Enid Wenban and Joan Wilson, who went into social work at a time of rapid expansion of welfare services and made satisfying and successful life-long careers. Education too could be a personally rewarding career choice. Bob Frost made his teaching career in primary schools where the 1967 Plowden Report had proposed a radical new child-centred approach to teaching methods and the curriculum. As the new young head of a Kent primary school, Bob benefitted from the 1960s school-building boom and set about making his mark.

My predecessor ran a very nice school. But she had her classes all arranged in a row, so I gradually changed that to [groups of] individual seats, six here, six here, and children of like ability, for example at maths, would sit there and those who weren't quite so able would sit there, so they could work at their own pace. Not everybody in the class has got to do the same darned thing, but for goodness' sake, do the best you can. And the school ran on those lines. I was trying to get from them the best they were capable of doing.

A late entrant to teaching, Joy Lofthouse started in a residential school for 'delicate' children and, like her second husband Charles, went on to spend the rest of her career in education.

Others chose to be active in local politics as their contribution to public life. Bill Graves was already well versed in union politics when he was elected as a Labour councillor in Bristol. At the other end of the political spectrum, Gladys Parry was about to launch into an unfamiliar new role in Manchester.

I was very involved in politics and being a true Conservative I couldn't see how some of these people that were putting up for government that had no experience, didn't even have a job some of them, could run a country. So of course I became a very ardent supporter. I got called in to the office of the local agent and he said, 'We've a mind to put your name forward as a magistrate.' So I said, 'Oh, aye?' I thought, What the hell's a magistrate? I'd heard of JPs [Justices of the Peace] but I didn't know what they did. My name was put forward; I thought, Go along with it. The first time I went, there was a guy in charge and I went up to him and I said, 'I've made a terrible mistake, I don't know a thing about being a magistrate, I don't know a thing about the law.' And he just patted me on the head and said, 'Let's hope you keep it like that.' And that's how I became a magistrate!

Gladys soon found her confidence, took advice and learned fast. Before long she was elected Chairman of the Bench.

I loved it. I thought to myself, Here I am from Hulme, if only my father was here today, he would really love this, he'd be proud of me. And here I am, and there were some toffee-nosed beggars on the bench, real snooties, and I could hold my own with them. And I loved that, because I was in charge! So I thought, right, so then I stuck that for 24 years. It was a lovely job and you meet heartbreaking people, heartbreaking stories, very sad cases but funny ones too. Like the man in the fines court. He came in. 'Are you paying your fine?' 'No, I'm not paying my fine.' 'Jail forthwith,' I said, and they'd grab him and he's kicking and shouting and getting dragged through the door, because you know, once they do that, they pay. So he paid. And he walked out and he looked at me and he said, 'You lot, you're all bent!' If I'd have thought at the time I would've grabbed him back but I was that shook that he'd done this, I couldn't help but laugh. Here's me putting him behind bars and he's calling me bent! It was all part of life, I enjoyed seeing it. I was very proud of the fact that, coming from Hulme, from a place where there wasn't much money, that I'd become a magistrate. I was more than proud, more than proud.

Others were making their contribution in different ways. Dr Bill Frankland was never a household name, but his invention of the pollen count scale and his research into common allergies have helped millions of people over the nearly 70 years he has practised in this area.

I started work by chance in the allergy department at St Mary's and I've been an allergist ever since. I have some hay fever myself, I've had it for 90 years, but just now I think I've finally grown out of it. I started the pollen count in 1951 and now you see it every day, it goes in the daily papers. I did the first double-blind controlled trial in allergic disease. I've produced over a hundred articles and written books and chapters of books, so I'm still very interested in anything medicine, particularly with the word allergy attached to it . . .

I always considered myself lucky [in the war] because I was

a doctor and therefore I hadn't got a rifle or a pistol or anything like that. My job wasn't to kill people but to help them get well. So this to me was a great privilege. I had the choice, thank goodness, of being a doctor and helping my fellow human beings.

◆

The 1939–45 war now seemed a distant memory. The Campaign for Nuclear Disarmament and the anti-war movement prompted by the long attrition in Vietnam created an atmosphere in which it seemed inappropriate to reminisce about Blitz spirit or pass on war stories of triumph and loss to younger generations. In any case, the war generation wanted to forget and the young didn't want to know. They were out on peace marches or wrapped up in their own all-absorbing pop culture, their parents often bemused onlookers.

Instead, for the generation who grew up in its shadow, there was new interest in the everyday experience of the First World War, sparked by the monumental BBC series *The Great War* in 1964. Marking the fiftieth anniversary of the outbreak of the war, for the first time this made striking use of veterans' testimony to bring home the reality of trench warfare. A more modest but ultimately more influential radio programme, *The Long, Long Trail*, broadcast on the BBC Home Service in 1961 was produced by Charles Chilton.

Charles had made his name in music programmes and was by now better known for his popular science fiction drama, *Journey into Space*. *The Long, Long Trail* was his passion project. While on holiday in France with his family he'd visited the Commonwealth war cemetery at Arras to look for the grave of the soldier father he never knew.

We were walking up and down, looking for my father's grave, and we couldn't find it. There was a man mowing the lawn and he turned out to be an ex-British soldier employed to look after the graves and he said, 'Have you looked on the wall on the monument? Inscribed there are the names of 35,000 soldiers who fought and died in the Battle of Arras and whose bodies were never found.' So I thought, 35,000 people never found! What did this mean?

For the first time Charles saw the scale of the sacrifice made by the young men of his father's generation, but he realised too how little he knew about the war. He started researching soldiers' songs and how these reflected their bloody experience with stoic black humour. *The Long, Long Trail* was the result. It caught the attention of theatre producer Joan Littlewood and Charles went on to work with her radical Theatre Workshop to create *Oh! What a Lovely War* in 1963, an innovative and highly stylised vision of the war that Richard Attenborough made into a landmark film in 1969. Together, they had the effect of reflecting and reinforcing the strong anti-war mood of a period dominated by the new 'peace generation'.

The stage production and film made a huge impact and, together with a renewed interest in First World War poetry, helped seed the popular idea of 1914–18 as a futile waste of human life – a simplistic view tempered over the years with time and education.

Despite the anti-war sentiment expressed by the post-war generation, this is not the way 1939–45 was ever perceived, or portrayed. Even so, there were aspects of Britain's war strategy that remained controversial for decades afterwards, especially among the young. For those who'd made and witnessed great sacrifice, for example in Bomber Command, it was bewildering and hurtful to have their experience criticised or devalued by a generation that had never known conflict or real hardship.

Russell Margerison, already distressed by the way Bomber Command and its efforts had been officially downplayed after the war, found he had to defend himself and British area bombing policy to post-war generations.

Churchill used to go round the 'dromes encouraging us to 'give 'em hell'. 'Give them one for me' and all this business. And it was all dropped like a hot potato at the end of the war. And when you think we lost, what was it, 56,000 killed? That's hurtful. That really is hurtful and I think it's extremely unfair . . . People didn't want to know about the damage we'd done, they didn't seem interested in the least as to what we'd done for the war effort. You didn't talk about it because it seemed like it was a taboo subject. Obscene. Particularly teenagers. 'You shouldn't have done it.' I've had that said to me. 'You should never have done all this damage to Germany. There must have been other ways.' I gave a talk in the local library and there was a student there got up and said, 'Don't you think what you were doing was obscene?' And I said to him, 'Well, what would you have done?' They're bombing us left, right and centre. Sheffield, Manchester, Liverpool, London, Coventry. The whole works, and yet they complain about us doing it to them. I can't come to terms with that. I can't understand that. What are we supposed to do? Sit at home and do nothing? Course you can't. You've got to retaliate. They don't see it. To them it's obscene. So yes, the students when they take that line, they annoy me. It's not fair and it's not on. I'd like to know what they would have done.

The process of education about – and reconciliation to – the Second World War started slowly. Representations of the war still tended to be heroic and two-dimensional, but alongside the dramatised heroics of *The Great Escape* and TV series *Colditz*, the gentle parody of a shambolic Home Guard platoon in Jimmy Perry and David Croft's *Dad's Army* allowed a family audience to look back to the war with laughter and affection. Jimmy's pilot script turned into a series so popular it ran for almost a decade until 1977.

What made me start *Dad's Army*? Simple. I wanted work . . . I thought, I'll write about the Home Guard. I dug out two training books from the Imperial War Museum library. Now what shall we do? We'll set it in a seaside town. I wasn't happy with the characters I thought up, they were wrong. They were sort of caricatures. Now, caricatures I have no time for. The first rule of comedy: you must have reality. I wanted to do the truth.

So he went back to the real characters he knew from his time as a teenager in the Home Guard, the bluff captain and the old-soldier sergeant. Its comic target was broader than just the war: part of its appeal lay in the way it satirised the class conflicts that were such a feature of the pre-war and early war years but were by then passing into folk memory.

> Class was always there. And anybody born in 1923, as I was, knew about it. The schooling, the factories, the domestic servants, the rules – invisible but nevertheless carried out. And we got on to that with a vengeance because [the cast] were so up for it.

Dad's Army gave post-war generations a benign view of the war as a counterweight to the comic-book heroics on the screen. In the absence of anything yet on school syllabuses, they were the only perspectives on offer. It wasn't until Thames Television's landmark series for ITV, *The World at War*, in 1973–74 and the attentions of the television historians that followed that the real task of public education began. The BBC was to play a major part in this endeavour, as it had done with *The Great War*.

The revelation of long-kept war secrets also helped public under-standing of the past and allowed the debt owed to the war gener-ation to be acknowledged at last with gratitude and pride. When a book about the Bletchley Park wartime code-breaking activities appeared in 1974, former Bombe-operator Jean Valentine was initially shocked.

> I was appalled, but it did mean that we could speak about what we did. It was a very strange feeling to be able to talk about it at last. In a way you felt a bit guilty because you said you wouldn't, but then the doors were open, you were able to do it. I certainly felt a little bit uncomfortable to start with. You see, having signed the Official Secrets Act, you feel bound by that. You made a promise, so when you broke your word, you felt uncomfortable. I did say to my husband, 'Oh, by the way, I actually worked there.' And he said, 'Oh, did you? I wondered where you were.' And it

just sort of passed off. He never really took an awful lot of interest. But then I think the more information that leaked out, the more he and other people became interested.

———◆———

The generation now in middle age bore witness to changes that were sweeping away much of what was familiar from their youth. The British Empire was history; the crowded nineteenth-century neighbourhoods replaced by high-rise blocks; the countryside colonised by new towns and overspill estates where the neighbourliness that had once sustained women like Gladys Parry was hard to come by. Much of the change was necessary and welcome, some the source of regret. Old ways, old landmarks, old friends started to disappear.

Dorothy Bohm, the teenage refugee who embraced Britain and London as her adopted home, always felt compelled to record changing times and preserve in her photographs what was about to be lost. She had made a name for herself with her candid portraits of ordinary people and places at particular points in time and her work was now regularly exhibited at venues such as the prestigious Institute of Contemporary Arts. When the Covent Garden market was due to vacate its eighteenth-century buildings in 1974, she was commissioned to photograph its last days and characters for a BBC documentary.

Covent Garden seemed to us so much part of all of our lives and it seemed terribly sad that it should go. I photographed it even before I knew that it was going to move and then of course the BBC asked me to photograph it at a time when it was disappearing. It belonged to the people, which was important, and I had great sympathy for the people who worked there.

With photography I am trying keep alive memories, things that happened to me and things that were happening around me. Because when I try to remember what I have lost and sometimes your memory is such that some of the very sad things I don't want to remember, so photography was a wonderful way for me of keeping things alive and continuous. The sort of photography I've done, I think is not only good pictures, which I hope, but it is also history because when I photographed London and Covent Garden, it has changed so enormously . . . it's really documenting a change and keeping it.

London, which she knew in the Blitz, is especially close to her heart.

London has changed unbelievably. I'm not surprised that there are so many tourists. It's a fascinating city and it's a good city . . . Everything was interesting in sixties London. I remember, for example, we went through a period when the young men would wear fancy uniforms, and I photographed quite a lot in the East End. I enjoyed that on a Sunday. So it was a labour of love. It never made money for me and it doesn't matter.

———————◆———————

By the end of the 1980s many of the war generation were well into retirement. Some struggled, especially women who'd never built sufficient National Insurance 'stamps' to qualify for a full state pension and had no other. At the other extreme, those who'd spent their working lives in industry or the public services and had guaranteed occupational pensions as well as their state pension enjoyed a level of financial security in old age their parents could only have dreamed of.

But the new affluence had been achieved at the cost of community spirit and national unity, the post-war consensus in favour of nationalisation, Keynesian economics and the welfare state, apparently broken under the weight of individual aspiration. Margaret Thatcher's firm leadership and unequivocal patriotism had many admirers among the war generation, but committed socialists like Bill Graves were distressed to see the gradual dismantling of their hard-won New Jerusalem.

The dreams that I had in 1945 have been shattered. The state that I helped to build was not maintained. It's gone, that welfare state, even the National Health Service is being privatised and it's being done by stealth. I know it. I can see it. I want to scream about it but I'm screaming in the corner by myself because nobody wants to know.

Divorce, to the regret of many in the older generation, became commonplace. With the stigma of illegitimacy finally vanquished in 1987 with a change in the law, the proportion of unmarried parents steadily rose to approaching 40 per cent by the end of the century. Families fractured and re-formed in unfamiliar configurations, yet those now retired and with time on their hands could take renewed pride in their children's achievements and discover new energy in the company of their grandchildren and great-grandchildren.

There were surprises in store for some. After two grown-up children, Kit Sollitt in Sheffield had an unplanned late baby at 48. She'd just gone to the post office to collect her first Child Allowance for month-old Diane and do some shopping.

Caught the bus. Came home. Unpacked all the food. Made a cuppa. Sat on the front steps drinking this tea and I'm looking at my washing. I'm thinking, Oh, that's lovely and white. And I realised they were nappies. And I thought, Oh my God, I've left the kid and she's been outside the post office for near an hour! I set off running, I had no coat on. I must have licked Seb Coe down that road. And she was still outside in her pram. Postmaster came to door and he says, 'We kept wondering whose kid it were.' I'd gone so long without a kid I'd forgotten I'd got one!

Kit was still collecting Child Allowance for Diane when she started her old-age pension.

Late in life too there were opportunities for some people to reconnect with family members estranged through war or circumstance. Connie Hoe had lost her English mother at eight and barely remembered her Chinese father, who had returned to Hong

Kong at about the same time for a family bereavement never to
return: 'Hong Kong in those days was another world. You couldn't
get there, and he was non-existent to me as a child.' Years later
and now a mother herself, Connie needed to rediscover her
Chinese roots. Though her father had since died, a visit to Hong
Kong with husband Leslie and daughter Christine enabled her to
meet close family members for the first time.

> I was so pleased, I met an auntie and uncle and of course all their
> families as well. It made me happier to know that I had blood
> relatives and I wasn't just alone.

Dorothy Bohm had last seen her parents on a station platform
in East Prussia in June 1939. She learned through the Red Cross
much later that her father had been deported to a Siberian work
camp. Eventually he was able to return to Soviet Europe, to her
mother and the sister she'd never met. With a slight thawing of
the cold war, Dorothy was allowed to visit them.

> I got a visa and the Foreign Office called me and said, 'But if you
> go there, we can't be responsible for you.' Anyway we did it and
> we met my parents . . . It was a tremendous heartbreak. I was
> particularly close to my father; if I'm anything worthwhile it was
> due to him. I wanted to hear more about life there [in Siberia].
> My mother told me that when he spoke to me he was all right,
> but at night he started to scream, and she told me not to try and
> make him talk about it. But if you met him, he seemed absolutely
> normal. The first time I saw them, they had already somewhat
> recovered. What I have learned is that people . . . it doesn't matter
> what they experience in their lives, they remain, because he was
> just the same as I knew him as a youngster, and so was my mother.
> They started recovering, it was fantastic.

There was heartbreak of a different kind for those who experienced the unnatural loss of a child in adult life. An early-morning
transatlantic call in 1996 brought Eileen Younghusband the

shocking news of her much-loved son's sudden and premature death.

> One day he was there and then he was gone. My only son. I've had to face so many different things that I'm not able to cry. I can't cry. And so I suppose you learn to face something. You can't do anything about it, so you have to overcome it, and you do that by taking your mind off in another direction.

The direction she chose was study. After two years at Cardiff University followed by an Open University course, she was finally awarded a degree in Spanish – and honoured for being the top OU student in Wales – at the age of 88, achievements of which she is justifiably proud.

> This has helped me by concentrating my mind on doing other things. I'm still sad, but not broken down by unhappiness. The only way to do it is to face it and to try and do something to compensate.

Fred Glover found it more difficult to displace his grief. The emotional reticence instilled in childhood prevented him from giving his wife Rita the support she needed at the worst time of their lives.

> We lost our youngest boy in a car crash . . . I seemed to become isolated, worrying about my own grief and not hers . . . Strange, I'd go off in the car and weep. Weep. And yet I couldn't express emotion in front of my dear wife, who I loved very much. I would have moved heaven and earth to protect her . . . There's no doubt about it, I did certain things that were quite wrong. I couldn't share that emotional side with my wife.

For Fred, this is a 'character defect' and a source of lasting regret.

Over these years of unprecedented change, there remained one indestructible symbol of continuity and stability. Unchanging, unknowable, dedicated to duty, Queen Elizabeth II remained steadfast, the consummate public servant. Margaret Rhodes recalls the lively young girl she spent holidays with at Birkhall, but that doesn't diminish her respect for the figure at the centre of public life in Britain for more than six decades.

> I don't think anybody ever appreciates what becoming the Queen really entails. It means giving up any pretence at doing what you may want to do, to doing what you have to do. Personal choice almost goes out of the window, except during the much-loved holiday times at Balmoral or Sandringham, when still the red boxes arrive and they have to be read every day. But that speech she made in South Africa on her twenty-first birthday encapsulated her feelings about it: that she was going to give her life to the country and, by golly, for 60 years she's done it all.

By 1990 Margaret had been widowed for nearly ten years and was living in a grace-and-favour house on the Windsor estate. At an age when her contemporaries were settling into retirement, she found a new role with her dear aunt, Queen Elizabeth the Queen Mother, by now in her ninety-first year and still undertaking public engagements.

> I was offered the job of lady-in-waiting to Queen Elizabeth, which I happily accepted. It was a wonderful idea because there's a danger when one's recently widowed, of just sinking into a sort of cabbage-like existence and not meeting people, so it made one dress oneself properly and have one's hair done to try and look good. I loved my years working for her. She was brilliant because she could go to the dullest event and somehow make it fun. Nothing pleases any of them more than when things go wrong. I mean, if there can be a disaster, you know, it's bliss, you can make good stories out of it. I loved her so much. She was just

like another parent to me really, and she once paid me the huge compliment of saying that I was like her third daughter, which I've always treasured.

The Hon. Margaret Rhodes, LVO carried on enjoying her role as a woman of the bedchamber until 2002 when the Queen Mother died at the age of 101. Margaret was at her aunt's bedside, with other close family members, at her passing.

———◆———

There were many accommodations and adjustments to be made in old age. Losing life partners, family and old friends was a painful and unavoidable late rite of passage. When Connie Hoe was interviewed she had only recently lost her husband Leslie. He'd had Parkinson's disease for the last 13 years of his life and she'd nursed him through all but the final months, when he was finally persuaded to go into a nursing home.

One day on my visit to him I was holding his hand, and I thought he fell asleep. He did fall asleep, but it was for ever. But I was pleased I was there, and he had a peaceful death.

Was it a happy marriage? She laughs: 'A very happy marriage. Well, 73 years, it had to be, didn't it?'

Bob Frost too cared for his wife Daphne in her last dreadful illness but despite everything, like so many bereaved partners left behind, he feels 'damned lucky' for the marriage he had, and some regret that he didn't show his appreciation more.

Fifty years being married to a woman who loved you to pieces, can't be much wrong with that, can there? We loved each other. They say you don't know what you've got till you've lost it. I believe in that now. She died a horrible death. Motor neurone. Totally paralysed but with an active brain. She couldn't do a thing. She couldn't eat, couldn't do anything other than bang keys on a typewriter. She'd been a secretary and knew the keyboard. And her last words were 'It's agony'.

Fred Glover's wife Rita had a distressing last year with throat cancer. In her final days she came home and Fred slept on a camp bed beside her. They'd been married for 62 years.

Worth her weight in gold. Always remember that. If you don't have memories, you really don't have anything. Memories that really matter. They matter to me. They matter to me.

At the turn of the new millennium, as our generation approached grand old age, many were adjusting to the last major changes of their lives. Reconciled to the past and counting their blessings, they felt ready at last to share with those too young to remember stories from a different century. We were ready to listen.

13

Looking Back, Looking Forward

Life is very good to me. I don't fear death but I want to go on living and doing all the things I'm doing now. I'm so busy, the day isn't long enough.

Dr Bill Frankland, 102

At the time of his interview for this book, in his 103rd year, Bill Frankland had just returned from a conference in Copenhagen, he was awaiting publication of his most recent scientific paper on a rare allergy and was looking forward to a trip to Singapore to attend the annual lecture in his name. From there he thought he might go on to Japan. He still sees patients – with another doctor present – and appears as an expert witness in court cases.

I want to continue working and researching because at present there's so much advance being made . . . DNA and genomes and people looking at cells and enzymes and genes, it's all very complicated. I can't keep up to date with it, but I do the best I can. The whole subject, it's rather like cancer research, it's bounding forward, advancing in so many ways. This to me is all fascinating . . . Why should I retire and what would I do if I retired?

Bill survived infantile TB, three years in a Japanese prisoner-of-war camp and self-induced anaphylactic shock in the cause of scientific research, but he doesn't have a prescription for his longevity.

Why have I lived so long? People often ask me this, especially
when I was 100. I say the main reason is luck. I've been near death
so many times but I've always escaped, so it's luck. But even so,
I have obeyed some of the simple rules . . . the sort of advice I
give to patients I feel I must do myself.

Few at anything like his age can match Bill's prodigious output
or his self-discipline, but it's clear from so much of their testimony
that having a purpose – and a passion to pursue it for as long as
possible – keeps even the most elderly of folk going.

John Harrison, born in 1914, survivor of the flu pandemic and
the mining of HMS *Belfast* in 1939, never lost his love of the water
and has belonged to swimming clubs for much of his life.

There's no rivalry in swimming. There's no jealousy in swimming.
It's the fact that if he can go faster than I can, how does he do it?
And that's why the clubs are so friendly.

But that doesn't mean he isn't still competitive. He joined the
navy swimming team at 78 and at 87 was shamed into learning
the butterfly by a 93-year-old woman. In 2014 he broke the world
swimming record in his class, an admittedly select group of
100–104-year-olds.

Well, I didn't realise what I'd done. All right, I did my best. I always
do. Why not? And when they told me what I'd done, they came
and hugged me. Most embarrassed, because of all the adulation.
I'd only done my swimming, that's all I'd done. I'd swum the best
I could, why not? That's what you're supposed to do in life, do
the best you can. And if you're not as good as the other person,
it doesn't matter. You tried. That's the principle.

It's a principle that has served this generation well.

Despite replacement knees and his 93 years, running for charity
keeps Jim Purcell going. 'Jarra Jim' ran his twenty-seventh Great
North Run in 2013 and took part in Sport Relief in 2014. He carried

the Commonwealth Games torch in 2002 and was immensely proud to be chosen as an Olympic torch-bearer in 2012.

> The reception was exceptional, not because of me, because of the torch. It was fantastic . . . all those people, men and women, young people what carried the torch. It was fantastic just being there, in their company.

So Jarra Jim is now a Tyneside celebrity.

> It doesn't matter when I go out. I can guarantee if I walk to Tesco's there's always ten people at least [say], 'Hiya, Jim!' Now that is satisfaction. Satisfaction that nobody's forgotten me. But on the other hand it's humbling to think that people still think good of me . . . I'm just Jim Purcell, old-age pensioner, live on Falmouth Drive. And of course when I'm out people do stop me in the street and talk to me. And once I get talking, I'm away. Once that happens, I'm out and should be back in five minutes. It's nearly an hour and a half before I get home!

Jim took up running as 'a cure for loneliness' after his wife Betty died at 54. He still runs with her wedding ring round his neck so that he feels she's with him, willing him on. He misses his 'Queen' still, but he's upbeat and extraordinarily fit for his age.

> Every morning I strip off, look at myself in the mirror – that's my first laugh of the day – step into that cold salt bath and slip down till I'm blinking right submerged underneath all the water, jump out, dry myself off, do a few exercises, come downstairs and have my breakfast. Tuesday and Thursdays I get on my rowing machine. I have it marked for three minutes. Every single day, seven days a week, I'm walking, maybe two mile, maybe more . . . Two weeks ago I passed every blood test, my blood pressure is great, my cholesterol is only 3.1, so according to my medical I'm only 26!

Keeping up old interests and finding new ones is as important for health and happiness in old age as keeping fit. Jean Valentine still does the cryptic crosswords that got her the job with the Bombes, though she prefers sudoku these days. After Bletchley Park opened to the public in 1993 Jean returned as a volunteer guide and stayed for 15 years, sharing her secrets with younger generations and learning much more about what went on beyond Hut 11. Earl Cameron, immensely proud to be appointed CBE in 2009, and sustained by his Baha'i faith, never really retired from acting. At the age of 92 he appeared in a cameo role painting Helen Mirren's portrait in the 2006 film *The Queen* and again at 96 in the 2010 sci-fi blockbuster *Inception*. Ron Jones worked his allotment until he was 94 and now, at 97, keeps busy supporting his local football club, Newport County.

> I was seven years old when my father put me on the little saddle on his bike and took me down to Somerton Park . . . and I've been a supporter ever since. They had me on their website the other day – 90 years a supporter of Newport County. They've made me vice-president down there. I've even got my own parking spot and everything.

At 97, Vera Lynn takes it easier these days and has time to reflect on her unique 80-year career.

> There was no way I couldn't have enjoyed it. Meeting people all the time and singing the songs they wanted me to sing and getting their reaction. It was quite an experience for a little girl from East Ham, suddenly doing important things, meeting important people. Not quite what I'd imagined I'd be doing as a child!

The old habit of public service dies hard and many are still volunteers, helping those often much younger than themselves. At 90, Bill Graves is still a fervent advocate of the NHS and a member of his local GP surgery's patient participation group.

We help support our doctors and the nurses in the practice . . . I go to the committee meetings, I give them any advice or knowledge that I've got. The lady who's our secretary, she's an ex-headmistress. Ain't my politics by a long way and she frowns at me a lot of the time, but she's smashing.

Judging by the number of times the phone rang during his interview, Baron Rix of Whitehall, CBE is still a busy man. An active crossbench peer, he's still campaigning on behalf of Mencap and the many other causes he works for.

I'm a happy person. I'm an optimistic person. The fact that I'm talking to you, aged 90, and I know that I'm going back to the House of Lords a week on Monday . . . straight back to work. In fact, I'm sure one of the phone messages is from our parliamentary department telling me what I've got to do! So I'm a happy person, yes.

After a career editing other people's work for the publisher André Deutsch, Diana Athill resumed her own writing, begun in the 1960s but then abandoned. She'd published *Instead of a Letter* in 1963, about her love affair with Tony during the war and his terrible betrayal. This was 'the most extraordinary therapeutic thing . . . like starting a new life', but it had the effect of making her believe she could only write in response to some traumatic event. Much later she was persuaded otherwise and, in her eighties and finally retired (she worked for Deutsch until she was 73), she started writing short memoirs about different periods of her life.

I didn't think I could, but I did. I was rather good at it and it all suddenly became enormous fun. It was such fun because it was so unexpected. I mean, there I was at 80, and having thought 'that's that', suddenly there's this new thing blooming all around me and I thoroughly enjoyed that.

Reflecting on her life over more than eight decades brought into focus how much society has changed, especially for women of her generation.

> I suddenly thought when I started, Goodness, how things have changed. How a little while ago if you were old you almost went into a uniform, you wore a certain kind of clothes and you looked in a certain kind of way and behaved in a certain kind of way and that will all be swept away, largely I think because make-up had improved so greatly that you could make up your face reasonably well without looking like a vampire bat. I remember after the war, *Vogue* started a feature called 'Mrs Exeter', which was a late-middle-aged lady wearing 'suitable' clothes, but nice clothes and quite soon 'Mrs Exeter' became unnecessary because everybody was wearing just what they wanted to wear, and that was an enormous improvement from the point of view of getting old. I mean, my grandmother certainly wore black dresses from the moment her husband died for the rest of her days . . . It was still quite common that you sort of deliberately made yourself unattractive once you'd decided you were old, and it wasn't really necessary to do that. So that was a great release.

Diana herself is impressively stylish at 97. She follows her own fashion with bold, colourful clothes, and jewellery and careful make-up that compliment her English complexion.

> I still spend too much money on clothes even now. I'm the world's leading mail-order person! I do think it's quite important to feel as good as you can. It is very, very important to remember that making yourself feel good has to be carefully watched, because you mustn't go on doing exactly what you did when you were young . . . You have to remember that you are old and you mustn't look ridiculous, you mustn't be mutton dressed as lamb. But you can be mutton dressed as quite a shapely sheep!

Her nineties have been times of change. Barry became ill and she looked after him until she was finding it difficult to cope and his family took him back to Jamaica to care for him. At 93 she decided to move from her London flat, where she'd lived for more than 40 years, to a communal home for elderly women run by a small charity. Here she is settled and content, still enjoying the world of books and occasional work assignments.

> I've made some very good friends here, which I'm very fond of and I still take pleasure in going to picture galleries . . . I read and read and read, and I like reviewing books.

Is there anything she misses? Alcohol now disagrees with her and 'it's quite a long time since I've minded not having sex'.

> The car is the only thing that I really had to say to myself: The time has come, you must give up the car, and that was hard and that I missed, but the drink and sex floated away sort of quite naturally really, luckily.

Diana seems to have made an almost complete accommodation to life in great old age. She is fortunate to have good health and to have found an agreeable new communal life where she can make new friends but retain her independence, something she has valued for much of her adult life. For those who have lost partners, living alone can be a challenge and a burden. Many widowers, like Jim Purcell, want to stay on in the homes where they spent their happiest years.

> The council want to move me. I said I'm too old for all that business, leave me be, I've been here since 1948. I'm not leaving.

Fred Glover feels the same way. He is still in the bungalow he built himself whilst working full-time, his family's first real home.

My world is in here. This is where it all happened, in here. I don't want to go somewhere else. Why should I?

Women sometimes feel differently. By the time she was 85, wartime anti-aircraft gunner Dorothy Hughes was widowed and finding it more difficult to cope with a house and large garden, but the prospect of a residential home filled her with horror, 'sitting in a chair playing bridge or whist or whatever, it wasn't me at all'. Then she saw a television programme about the Royal Hospital Chelsea and read an article in the British Legion magazine about its planned new facilities for women. She discovered that, as a Women's Royal Army Corps pensioner, she was eligible to apply.

My daughter thought I was crazy. She said, 'You'll never get in.' I was asked to go there in January 2009 for a four-day assessment. You see if you like it and they see if they like you.

Dorothy liked Chelsea and they liked Dorothy. Within six weeks she'd sold her house and become the first woman Chelsea Pensioner.

I didn't know the reception I was going to get because it's been a men's home for 317 years and having women in, I felt guilty, it was splitting up. Then I felt: No, why shouldn't I open the door for other women to be able to come? Anyway, when I got here, two of the men said, 'What regiment were you in?' So I said, 'Royal Artillery.' 'Ah, you're a gunner. That's all right.' And I was accepted there and then.

After five years she is still one of only eight women but Dorothy, secure in her comfortable 'berth' and with like-minded people around her, loves it.

When I came to Chelsea I had the feeling, I'm coming home. You're not regarded as men and women, you're a soldier, full stop. And it was wonderful because, although you know that it's probably your last post and you're going to die anyway, you're not alone. In wartime you backed each other up. You were teams. And you're teams here . . . I think if I hadn't come to Chelsea, I would have ended my life in 2005 because I'd really got to the stage where it's very difficult making friends when you're older, being a woman on her own. Here it's been a completely different life. I've met so many interesting people. I've had so many generals kiss my hand, and if it wasn't for my scarlet coat, they'd ignore me!

Old age is often a time for reconciliation and resolution – of family rifts, with old enemies and past demons. Diana found catharsis through her writing. Connie Hoe and Dorothy Bohm managed to reconnect with their estranged families abroad, resolving painful gaps in their lives. After coming out in the 1980s, George Montague was at last able to live the life he wanted. Shortly before his seventieth birthday in 1997 he met his Thai partner Somchai and they entered into one of the first transracial civil partnerships after these were introduced in 2004. A lifelong Labour supporter, he now admires David Cameron for pushing through gay marriage, though civil partnership is enough for them. Since moving to Brighton with Somchai and taking part in Gay Pride parades on his mobility scooter as 'the Oldest Gay in the Village', 91-year-old George has become something of a celebrity and a gay icon. He has lived through discrimination and persecution, the age of AIDS, and a sea change in public attitudes and policies, but there are no regrets or recriminations.

I suppose, if there was a heaven and I'd gone there and I was sitting up there and I was looking down, I'd have thought, Well, no, I don't think I'd change anything. I'd leave it as it was. It's good enough, and getting better.

There is belated recognition for the wartime women steel-workers in those satanic Sheffield foundries. Kit Sollitt's talks to schools about her war work sparked a full-blown campaign sponsored by a local newspaper for a statue to honour Sheffield's wartime women. Fund-raising began in 2009 and Kit was one of the key movers and shakers.

> We've done 12 different projects and we got the money – £170,000. It's made of bronze. The core inside is solid steel and it's two ladies, both in boiler suits. I think one's carrying a spanner and one's carrying summat and they've both got boots on. Me, I was fitted up with clogs, but some wore boots . . . The sculptor said it'll be there for ever, it'll be too heavy for anybody to ever move. I doubt that. They can shift owt if they want.

In January 2010 they were invited to meet Prime Minister Gordon Brown in Downing Street. Kit was very impressed by the champagne they were served on the train travelling down to London at 8 a.m., but was she impressed with the Prime Minister?

> We went into the White Room in Downing Street and he came in . . . We all had a good chat. He's a lovely chap, and his little boy came running in and played with us and we thought that was lovely . . . Just like a normal bloke. We thought he were lovely. If you weren't a Labourite when you went in, you were one when you came out.

It is a great achievement and will be a fitting tribute to Sheffield's 'women of steel'.

> It's good, really, because we slogged for them for six years, most of us, and at the end of the war they all got dismissed without a thank you as the men came back. So yes, it'll be nice to see. It shows we'd done it.

The men of the Arctic convoys too had to wait a long time for recognition. 'It hurt,' says Austin Byrne, that they got no campaign medal from the British after the war. He wrote to the War Ministry but by then relations with Russia had hardened and he got 'some sort of "go away, little boy" answer'.

Finally, nearly 70 years later they, or their surviving families, were entitled to apply for the Arctic Star and also to accept the Ushakov Medal, awarded by the Russians some time before.

It's great to get this one. I've got the British medal and I've got the Russian medal . . . so I'm really pleased now. In short, I'm on a high. And it's nice to know that the lads who went down with [*Induna*], their people will have been able to get them . . . A saying of mine is: if blood were the price of freedom, the merchant ship sailors paid it in full.

Sid Graham hasn't been able to claim his convoy medal because his pay book went down with the *Scottish Star*. This still rankles with his family, who are fighting on his behalf, now that he is in his nineties and frail, for proper recognition of his war service.

For the former crews of Bomber Command too, reconciliation has been more difficult. Recognition finally came, too little, too late for some, in the form of a memorial unveiled in Green Park, London, in 2012 and the following year the award of a clasp, rather than the full service medal they'd been denied after the war. Bob Frost is bitterly disappointed.

They've just issued a thing called a clasp that we could put on our 39–45 Star. I heard it described by somebody as being like something out of a Christmas cracker. I've got the form to fill in to apply for it but I don't think I'll bother.

Russell Margerison doesn't think he will, either.

I personally don't attach too much importance to medals. But I think we should have earned due recognition and had a campaign medal for Bomber Command. We just didn't. All the forces got some kind of campaign medals and we never did.

The hurt lingers. Bob used to return to Europe every summer with his family to visit the brave people who helped him escape on the *Comète* line. Some of them ended up in concentration camps and lost relatives there. Their experience has left a lasting impression and Bob refuses to be apologetic for his part in the war.

> I'm not in the least sorry that we put a stop to that. I make no excuse whatsoever for stopping this country becoming a concentration camp. I don't regret that at all, I'd do the same again . . . We didn't win the war, nobody wins at war, somebody comes off worse than the others and thank God they came off worse than we did. It's not pride. I'm angry. I'm not proud of it. But, by God, I didn't want it to happen, not here. I wanted my children to grow up with their heads up.

Russell feels much the same way, but he does feel pride.

> Total war is a nasty, horrible business. We don't want wars but once you get involved in a war it's got to be all out, hasn't it? There's no half measures in wars. Got to be all out, and it was . . . Yes, I do feel a sense of pride. We did win the war, and we had no intention *not* to win the war. We *knew* we were going to win the war. Purely a question of time. And yes, I was proud to be part of it and I'm glad I was and I would do it all over again. It was a wonderful experience really, a wonderful experience. You go away as a boy and come back as a man.

That sentiment is echoed by many other combatants, even those like Frank Rosier who were horribly injured.

> It was a terrific time to have lived, in many, many ways. And I thank the good Lord I lived through it and was part of it. Made a man of me. Made a man of me.

For all former prisoners of war, especially those in the Far East, reconciliation is an ongoing process that perhaps can never be fully complete whilst painful memories remain, however far buried they are below the surface. The post-war symptoms of stress may be long gone but the experience itself can't be erased; it will always be part of who these men became and are still. Each found their different ways of coming to terms with the past. Fergus Anckorn has always taken a rational view. He knows that generosity of spirit is more likely to aid healing than hatred.

> I don't hate the Japanese . . . It was the fault of having a war that I got to see the Japanese, so I don't blame them. I know they were horrible to us and the beastly tricks they got up to, but I would never have seen any of that had there been no war . . . I used to get bashed around an awful lot, merely because I didn't understand what they were saying, so I thought, When the war is over, I'm going to visit Japan – because I'd heard it was a nice place – and I'm going to learn Japanese so that if there's another war I'm going to be the interpreter, I'm not going to get bashed.

He went to evening classes, found Japanese straightforward to learn and even passed some of his new knowledge on to his granddaughter. As a result, she is now studying Japanese at university. 'She's well into it,' he says, 'so she'll end up teaching me.' Visits to Japan and Thailand and reconciliation events at the Japanese Embassy in London have all helped the healing process.

Bill Frankland coped by setting his face to the future and deciding not to talk to anyone about his war experience, a policy he kept up for more than 60 years. He has since returned to Singapore. Blakang Mati – since renamed Sentosa ('Isle of Tranquillity') – where he spent some time and which the POWs called Hell Island 'is unrecognisable now – golf courses and five-star hotels and all sorts of things'. He never hated the Japanese because of the lesson on hatred his father taught him in early childhood, and he is proud of the medical work he was able to do in the camps. But bad memories can't be blotted out entirely. In December 2013 he was invited to the London premiere of *The Railway Man*, the film of Eric Lomax's experience on the

Burma–Siam railway and the dramatised story of his own journey of reconciliation.

> It was so far from the truth but it doesn't matter, it was a good film. That night I got to bed just after 1 a.m. and for the first time for 70 years I actually had a nightmare about prisoner-of-war life . . . Presumably my psyche won't forget about it.

These days there is pleasure to be taken – and given – in talking about the past. Fergus has shared his story with schools, historical societies and young officers from his old regiment, the Royal Artillery. Almost all of those interviewed have given talks or visited schools since 2000 to share their experience of living through the twentieth century. They are energised by these exchanges, find their audiences attentive and engaged, and they learn new things themselves. It is a joy and a relief to discover that people are interested and value what they have to say. After decades of self-imposed silence, they have given themselves permission to speak, not reluctantly but wholeheartedly, as if impelled to take this last opportunity to share with others the fruits of their long experience, the dark times as well as the light.

For Eileen Younghusband, as for many others, it is a mission of national importance.

> It's not a question of self-glorification, it's a question of recording what so many young women and young men went through in those terrible years when we had to fight for our lives. I feel that those of us that can write or can talk, we must record this for future generations because, after all, it's the history of our nation.

Vera Lynn no longer goes into schools, but she agrees.

> I used to go into schools and talk about Burma and they'd ask, 'What was it like?', 'What did we eat?' People can't understand what it was like. People didn't want to talk about it [after the war], which was strange. It's a big and important part of their lives when

they were young. I think children should be taught what it was all about because it's very important and it does them good to know what went on in their grandparents' and great-grandparents' lives.

Centenarian Gus Bialick is a volunteer with Intergen, a project bringing older people together with students in London primary and secondary schools. There he talks about his life experiences, 'the things you may not read in the history books'. The aim is to build intergenerational relationships and challenge the stereotypes that sometimes keep the generations apart.

The times that we live in today and the times that we lived through were so different, that the talk that I give about my experiences can only be conveyed by somebody who'd actually been through them. To read about it in books is not the same thing. To experience being afraid while bombing is taking place is another feeling. When it's over and you can talk about it, you feel that you've achieved something by helping the young people to understand what went on, and let them think that even though they're living at a time like this, now, with its peacefulness, these things can happen again. What happened in the past can happen in the future, so we must try and understand how to avoid these things happening. For instance, we have different peoples living in the country now, from different parts of the world, different colour skins, different upbringing, different attitudes to life. We must learn to understand them better. We're all human beings and we must learn that it's not too hard to understand another person if you want to. We must forget prejudice, we must forget religion. Basically, we're all human beings and we must learn to live with each other and respect each other's point of view if we can.

There's no doubt in my mind that the things I talk to the younger generation about must be of benefit to them, and to anybody who listens to what I have to say, because to learn from other people's experiences still counts for a lot.

As well as answering the questions children always ask (What did you eat? What did you wear? Did you kill anyone? Were you scared?), there's a point to these talks beyond relaying facts and feelings. Like Gus, Freddie Hunn wanted to get a wider message across:

> Lots of schools ask me if I'll go and tell them about the war, and I take as many pictures as I can. But I think it's important that they know the horrors of war. Wherever I talk, I say, 'War is not the answer,' and I impress it on children. It's not a glorious thing, war. It's a terrible thing. If you can avoid war and make peace, and do good, it's far better than killing people. I try to tell people, 'Don't think it's heroic.' I know there's heroic things done in war, but there's no great joy in killing people. It's terrible.

After his interview in 2014 he was filmed in lively conversation with a group of Brownies and Beaver Scouts. Two days later Major Freddie Hunn, MBE died aged 94 while visiting his son in France. His family said he was delighted to have been able to tell his story on film – and now in print – for the first time.

Freddie's message to young people was one Hetty Bower passionately believed in and spent much of her life campaigning for. Possibly the most active of those years were her last ones. At 102 she was asked to address the Hiroshima Day commemoration in London, her first ever public speaking engagement. She made such an impression that afterwards she was in demand by schools and universities, at rallies and peace marches, and for media interviews. Though her sight and hearing were failing by then, her legs and her determination were still strong.

> I'm able to be active. There are a lot of people that can't be. My legs are good and can still carry me and therefore I feel I should use them to good purpose. And the good purpose is no more bloody war . . . My one aim is to work for peace on earth and no more war . . . We can't make progress, eliminate poverty amongst the humans who inhabit this planet, unless we have peace in which

to do it. That's the first essential, and then we have to tackle poverty. And I want and hope that it is coming yet for all that, that the world could say no child in our planet cries because of hunger and there is no food to give it. So it's not a big wish. Or is it?

Having recently spoken at the Labour Party Conference, Hetty was on her way to talk to children at a primary school when she had a stroke and died three weeks later, in November 2013. She was 108. In her interview, one of the last before she died, she said the thing that kept her going was watching her great-grandchildren grow, but death didn't worry her.

> It wouldn't matter if I went to sleep and didn't wake up tomorrow.
> It really wouldn't make a great deal of difference. But as I'm here,
> I have to do something, and that something is working for peace
> on earth.

The end of life for people who've lived the best part of a century or more is feared by few, welcomed by some. Many still feel they have useful lives and work still to do. Vera Price, in her 110th year when interviewed, is one of the very few who has had enough.

> I personally welcome death now. Not that I'm morbid, but I've
> had my day and life is very uncomfortable at the moment. I'm no
> use to anybody and I think it will be just lovely to die.

As a lifelong Christian, Vera has no doubt that this won't be the end, though she won't speculate on what might come next: 'You mustn't make guesses about that sort of thing.' Religious belief, her formative childhood experience of seeing an infant flu victim dead but beautiful on her purple cushion, and experiencing supernatural episodes at key moments of her life give her supreme confidence that death is merely release into a better world.

Matthew MacKinnon-Pattison, now 90, learned religion young at his Quarriers Homes orphanage in Scotland. Though belief has come and gone over the years, it has returned to give him comfort and certainty in old age.

> I know where my God is. And I know that when this life is over, He's promised me that I'll be with my lovely wives again and the old folks and all the people I love, but I've also got to think that I'm just going to keep going until He calls me.

Dr Bill Frankland is a scientist and a Christian, though he's less sure about the hereafter.

> I hope there will be an afterlife and I can meet my wife and so on, but I'm not absolutely certain about it. But it's not something that worries me, so death doesn't worry me.

The thought of reunion with loved ones is a comfort for many. Jim Purcell kisses Betty's wedding ring night and morning.

> She keeps me going in everything . . . When I met her, everything changed. I was my own king, and she was my Queen. And it's never blinking left me, and it never will, till we're together again. I've got faith in that as well, see. It's fantastic. I canna grumble at all.

That hope is so important to Fred Glover that he decided to be baptised and confirmed for the first time at the age of 91, just to make sure.

> I thought, If I'm not careful, she's going to be there and I'm going to be somewhere else. If there is any future life, I want it to be with my dear Rita, for ever.

It isn't death but incapacity and loss of independence that many fear. Photography has been Dorothy Bohm's life and it still sustains her now she is in her nineties, but she is aware that life is finite.

Now people are interested in my prints and I'm hoping to leave some of my work with the V.&A. [Victoria and Albert Museum] because it will be a record of what has gone. But I'm also aware that my life has got to come to an end. I feel I've had a very, very full life and I'm not afraid of death, not at all. I dread the thought of being a nuisance to my family . . . I'm afraid I'm against keeping people alive who are not really alive any more.

Bob Frost agrees:

Just let me go quietly. I don't want to end up a useless old thing stuck in bed unable to do this, that or the other for himself, dependent on other people nursing him along. I'd much rather be knocked down by a number nine bus.

After a major stroke, and now with dementia, former merchant seaman Sid Graham, 94, can no longer tell his story. But supported by his wife Esther and surrounded by his 9 surviving children, 33 grandchildren and 61 great-grandchildren, he still takes great pleasure in looking at family photo albums and watching himself in a television interview he did for a 1997 BBC series on Britain's maritime history. His 11 (and counting) great-great-grandchildren will no doubt continue to tell his story of another way of life and another century in years to come.

Although 'life is still very much worth living', Diana Athill now thinks quite a bit about death. She has no religious belief but she does lean to the view that we all leave a trace – good or bad – behind. She isn't frightened – death after all is 'very ordinary' – but she does worry about becoming ill and suffering in death. She should take comfort in Fergus Anckorn's experience, born of close proximity to the dead and dying in the POW camps, which has given him a pragmatic, humanist perspective.

I have no religious beliefs. People say to me, 'Someone up there was looking after you.' Oh yes? What about my friends? He didn't look after them. So when they say [that], I say, 'No, they're not.

I'm just living and lucky to be alive. And as for dying, I've seen hundreds of people die, blown up, shot, dying in the prisoner-of-war camps from malnutrition and disease. I've held the hands of dozens of people when they're dying and it's nothing to fear.

When you die the pain goes away and furthermore, you don't know you're dying . . . so death is nothing to be frightened of. You don't know when it comes; it comes when you're not expecting it. I've seen all these horrific deaths and I've never yet seen anyone die in pain. Gradually the pain goes away altogether.

Yes, I'm not worried about death at all. I'm waiting for it. All my friends are dead, they're all gone. It's time I went with them and when the time comes, it won't worry me in the slightest. I'm a bit like the Japs, ready for it, looking forward to it.

Until then, life for 95-year-old Fergus goes on: there are well-rehearsed magic tricks to confound new audiences and commitments to schools and veterans associations to honour. If life is occasionally physically tiresome for these very elderly people, their instinct is to give themselves a good talking-to, rather than give in to complaining infirmity. Joy Lofthouse, 91, former ATA pilot and retired teacher, epitomises that spirit:

You either go on or you don't, and we learned to go on during the war with people dying around us. You can't help getting old, but you can help being a miserable old lady. So I decided I wasn't going to be a miserable old lady . . .

The way I was brought up and my whole childhood gave me confidence. It made me self-confident, made me believe in myself that whatever I attempted, it was possible to do. In fact, I still often quote the motto from my primary school that says: 'I can. I will. I must.' I still say that to myself sometimes when, you know, I'm walking with a stick, a little more decrepit, I say, 'Come on. I can, I will, I must.'

Looking back on their lives and all the changes they've seen since the war, there are some predictable grumbles: young people tapping on their phones rather than talking face to face; automated checkouts; waste; politicians.

There is fear for their grandchildren and great-grandchildren's prospects as good, secure jobs – the kind they had – become scarcer. The benefits of the welfare state they enjoyed in adult life and rely on in old age seem unlikely to outlast their children's lifetime, much less their grandchildren's. They feel lucky to have had them and regret what they see as the gradual erosion of the New Jerusalem they helped build.

There is sadness too that the lessons of the war haven't been learned and probably never will be. The rise of religious intolerance is a particular worry, and that old fear of the incomer is still there: 'Our tolerance allows the intolerance of others' is a common view. However, the suggestion that Britain or its constituent nations should become more separate is seen by some as a threat and a stupidity. They are patriots but they believe in the idea of Europe as a bulwark against future conflict; UKIP has plenty of support among the elderly – but perhaps more for its policies on immigration than on Europe. They can be passionate English, Welsh, Scots or Irish but many elderly Britons are proud, still, to be part of the Union and many still refer to it as Great Britain, a usage little heard these days.

Proud Scot Matthew MacKinnon-Pattison, interviewed just before the 2014 Scottish Referendum vote, offered his own heartfelt analysis of how his generation got to here.

My generation has come up through the tail end of the First World War. We could see the soldiers from that walking along the street, begging. We came up through the General Strike. We were babies then, but it must have had some effect on our parents. Then we seen the hunger marchers coming over the hill heading for London or Glasgow or wherever they're going, people who had no work. We came through the Depression in the thirties. Then suddenly war is thrown at us. We fight that war and we come out of it. We tidy up everything. We say we're going to have no more depressions. We're going to have no more sickness and illness that are not being looked after. We're going to have things running properly. We're not going to have people just making profit out of trains and railways and things like that just for the sake of making a profit. Things are to be run to help the people. Then my friend Harold Wilson come along one day and he said, 'Buy British.' Maggie Thatcher come along and she sold the flipping lot to everybody outside Britain. Every part of nationalised industry's gone abroad. And we all sit back and said, 'Oh, I never noticed!'

No. You see, if we don't keep an eye on things we're going to lose them. And my old country right now is in the throes of a stupid idea of breaking away. Why I do not know, except greed, hatred or something else. What good's it going to do? We're trying to unite the world. We're trying to bring countries together. We got into the European Union – marvellous! We don't fight Germany any more, we don't fight France. We've knocked the dickens out of all of them anyway at sometime or another, but we're trying to get together and then you start getting other people wanting to fragment it, break away a little bit here, a little bit there . . . Our generation has had its day. We've done our best. We've handed it over . . . So God bless you all!

The 1939–45 war remains the central formative event of their lives. It is the period they remember most clearly and still feel most strongly attached to. Whether in action, on the home front or in a POW camp, they endured much and achieved much. Though they may regret the war having to be fought and still mourn lost friends and family, no one regrets having been part of it. The heightened awareness, the ever-present threat of danger and that unique unity of purpose were powerful and exhilarating forces that made it a special time for many, like Joy Lofthouse.

I still look back on that as the most exciting time of my life. But I'm sure many people, whatever they did in the war, do the same, because somehow one was alive. One was fighting for something. There was some meaning to life. Everything meant something. Certainly there was propaganda, not brainwashing, but propaganda which made us feel it was worthwhile what we were fighting for. So yes, there was a great meaning to life.

Pride in their efforts is closely bound to pride in Britain and this seems to be felt especially keenly by second-generation immigrants like Gus Bialick.

We went into the army as civilians, and we came out as patriots for Great Britain. I can tell you that each one of us thought of England as our home, and the place we were born in, the place we wanted to live in for the rest of our lives. We thought of that whilst we were in places like Italy and Sicily, and in Algiers and places in North Africa . . . Each one of us knew exactly what we were about and why we were [there]. We knew that we were doing something which would help every one of us to live decently.

Austin Byrne, 92, has a flagpole in his garden in Bradford, improvised from aluminium tubes discarded by the mill where he used to work. Every year, a few days before Remembrance Sunday he raises the Union Jack and leaves it there for the week of 11 November.

I'd go out each morning, salute it, say my prayers and bow to it and sing 'Land of Hope and Glory' and then I come in and have my breakfast. And then, say, if I'm having a drink at night, I'll go out and toast it. But each night then I go out, salute it, say my prayers and come in.

In March each year, for the anniversary of the sinking of the *Induna*, he does the same with the Red Ensign, the flag of the British Merchant Navy.

I put it up the day before we was sunk and I leave it up for the four days we were in the boat and take it down on the fifth day. But I go out twice a day and say a prayer for the boys that weren't lucky enough. But when I say my prayers now, I do it the Orthodox way when I'm finishing because it's Russia that they're in . . . Each time I look at that flag and think about it and say my prayers, it brings all the men back to me. And I do feel their spirits are in that garden with me. I know it sounds silly but that's how I feel. It makes me feel very, very full. My eyes are wet and everything. But it's very satisfying and I'll do it as long as I can.

Though reconciliation may be all but complete, that old reticence about enquiring into private grief or sharing one's own, especially when it comes to war memories, is still evident in much of the testimony. Joy Lofthouse explains this as self-control:

Looking back on the war, I realise we learned to control our emotions, because you didn't know a family that hadn't lost someone. If one was ever expressing emotions too much or being very emotive, I don't think we'd have ever won the war. You know, we had to have that wartime spirit and I know anyone you interview of that generation will probably say the same. This is a completely different world now, when everyone has to open up and express their feelings and everyone has to know how you're feeling.

There are lingering sensitivities, as Enid Wenban found at her ninetieth-birthday celebrations;

I found myself sitting between two of my friends, one German, one French, both married to Englishmen, and I quite spontaneously said, 'I was working in London right through the Blitz. Where were you, Laura?' And she said, 'I was in Hamburg and the bombing was awful.' And I said, 'Where were you, Claude?' 'I was in Paris and we didn't have enough food and it was awful.' I didn't pursue the conversation any further. I'm sure neither of them would have wanted to talk about their experiences from those days.

Some war memories are perhaps best left unspoken, unshared.

Do *they* think they are Britain's greatest generation? Emphatically not. They don't see themselves as anything special, or having done anything that anyone wouldn't do under similar circumstances. Vera Lynn has confidence in the rising generation.

> We put up with a lot of things but I'm sure the young people of today, if anything like that should happen, they'd be quite capable of doing the same thing as we did, coping with the bombs and the Blitz and the food and the clothes coupons.

Some, like Connie Hoe, look to their parents' generation, who came through the 1914–18 war, as more deserving of the accolade.

> Maybe the generation before us with the First World War was perhaps greater, because the people in the 1910s, the conditions under which they worked and were housed was far below our generation, so perhaps really it's that generation that was the greatest.

They will admit to having endured a great deal, and that this perhaps marks out their generation, particularly from those that followed. Connie says:

> When I say to my great-grandchildren, 'How would you like it if you had to go and sleep in a hole in the garden with the air raids on and then have to go to work the next day? And wash in cold water – if you had water?' And they are amazed. They can't believe it.

As Joy Lofthouse says: 'So we were a different generation, but I don't say we were better or worse than anyone else. Different and thankful for it.'

But if the question is put rather differently – 'Are you proud to have been part of your generation?' – then there's no hesitation. There is overwhelming pride in having been a small part of something momentous, a great struggle, and having done their best to overcome all obstacles and then going on to help make a better world for their children. Eileen Younghusband has no doubts:

Despite all the tragedies and trials and unhappiness that we had to face, I'm proud I'm a member of that generation that managed to fight their way through those terrible years and the post-war years and still manage to hold our heads high. I'm definitely proud of our war generation.

Chelsea Pensioner Dorothy Hughes agrees.

We had to struggle, and it was a hard struggle. Nothing was made for us, you had to look after yourself . . . I'm proud to think that we stuck together, that as a nation we got through it and we tried to make a better country to live in than it was before the war.

Ninety-year-old Gladys Parry, the working-class lass from Hulme who never had the luxury of learning polite reticence, believes there *is* something special about her generation.

Yes, I do. Because we learned how to stretch a penny into a pound. We were stronger in every way because of bombing of a night-time, we got used to it. But no, we stood up, we stood up and we were strong. The women were strong and you see the old dears today and the old men. They're still strong. They can stand up and fight still.

'And I do!', she says, laughing.

Who's Who

Anckorn, Fergus

Born 1918 in Kent. Served in the Field Artillery 1940–45. Captured by the Japanese in the fall of Singapore. POW 1942–45. Member of the Magic Circle since the age of 18 and still a practising conjurer. Widowed, two children. Lives in West Sussex.

Athill, Diana OBE

Born 1917 in Norfolk into a wealthy family. After a long and successful career in publishing, established herself in later life as a gifted memoirist and commentator on ageing. Unmarried. Lives in London.

Bialick, Gus

Born 1914 in London's East End, the son of Polish Jewish immigrants. War service in the Pioneer Corps, serving in north Africa and Italy. Widowed, one son. Still lives in London where he talks to schoolchildren about his life for the charity Intergen.

Bohm, Dorothy

Born to Jewish parents in what is now Russia in 1924. Arrived in Britain as a 15-year-old refugee. Distinguished career in photography, specialising in people and places at particular moments in time. Married, two daughters. Lives in London.

Bower, Hetty

Born 1905 in Hackney, into an Orthodox Jewish family. Lifelong socialist and pacifist. Two daughters. Came to public attention late in life as a public speaker and peace campaigner. Hetty died in 2013 aged 108.

Byrne, Austin

Born 1922 in Bradford and still lives there. Served in the Merchant Navy 1941–46 on Atlantic and Russian convoys. Survived a torpedo attack in 1942. Worked in Yorkshire woollen mills after the war. Widowed, one son.

Cameron, Earl CBE

Born 1917 in Bermuda. Arrived in Britain in 1939. Served in the Merchant Navy. One of the first black actors to break the 'colour bar' and star in a British film (*Pool of London* 1951). Still working in his nineties. Widowed and remarried, six children.

Chilton, Charles MBE

Distinguished BBC radio drama and music producer, born in King's Cross, 1917. Wrote and co-produced *Oh, What a Lovely War!* with Joan Littlewood's Theatre Workshop in 1963. Married, two children. Charles died in 2013 aged 95.

Craig, David

Born 1925 in Poolewe, north-west Highlands. Served in the Merchant Navy from 1943 and campaigned for official recognition for those on the Russian convoys with the Arctic Convoy Association. Lives in Kilmarnock.

Elston, Ellen

Born 1908 in London, the eldest of six children. Her father was killed at Passchendaele in 1917. She later married and settled in Devon. Ellen died in 2008 aged 99.

Frankland, Dr Bill

Born 1912 in Sussex, one of twins. Trained at Oxford and St Mary's Paddington before enlisting in RAMC in 1939. POW of Japanese 1942–1945. Widowed. At 103, Bill is the world's oldest medical practitioner and allergy specialist.

Frost, Bob

Born 1923 in London. Messenger boy with the London Fire Brigade, then a rear gunner with Bomber Command. Shot down in Belgium 1942 but escaped back to Britain. Widowed, two adopted children. Post-war career in teaching. Lives in Kent.

Glover, Fred

Born 1923 in the Kentish Weald. Never knew his parents but grew close to his foster-mother. Boy soldier before joining the Parachute Regiment in 1943. D-Day veteran. Widowed, three children.

Graham, Sid

Born 1920 in Barbados. Served in the Merchant Navy during the war. Survived a torpedo attack in the Atlantic. Despite a major stroke, still enjoying his large extended family. Married, nine surviving children.

Graves, Bill

Born 1924 in Bristol into a strong socialist family. Joined Home Guard and then war service in the Navy. British Rail driver after the war and active in trade union and local politics. Widowed, three children. Still lives in Bristol.

Harrison, John

Born 1914 in Farnborough. Young musician and keen swimmer. Joined Navy in 1938 and survived the mining of HMS *Belfast* in 1939. Worked in Nigeria after the war. Widowed, one daughter. World champion swimmer in his age category (100–104).

Hoe, Connie

Born 1922 in Limehouse, of Chinese father, English mother. Effectively orphaned at 8. Married at 19 and delivered her baby alone. Reconnected with Chinese relatives in Hong Kong later in life. Widowed, one daughter.

Holsgrove, Richard

Born 1923. After braving the London Blitz as a Junior Fireman in the Auxiliary Fire Service, volunteered for the Navy in 1941 and served on North Atlantic convoys for much of the war. Married with children. Living in Essex.

Hughes, Dorothy

Born 1923 in Swansea. War service in ATS on anti-aircraft batteries in London and the South-East. Remained in the WRAC after the war and in 2009 at the age of 85 became the first female Chelsea Pensioner. Widowed, one daughter.

Hunn, Major Freddie MBE

Born 1919 in Great Yarmouth, one of seven. Joined the 12th Royal Lancers underage. Evacuated with the BEF at Dunkirk. Saw action in North Africa, Italy and Palestine. A career soldier after the war. Married, four children. Freddie died in 2014, aged 94.

Jones, Ron

Born 1917 in the Welsh valleys. Called up in error and captured in north Africa. POW in Italy and Germany. Captive labourer at the IG Farben factory at Auschwitz III, Monowitz. Widowed, one son. Lives in Newport, Gwent.

Lofthouse, Joy

Born 1923 in Gloucestershire. Worked in a bank until she joined the Air Transport Auxiliary, flying new aircraft to wherever they were needed. Post-war career in teaching. Divorced, three children, remarried and widowed. Lives in Gloucestershire.

Lynn, Dame Vera

Born 1917 in East Ham. Started performing at seven. Seventy-year career as radio and recording artist, her songs are particularly associated with the Second World War. Had a number one album at the age of 92. Widowed, one daughter. Lives outside Brighton.

McCoy, Mabel

Born 1921 in Manchester into a middle-class family with a war-disabled father. Did well at school, studied Chemistry at Manchester College of Technology and became a research chemist.

MacKinnon-Pattison, Matthew

Born 1924, brought up in a Scottish children's home. Joined the Argyll and Sutherland Highlanders and served at the Battle of Monte Cassino. Methodist lay preacher. Twice married, twice widowed, two children.

Margerison, Russell

Born 1924 in Blackburn. Last surviving child of six. Volunteered for RAF aircrew at 17. Rear Gunner with Bomber Command. Shot down in 1944, captured and imprisoned. Married, four sons. Russell died in 2014 aged 89.

Montague, George

Born 1923. War service as RAF PT instructor. Married with three children but led a clandestine life as a homosexual. Finally came out in 1982. Civil partnership 2004. Lives in Brighton where he is 'the Oldest Gay in the Village'.

Mowatt, David

Born 1921 in Dornoch, Scottish Highlands. Joined the Seaforth Highlanders as a reservist. Captured at Dunkirk with the 51st Highland Division and spent the rest of the war as a POW in Europe. Married, three daughters. David died in 2014 aged 93.

Neil, Wing Commander Tom DFC★ AFC AE

Born 1920 in Bootle. Battle of Britain fighter pilot. Saw later action attached to the USAAF, at the Battle of Normandy and in Burma. After the war, continued in the RAF as a test pilot until 1964. Widowed, three sons. Lives in Norfolk.

Overall, Donald

Born 1913, he barely knew his father who was killed in 1917. Attended the unveiling of the Cenotaph in 1920 with his mother. Donald died in 2012 aged 99.

Parry, Gladys

Born 1926 in Hulme, Manchester. Father captured at Dunkirk. Drafted into Avro aircraft factory at 15. Hard early life. Active in local politics and appointed a magistrate. Widowed, two boys. Retired to Spain but returned to the UK.

Perry, Jimmy OBE

Born 1923 in Barnes, London. Actor and screenwriter. Using his own experience he co-created some of the most successful television comedies of the 1970s and 1980s: *Dad's Army, It Ain't Half Hot Mum* and *Hi-de-Hi!* Married, he lives in London.

Pickering, Squadron Leader Tony

Born 1920 in Leicestershire, one of eight children. Joined RAF Volunteer Reserve at 18 whilst an engineering apprentice. Battle of Britain fighter pilot. Demobbed 1945 with rank of Squadron Leader. Twice married, two children. Lives in Rugby.

Price, Vera

Born 1905 in Bath. Worked for the Foreign Office as a cipher clerk and travelled widely. Returned in 1951 to work for the new National Assistance Board. Widowed, Vera lives in Bristol and celebrated her 110th birthday in January 2015.

Purcell, Jim
Born 1921 in Jarrow. Impoverished childhood. Joined the Territorial Army (Royal Engineers) at 18. Evacuated at Dunkirk and captured in north Africa 1943. Widowed, five children. Still lives in Jarrow and runs marathons as 'Jarra Jim'.

Rhodes, Hon Margaret LVO
Born 1925 in Scotland, the youngest daughter of Lord Elphinstone. Her aunt became Queen Elizabeth on the abdication of Edward VIII, and Queen Elizabeth II is her cousin. Widowed, four children. Lives on the Windsor Estate.

Rix, Baron Brian of Whitehall CBE DL
Born 1924 in Yorkshire. Distinguished career as farceur and actor-manager of the Whitehall Theatre, and as a learning disability rights campaigner for MENCAP. Widowed, four children. Still campaigning as an active peer. Lives in Surrey.

Rosier, Frank
Born 1925 in Chelsea. Lost two brothers in the war. Joined the Glosters at 17. D-Day veteran. Lost an eye in the Battle of Normandy. Post-war worked as a postman then studied and became an auditor. Widowed. Lives outside Portsmouth.

Sollitt, Kit
Born 1919 in Sheffield, one of eight children. Conscripted into a steel foundry at 20. Married a fellow worker in 1944, four children. Author of two novels about Sheffield steelworkers. Still lives in Sheffield.

Valentine, Jean
Born 1924 in Perth. Joined the WRNS in 1942 and was trained to operate 'Bombes' – decrypting machines – at Bletchley Park where she much later volunteered as a guide for 15 years. Widowed, two children. Lives in Henley.

Wenban, Enid

Born 1920 in Surrey. After working in a reserved occupation joined the ATS in 1943. Trained as a Special Wireless Operator intercepting enemy traffic. Long and varied career as a social worker. Unmarried. Lives in Bognor Regis.

Wilson, Joan

Born 1923 in Croydon. Worked as shorthand typist in pre-welfare state Public Assistance. Briefly in the ATS. Post-war trained as a child care officer and spent her career in the social services. Unmarried. Lives in Chichester.

Wiseman, Andy

Born 1923 in Berlin, to Polish-Jewish father and American mother (father died in death camps). Evacuated to Britain in 1939. Joined RAF underage and trained as a bomb-aimer. Shot down 1944 and captured. Widowed, four children.

Younghusband, Eileen BEM

Born 1921 in in north London. Joined the WAAF 1941 and trained as a filter plotter. After the war spent many years in the hospitality business. Widowed, one son (d). Keen poet, published author and prize-winning Open University graduate. Lives in Glamorgan.

Helping older generations
leave their mark

We spoke to hundreds of men and women aged between 85 and 110 for this book and the television series it accompanies. Inevitably, only a small selection could be included, but what impressed us in all our conversations – on the phone, in person or on camera – was the extraordinary richness and variety of their experience from a century when Britain changed more dramatically than at any time in its long history.

But this rich experience is rapidly slipping beyond living memory. Within a decade even the youngest surviving Second World War combatant will be gone. That is why it's so important to record this treasure trove of living memory before it disappears.

This isn't just a job for professional historians and programme-makers; it can be an immensely rewarding labour of love for anyone with elderly relatives or friends. Some families know surprisingly little about the detail of their loved ones' wartime experience. This is often because of a misplaced concern that it might be too painful, upsetting or embarrassing for them to talk about their experiences. After 1945 there was an understandable reluctance to talk openly about military operations or the sorrow and tragedy of war. 'Not making a fuss' and keeping a check on emotions was often how this generation coped with traumatic events and complex feelings. For those bound by the Official Secrets Act, the added duty of silence was so ingrained it became a habit – even after the 30-year limit. But these restrictions and taboos have long gone: what was once private is now public. In very different times, many of the oldest generation feel more than ready to talk openly about what were often the most intense, dramatic and exciting years of their lives.

In our experience elderly people love to share their stories. In old age many people take great comfort and pleasure in reflecting on the distant past. This is sometimes known as 'life review' and it is the memories of childhood and youth that often appear most vividly. Recording these can be a source of pride for interviewer and interviewee and a bonding experience for both. It is an opportunity for secrets to be revealed, long-suppressed emotions to be released and past pains to be resolved. The finished result is a permanent record of the lives, memories and personalities of those we love and want to remember.

But they are unlikely to offer; they need to be asked. So it is up to those who know and love them to ask.

Anyone from primary-school-age children upwards can conduct and record life-story interviews: often the youngest can bring out the best in the oldest. But anyone can do it with some basic equipment and careful preparation.

Following some simple rules will help ensure the best results:

1. Prepare beforehand

First, it's important have a clear idea of what you want to find out from the person you are interviewing. Preparation is key and this may involve reading around the subjects – perhaps a particular battle, school life in the 1920s or wartime rationing – that you want them to talk about. What you need to unravel is the personal experience of the historical event or aspect of life in the past. It may turn out to be very different from the received wisdom, which is one reason it could be so interesting. Life stories are of course subjective, they are a unique personal perspective on the past and not everyone else will agree with them. But again, this is why they are valuable, especially for family members.

2. List the main questions you want to ask

These will form the spine of the conversation you will record. Give your questionnaire a logical shape, arrange it – perhaps in chronological order – so that there is a clear sequence of topics or events and the questions move smoothly from one to another. This will give the interview a more natural flow and help interviewees focus their thoughts on a particular subject. Your questions will shape your interview but don't follow your questionnaire too rigidly: some of the best things you find out will be unexpected so it is important to give your interviewee the space to tell you what they think matters. Specific, detailed questions are often better at triggering memories than general ones. There are simple guides to questionnaires and interviewing provided by the Oral History Society that can be found online at www.ohs.org.uk.

The best published guide to questionnaires, and to all aspects of life-story interviewing, is *The Voice of the Past: Oral History* by Paul Thompson, the founding father of oral history in Britain, published by Oxford University Press.

3. Make your interviewee feel at home

The art of good interviewing is getting someone to talk in an honest and open way about the experiences you want to explore. To do this you need to make them feel relaxed. There are some basic dos and don'ts to achieve this.

> *Do be reassuring*: often people will say they are very ordinary and boring and have nothing to say that will interest anyone else. Reassure them that their lives, experiences and memories are fascinating and important to younger generations.
>
> *Do be clear*: phrase questions in a simple way using short, easily understood questions.

Do show interest: this is best done by non-verbal means such as constant eye contact, nodding and smiling.

Do sit as close to your interviewee as you can, close enough to touch and hold hands. It adds to the intimate atmosphere that is so important in getting your subject to relax and open up.

Do use cue words and phrases to get a fuller account or explanation: 'Why?', 'Why not?', 'Tell me more about that', 'What happened next?' and 'How did you feel about that?'

Do learn to use silence whilst interviewing. Sometimes at an intimate or emotional moment a little silence can help. Your interviewee will often fill it and add another thought or story. But silences that are too long or used too often can break the flow of the conversation and ultimately undermine the interviewee.

Don't talk too much – be a good listener.

Don't interrupt. If you stop a story in midstream because you think it is boring or irrelevant you may block the flow of further recollections. After a digression return to the point by using a phrase like 'Just going back to . . .' or 'Earlier on you were saying that . . .'

Don't contradict or argue. If you disagree with opinions expressed take a neutral stance: a heated discussion may undermine the relationship of trust on which the interview is based.

4. *Look at documents and photographs together*

Before or after the interview, ask to see any documents or photographs your interviewee may have. These can be priceless assets in a family or community history project. Looking through them together and asking questions about people and places may prompt powerful memories, so it is sometimes best to see these before the interview begins. On the BBC television series *Who Do You Think You Are?*, the most telling sequences are often when the celebrity subject holds an old document or photograph. It is in that moment of physical contact with the past that the true emotional significance of the story is brought home to them.

This, as the programme-makers know very well, is the moment when they are most likely to shed a tear.

5. Choose your recording medium carefully

The basic rules of interviewing are the same whatever recording medium you use, whether film or audio only. Today most of us can use the latest digital technology to instantly film interviews using a smartphone or tablet. There are many different recording formats available, ranging from cassettes to digital voice recorders and recorded Skype interviews, but remember that in the longer term they may all have a limited life which will make it difficult to save the recording for the future, so it is well worth giving serious thought to the best format to use. This will depend on what you want to use the recording for. Is it simply a treasured record for the family, or will it be part of an exhibition, school or community project, radio programme, website or publication that may have a shorter life? There are lots of exciting possibilities, so before you start, be clear about its purpose and research your best options before buying any expensive equipment.

Whatever the final form of your interview, you'll have the satisfaction of leaving a precious record of the past to be appreciated by current and future generations, and of helping an elderly person leave their own mark, in their own words. This is what we set out to do in celebrating the lives and achievements of Britain's greatest generation. You can too, in your own way and with the older people you know and love.

Further reading

MEMOIR

Athill, Diana. *Life Class*. Granta Books, 2009.

Fyans, Peter. *Conjuror on the Kwai: Captivity, Slavery and Survival as a Far East POW*. Pen & Sword, 2011.

Johnson, George 'Johnny'. *The Last British Dambuster*. Ebury, 2014.

Jones, Ron with Joe Lovejoy. *The Auschwitz Goalkeeper*. Gomer Press, 2013.

Lynn, Dame Vera. *Some Sunny Day*. Harper Collins, 2009.

Margerison, Russell. *Boys at War*. Northway Publications, 2005.

Montague, George. *The Oldest Gay in the Village*. Metro Publishing, 2014.

Neil, Tom. *Gun Button to Fire: A Hurricane Pilot's Dramatic Story of the Battle of Britain*. Amberley, 2010.

Rhodes, Margaret. *The Final Curtsey*. Birlinn/Umbria Press, 2012.

Rix, Brian. *Farce about Face*. Hodder & Stoughton, 1989.

Wellum, Geoffrey. *First Light*. Penguin, 2009.

Younghusband, Eileen. *One Woman's War*. Candy Jar Books, 2013.

FIRST WORLD WAR AND INTERWAR PERIOD

van Emden, Richard. *Meeting the Enemy: The Human Face of the Great War*. Bloomsbury, 2013. *The Quick and the Dead: Fallen Soldiers and Their Families in the Great War*. Bloomsbury, 2012.

van Emden, Richard and Steve Humphries. *All Quiet on the Home Front: An Oral History of Life in Britain during the First World War*. Headline, 2003.

Gardiner, Juliet. *The Thirties*. Harper Press, 2011.

de Groot, Gerard. *Back in Blighty: The British at Home in World War One*. Vintage, 2014.

Hanson, Neil. *The Unknown Soldier: The Story of the Missing of the Great War*. Corgi, 2007.

Shephard, Ben. *A War of Nerves: Soldiers and Psychiatrists 1914–1994*. Jonathan Cape, 2000.

White, Jerry. *Zeppelin Nights*. Bodley Head, 2014.

SECOND WORLD WAR

Addison, Paul and Jeremy Crang. *Listening to Britain: Home Intelligence Reports on Britain's Finest Hour*. Vintage, 2011.

Bourne, Stephen. *The Motherland Calls: Britain's Black Servicemen and Women, 1939–45*. The History Press, 2012.

Calder, Angus. *The Myth of the Blitz*. Pimlico, 1991. *The People's War: Britain 1939–1945*. Pimlico, 1997.

Connelly, Mark. *We Can Take It*. Pearson, 2004.

Elliott, Sue with James Fox. *The Children Who Fought Hitler*. John Murray, 2009.

Gardiner, Juliet. *The Blitz: The British Under Attack*. Harper Press, 2010. *Wartime Britain*. Headline, 2004.

Gillies, Midge. *The Barbed-Wire University: The Real Lives of Allied Prisoners of War in the Second World War*. Aurum, 2012.

Goodman, Susan. *Children of War*. John Murray, 2012.

Harrison, Tom. *Living Through the Blitz*. Penguin, 1990.

Hickman, Tom. *Called Up, Sent Down: The Bevin Boys' War*. The History Press, 2010.

Hylton, Stuart. *Careless Talk*. The History Press, 2010.

Levine, Joshua. *Forgotten Voices of the Blitz and the Battle of Britain*. Ebury, 2007. *Forgotten Voices: Dunkirk*. Ebury, 2010.

Longden, Sean. *Dunkirk: The Men They Left Behind*. Constable, 2008.

McKay, Sinclair. *The Secret Life of Bletchley Park*. Aurum Press, 2010.

Mortimer, Gavin. *The Longest Night: 10–11 May 1941, Voices from the London Blitz*. Weidenfeld & Nicholson, 2005.

Nichol, John. *Home Run: Escape from Nazi Europe*. Penguin, 2007.

Nicholson, Virginia. *Millions Like Us: Women's Lives During the Second World War*. Penguin, 2012.

Summers, Julie. *The Stranger in the Home: Women's Stories of Men Returning Home from the Second World War*. Simon & Schuster, 2008.

Taylor, James and Martin Davidson. *Bomber Crew*. Hodder & Stoughton, 2004.

Whittell, Giles. *Spitfire Women of World War II*. Harper, 2007.

POST-WAR PERIOD

Addison, Paul. *Now the War is Over*. Jonathan Cape/BBC, 1985.

Akhtar, Miriam and Steve Humphries. *The Fifties and Sixties: A Lifestyle Revolution*. Boxtree, 2001.

Marwick, Arthur. *British Society Since 1945*. Penguin, 2003.

Hennessy, Peter. *Having It So Good: Britain in the Fifties*. Allen Lane, 2006. *Never Again: Britain 1945–51*. Allen Lane, 1992.

Kynaston, David. *Austerity Britain 1945–51*. Bloomsbury, 2008. *Family Britain 1951–57*. Bloomsbury, 2009. *Modernity Britain, 1957–62*. Bloomsbury, 2014.

Sandbrook, Dominic. *Never Had It So Good: A History of Britain from Suez to the Beatles*. Little Brown, 2005. *State of Emergency: The Way We Were: Britain 1970–1974*. Penguin, 2011. *White Heat: A History of Britain in the Swinging Sixties*. Abacus, 2008.

GENERAL

d'Ancona, Matthew (ed.). *Being British: The Search for the Values That Bind the Nation*. Mainstream, 2009.

Thompson, Paul. *The Voice of the Past: Oral History*. OUP, 2003.

Weight, Richard. *Patriots*. Pan, 2002.

Weightman, Gavin and Steve Humphries. *The Making of Modern London: A People's History of the Capital from 1815 to the Modern Day*. Ebury, 2007.

Index

Personal names in **bold** are for the interviewees. War references are to World War II unless specified as World War I.